THE INHERITANCE AND INNATENESS OF GRAMMARS
Edited by Myrna Gopnik

Vancouver Studies in Cognitive Science is a series of volumes in cognitive science. The volumes will appear annually and cover topics relevant to the nature of the higher cognitive faculties as they appear in cognitive systems, either human or machine. These will include such topics as natural language processing, modularity, the language faculty, perception, logical reasoning, scientific reasoning, and social interaction. The topics and authors are to be drawn from philosophy, linguistics, artificial intelligence, and psychology. Each volume will contain original articles by scholars from two or more of these disciplines. The core of the volumes will be articles and comments on these articles to be delivered at a conference held in Vancouver. The volumes will be supplemented by articles especially solicited for each volume which will undergo peer review. The volumes should be of interest to those in philosophy working in philosophy of mind and philosophy of language; to those in linguistics in psycholinguistics, syntax, language acquisition and semantics; to those in psychology in psycholinguistics, cognition, perception, and learning; and to those in computer science in artificial intelligence, computer vision, robotics, natural language processing, and scientific reasoning.

VANCOUVER STUDIES IN COGNITIVE SCIENCE
forthcoming volumes

VOLUME 7   *Modeling Rationality, Morality and Evolution*
            Editor, Peter Danielson, Philosophy
            University of British Columbia

VOLUME 8   *Attention*
            Editor, Richard Wright, Psychology
            Simon Fraser University

D1622669

the
inheritance
and
innateness
of
grammars

edited by Myrna Gopnik

New York   Oxford
OXFORD UNIVERSITY PRESS
1997

Oxford University Press

Oxford   New York

Athens   Auckland   Bangkok   Bogota   Bombay   Buenos Aires
Calcutta   Cape Town   Dar es Salaam   Delhi   Florence   Hong Kong
Istanbul   Karachi   Kuala Lumpur   Madras   Madrid   Melbourne
Mexico City   Nairobi   Paris   Singapore   Taipei   Tokyo   Toronto

and associated companies in
Berlin   Ibadan

Published by Oxford University Press, Inc.
198 Madison Avenue, New York, New York 10016

Oxford is a registered trademark of Oxford University Press

Library of Congress Cataloging-in-Publication Data
The inheritance and innateness of grammars / edited by Myrna Gopnik.
p.   cm. — (Vancouver studies in cognitive science : v. 6)
Includes bibliographical references.
ISBN 0-19-511533-3; ISBN 0-19-511534-1 (pbk)
1. Innateness hypothesis (Linguistics)   2. Biolinguistics.
3. Language disorders.   4. Language acquisition.
5. Language and languages—Origin.   I. Gopnik, Myrna.   II. Series
P37.5.I55I54   1997
401—dc21   97-1876

1 3 5 7 9 8 6 4 2

Printed in the United States of America
on acid-free paper

Contents

Contributors

Shanley E. M. Allen, Max-Planck-Institut für Psycholinguistik

Harald Clahsen, Department of Language and Linguistics, University of Essex

Martha B. Crago, School of Communication Sciences and Disorders, McGill University

Jenny Dalalakis, Department of Linguistics, McGill University

Shinji Fukuda, Department of Linguistics, McGill University

Suzy E. Fukuda, Department of Linguistics, McGill University

Myrna Gopnik, Department of Linguistics, McGill University

Detlef Hansen, Department of Speech and Language Disorders, University of Hannover

Wendy P. Hough-Eyamie, School of Communication Sciences and Disorders, McGill University

Judith R. Johnston, School of Audiology and Speech Sciences, University of British Columbia

Patricia K. Kuhl, Department of Speech and Hearing Sciences, University of Washinton

Andrew N. Meltzoff, Department of Speech and Hearing Sciences, University of Washinton

Laura Ann Petitto, Department of Psychology, McGill University

Steven Pinker, Department of Brain and Cognitive Sciences, Massachusetts Institute of Technology

Harvey M. Sussman, Department of Linguistics, University of Texas

J. Bruce Tomblin, Department of Speech Pathology and Audiology, University of Iowa

the
inheritance
and
innateness
of
grammars

1

Introduction

Myrna Gopnik

One of the puzzles about language is the fact that children do not speak when they are born, but by the time they are two they are using language and by four they are fluent speakers. How do they accomplish this amazing feat? Charles Darwin suggested that humans had an "instinct" to learn language. This biological view was supplanted in the early part of this century by the view that language was a sociocultural phenomenon and that children learned language in the same way that they learned the other forms of their culture. In the early 1960s Noam Chomsky proposed a radically new explanation: a child learns language in the same way that he learns to walk upright, because it is part of his nature and not because it is part of his culture. The development of the ability to speak, or to walk upright for that matter, does not happen instantly. It follows a natural course of development. Though no two children are precisely alike in their development, they all exhibit the same general pattern of development within the same general time frame. On the basis of limited exposure to language and with the help of their natural instincts for language they can quickly and accurately build the correct grammar of their language. This grammar allows them to produce and to understand new sentences that they have never heard before.

This way of thinking about language and language learning is certainly provocative. But is it accurate? Do humans have a special biological endowment for language or is language learned in the same way as anything else is learned? The debate continues. Several different consequences follow from the hypothesis that language is part of the innate biological endowment of humans. These consequences can give us some direct ways to test this hypothesis. The first comprehensive review of evidence relevant to this hypothesis was presented by Lenneberg in his book *Biological Foundations of Language* (1967). Since that time many studies of various kinds have investigated this question. This volume grows out of a conference on the Biological Foundations of Language held at Simon Fraser University in Vancouver in 1993. That conference brought together experts from several different fields who presented some of the new kinds of evidence relevant to this question.

If children are biologically primed to pay particular attention to language then there also should be some special mechanisms that help them select the variables that are crucial for representing language and to ignore information that is not relevant to language itself. P. Kuhl and A. Meltzoff present evidence from babies that shows that even before children are speaking they exhibit special abilities that enable them to construct particular representations for language. They suggest that "the indelible mark of early learning may be traceable to a biological preparation for receiving language input from other humans during the first years of life." In a similar vein L. Petitto presents evidence from deaf children whose linguistic input is sign language. She argues that the innate principles that govern the ability to learn language are independent of the medium in which language is presented to the baby. She shows that signing babies follow the same developmental path in learning language that speaking babies do. They appear to be sensitive to certain patterned regularities in the input that both spoken and signed languages share. Her work suggests that the biological endowment of humans enables the infant to pay particular attention to these linguistic regularities no matter what medium they are encoded in.

If, on the other hand, it were the case that there were no special language-learning abilities, then children who are exposed to more language earlier should have an advantage over children who get normal, but limited input. M. Crago et al. present just such a case. They show that within Inuit culture, as opposed to general North American culture, young children are rarely spoken to and are not encouraged to speak. Yet even though these children receive very limited language input, they show the same timing and pattern of language development as that of their more talkative neighbours to the South.

If there are innate, biological mechanisms that guide children in their task of acquiring language then it is reasonable to suppose that these mechanisms might be interfered with if there were a mutation that changed this biology. Another set of papers discusses precisely the case in which children do not learn language in the normal way though they do not seem to be impaired cognitively, neurologically or emotionally. Tomblin presents evidence that shows that this disorder aggregates in families and is more concordant in monozygotic twins than in dizygotic twins. The data that he presents strongly argues that some genetic factor (or factors) is responsible for this disorder. Gopnik et al. and Clahsen and Hansen present evidence to show that this disorder directly affects the child's ability to construct a grammar. The two essays differ slightly, however, in the precise parts of the grammar that they believe are affected. The chapter by Johnston discusses a similar population, but comes to a quite different conclusion. She argues that certain information-processing capacities are at risk in these children. She suggests that it is these processing deficits that may account for the delay in language learning. The problem is that there is no demonstrated law-like connection between the processing deficits observed in some of these children and the pattern of linguistic deficits that they display cross-linguistically. Therefore it is still unclear whether the cognitive and the linguistic disorders are causally connected or simply co-occur in some subjects.

The other two essays in this volume address the issue of the innateness of language in a broader context. Pinker looks at the way in which natural selection could have resulted in a genetic predisposition for language in humans. He suggests that the biological specialization for language in humans is no more miraculous than the elephant's trunk or the bat's echo-location; all are special yet all are the result of known evolutionary processes.

Sussman's essay also is concerned with evolutionary processes. He suggests that the neurological structures that enable humans to construct phonemic categories from variable characteristics in the auditory input evolved from earlier auditory systems that had to solve a similar problem. Therefore, he argues, the ability of humans to do phonemic categorization can be elucidated by neuroethological studies of other creatures, such as the barn owl, that have to solve a similar problem.

Two other papers at the conference were directly concerned with discovering the neurological properties of human brains that appear to deal with language. At the conference Al Galaburda and John Marshall presented evidence from developmental and acquired disorders of language that showed that there is some neurological substrate that subserves language. Unfortunately, neither paper was available in time for this volume.

Two important kinds of evidence that have been used to support the innateness of language are not included in this volume: evidence from the study of existing languages and from the normal acquisition of language. Though this evidence is interesting and important, its force depends on understanding the details of the specific principles of grammars and of seeing the ways in which these principles are instantiated. Providing a comprehensive view of this evidence would take us well beyond the scope of a single volume, and furthermore the work is already widely available. Though there are no chapters that specifically address these issues, their influence is evident in several of the other essays.

I would like to thank all of the participants in the conference and the contributors to this volume. Their work has been crucially important

in the elucidation of these issues and they all contributed enormously
to what was a very interesting conference. I would also like to thank
Prof. Steven Davis for inviting me to organize the conference on the biology of language and to edit this book. His help and encouragement
have been invaluable. I would also like to thank the Social Sciences and
Humanities Research Council (SSHRC) of Canada, the publication
committee and the Dean of Arts of Simon Fraser University for supporting this work, Tanya Beaulieu for her work on the on-site arrangements and the organizing committee of Vancouver Studies in Cognitive Science. For their assistance in the preparation of this volume I
would like to thank Lindsey Thomas Martin, Eleanor O'Donnell and
Jenny Dalalakis. For everything I thank my husband Irwin.

Reference

Lenneberg, E.H. (1967). *Biological Foundations of Language.* New York: Wiley

2

Evolution, Nativism and Learning in the Development of Language and Speech

Patricia K. Kuhl and Andrew N. Meltzoff

Introduction

Infants acquire language like clockwork. Whether a baby is born in Stockholm, Tokyo, Zimbabwe or Seattle, at 3 months of age, a typically developing infant will coo. At about 7 months the baby will babble. By their first birthday, infants will have produced their first words, and by 18 months, 2-word combinations. Children of all cultures know enough about language to carry on an intricate conversation by 3 years of age.

When our own daughter began to produce the "bababababa" characteristic of canonical babbling, we were struck by the regularity of its form and the precision of its timing. Having occurred on schedule rather than being accelerated by our ever-constant modelling, we were reminded that the milestones of human language occur at the appointed time regardless of the language in which the child is being reared, the educational background of the infant's parents – and, apparently, regardless of parental prompting or the theories they hold.

Such observations seem to support Chomsky's nativist view that language milestones occur at pre-specified times, as do the eruption of teeth or the onset of puberty. Recent discoveries, however, require revisions to this idea. The emerging view remains strongly nativist, to be sure, but suggests a critical role for language input. The new view provides some insight into how one *particular* language rather than another is acquired. Not only the fact that infants are language-generalists needs explanation (Chomsky's forte), but also the process by which they so quickly become culture-bound language-specialists, adopting a particular "native tongue" that permanently marks them. This indelible mark presents one of the deepest mysteries of early language development: try as one might, unlearning the accent or phonology of one's native tongue is virtually impossible. Henry Kissinger was not born with a German accent, nor Chomsky born with a Philadelphian one. These are not innate characteristics; once acquired, however, they have persisted over decades. Such is the mark of early learning.

The new data also suggest another shift from the standard nativist view. During early development, there is no compelling reason to postulate that the linguistic system functions independently of other cognitive and social systems. We will argue that although the language system may become modularized with development, infants do not begin life with a fully organized language module that is isolated from other aspects of cognition (Fodor 1983).

We will suggest a view that incorporates evolution, nativism and experience in the development of language. Our view embraces the notion that infants are born with abilities highly conducive to the development of language. We are nativists in this sense. These innate abilities *initially structure* the acquisition of language. However, infants' innate abilities do not *solely determine* language. Linguistic experience alters the system in profound ways. It fully restructures the system, and does so quickly, relatively permanently, and via an interesting mechanism that will be described here.

The theory and the arguments we present primarily address the phonetic level of language, the perception and production of the most basic units of language, the consonants and vowels of human speech. The phonetic level has advantages: one can study the comparative, developmental and cross-cultural aspects of the perception and production of speech. Even machines' capabilities to categorize the sounds of language can be tested. It therefore allows a comprehensive look at the underpinnings of humans' linguistic capacity. Our hope is that study of the phonetic level of language may inform theories of language acquisition at other levels.

The more specific goal is to elaborate further the *Native Language Magnet* theory of speech development first described by Kuhl (1992a, 1992b, 1993a, 1993b, 1994). A three-step process in the acquisition of speech is postulated: (a) innate perceptual boundaries exist that are tailor-made for language processing at the phonetic level; (b) exposure to ambient language results in stored representations that reflect the distributional properties of a particular language; and (c) the stored representations act recursively to alter the innately specified boundaries; they profoundly influence the subsequent perception and production of speech in relatively permanent ways. We believe that in early infancy, language acquisition is underpinned by a more general cognitive representational ability like the one described by Meltzoff (1990). This early representational system is polymodal – it is one to which all sensory modalities as well as the motor system has access. Moreover, the type of experience that influences speech representation entails a rather special interaction that occurs with conspecifics (Meltzoff and Gopnik 1993; Meltzoff and Moore 1995); a tape recorder presenting the sounds of language would not trigger it. The specific interweaving of what is "given by nature" and what is "gained from experience" is the story we will tell.

Nativism: Initial Structure for Phonetic Categorization

Infants have innate perceptual abilities that support the acquisition of language at the level of speech. Two pieces of evidence stand out: (a) categorical perception, a phenomenon showing that infants' perceptual systems partition sound to roughly define the phonetic categories of language; and (b) talker normalization, a phenomenon demonstrating that infants perceive their own vocalizations as "matching" adults' vocalizations, even though the two are physically very different. Even the most sophisticated computers have not succeeded in this special capacity for talker normalization. Yet human infants do so with ease. Such a biological endowment is necessary for infants to acquire the ability to speak themselves.

Categorical Perception

Tests of categorical perception (CP) use a continuum of speech sounds as stimuli. A series of sounds is generated by altering some acoustic variable in small steps. On one end of the series the sounds are identified as one syllable, the syllable /ba/ for example; on the other end of the continuum the sounds are identified as another sound, the syllable /pa/ (Liberman, Cooper, Shankweiler and Studdert-Kennedy 1967) (Figure 1).

Tests of CP ask listeners to identify each one of the sounds in the series. Early researchers expected that the sounds in the series would be perceived as changing gradually from /ba/ to /pa/, with many sounds in the middle of the series sounding "ambiguous" or a poor mixture of the two. That did not occur. Adults reported hearing a series of /ba/'s that abruptly changed to a series of /pa/'s. There was no in-between. When researchers asked listeners if they could hear the difference between two adjacent /ba/'s (or /pa/'s) in the series, they could *not* do so, even though the two /ba/'s (or /pa/'s) were physically different. Listeners did not hear differences between adjacent stimuli in the series until they heard a sudden shift – the change from /ba/ to /pa/. The fact that listeners' responses were "categorical" gave the phenomenon its name.

CP is sensitive to linguistic experience (Miyawaki, Strange, Verbrugge, Liberman, Jenkins and Fujimura 1975). For adults, CP occurs only for sounds in their native language. When Japanese listeners were tested on a series of sounds that ranged from /ra/ to /la/ (a distinction that is not phonemic in Japanese), they did not hear a sudden change

An acoustic continuum
with equal physical steps

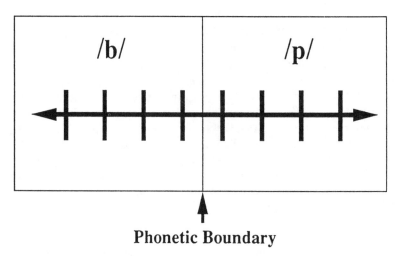

Phonetic Boundary

Figure 1: Categorical perception is tested using sounds from a computer-generated series. The sounds vary in equal steps along an acoustic dimension; however, perception changes abruptly at the location of the phonetic boundary between the two categories.

at the boundary between /ra/ and /la/. They heard no change at all. (This is why Japanese speakers tend to substitute /l/ for /r/ in speech.) Nonetheless, American listeners reported hearing a series of /ra/'s that changed suddenly to a series of /la/'s (Figure 2, top). The bottom half of Figure 2 compares the American and Japanese discrimination data. American listeners showed the characteristic peak in discrimination at the location of the /r-l/ boundary; Japanese listeners did not show this peak in discrimination at the phonetic boundary. Their performance in discriminating /ra/ from /la/ was at chance throughout the series (Figure 2, bottom).

The Americans were unlikely to have one set of innate endowments (a /ra/-/la/ detector) and Japanese another; that CP was language-specific suggested that it might be learned. Perhaps this learning arose as a result of hearing words with different referents contrasting /b/ and /p/ – like "bat" and "pat." If so, then very young infants would not be expected to show CP.

The relevant study was done by Eimas, Siqueland, Jusczyk and Vigorito (1971). Infants' responses to a /ba-pa/ series were monitored using a specially designed technique that relied on the measurement of sucking. The results showed that young infants demonstrated CP. Moreover, infants demonstrated the phenomenon not only for the

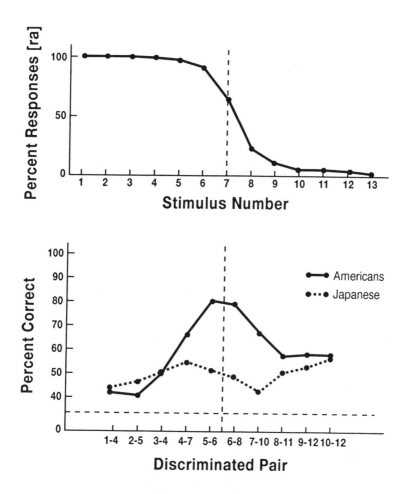

Figure 2: An example of categorical perception for the syllables /ra/ and /la/. American listeners identify sounds in the series (top) and show the characteristic peak in discrimination at the location of the phonetic boundary (bottom). Japanese listeners do not show the peak in discrimination. Redrawn, with permission, from K. Miyawaki, W. Strange, R. Verbrugge, A.M. Liberman, J.J. Jenkins and O. Fujimura (1975), An effect of linguistic experience: The discrimination of [r] and [l] by native speakers of Japanese and English. *Perception and Psychophysics* 18: 331–40.

sounds of their own native language, but also for sounds from many foreign languages (Streeter 1976, Lasky, Syrdal-Lasky and Klein 1975). Although adults were "culture bound," infants were not: they were primed to be members of any linguistic culture, "citizens of the world."

It can be concluded that infants' auditory perception is tailored to language processing at birth. Moreover, this does not depend on experience. Infants behave this way even for sounds they have never before heard. The puzzle that remains (to be discussed later) is when, why and by what mechanism adults "lose" a language-related ability that is present at birth.

Talker Normalization

The studies on CP show some rudimentary structure available to infants that helps them partition the perceptual space into gross divisions. However, perception of a phonetic category requires something more. In order to perceive a phonetic category, infants have to be able to perceive *similarity* among sounds that belong to a particular category, even though they are discriminably different. When different people produce the same vowel sound, one can hear the differences between them but one can also hear their identity. This is phonetic constancy despite auditory discriminability, categorization that renders discriminably different things equivalent.

This categorization ability is critical to infants' acquisition of speech. Infants' vocal tracts cannot produce the frequencies produced by an adult's vocal tract, so they cannot create the exact frequencies that an adult produces. Infants must hear the commonality between the vowels they are capable of producing and those produced by adults in order to learn to speak. Computers cannot yet be programmed to "perceive" these kinds of similarities across a wide range of talkers. Would naïve infants outperform the smartest computers in perceiving a perceptual similarity, *constancy*, for the same vowel produced by different talkers?

Kuhl demonstrated that infants have the ability to sort vowels by phonetic category regardless of the talker producing the sound (Kuhl 1979; 1991b). Figure 3 shows the results of two studies. Shown in the top panel are infant data from an /a-i/ categorization experiment (Kuhl 1979), and in the bottom panel, results from an /a-ae/ categorization experiment (Kuhl 1991b). In both, infants were initially trained to produce a head turn to a single vowel from Category 1 produced by a male speaker, but not to produce the head turn to a single vowel from Category 2 by the same speaker. The first and third panels show the results of the training data; infants master this task at the 90% correct level in short order. During the test phase of the experiment, novel exemplars are presented from both Category 1 and 2, produced by new male, female and child talkers. The results of these studies (second and fourth panels) demonstrated that infants generalize their head-turn response to the novel vowels of Category 1, but not Category 2, which is predicted by the hypothesis that infants are capable of perceptually sorting the novel vowels into two phonetic categories.

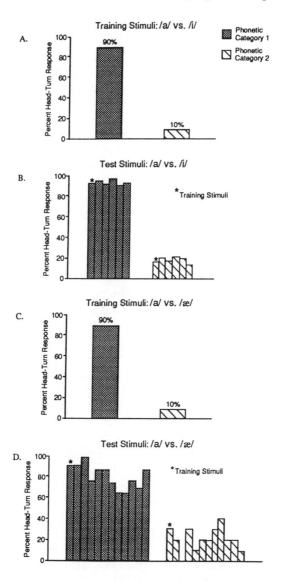

Figure 3: Categorization data from 6-month-old infants. Infants are trained until they reach 90% correct performance on the discrimination of two vowels spoken by a single speaker, panel A (/a/ vs. /i/), panel C (/a/ vs. /ae/). Infants were then tested using vowels produced by many speakers, including new male, female, and child speakers (panels B and D). Performance indicates that infants can perceptually sort vowels into phonetic categories regardless of the speaker who produces the vowel. From P.K. Kuhl (1991b), Perception, cognition, and the ontogenetic and phylogenetic emergence of human speech. In S.E. Brauth, W.S. Hall and R.J. Dooling (eds.), *Plasticity of Development*, 73–106. Cambridge, MA: MIT Press.

Infants succeeded for both relatively easy vowel contrasts such as /a/ versus /i/, and difficult contrasts such as /a/ (as in "pot") versus /ae/ (as in "pat"). In the /a -ae/ case, the vowels were naturally produced by 12 different men, women and children. Voices that sounded very different were purposely chosen. Women with exceptionally high voices, men with deep voices, even people with colds who sounded very nasal but could be understood. The stimuli would have confused even the most complex computer designed to categorize phonetic units. Infants had no trouble sorting these vowels into categories despite these acoustic differences. Talker normalization has now been shown in 2-month-old infants (Marean, Werner and Kuhl 1992) and newborns (Walton, Shoup-Pecenka and Bower 1991).

These two perceptual abilities – CP and perceptual constancy – are innate foundations for speech and language learning. The CP phenomenon shows that infants parse the sound stream in a way that segments the basic units of speech. CP provides "basic cuts" in the acoustic stream that coincide with linguistic categories. Talker normalization provides another benchmark. The physical (acoustic) disparity between the voices of different individuals is so extreme that it prevents computers from correctly categorizing speech across a wide range of talkers; it is still unknown what makes for "/i/-ness" in a vowel sound spoken by different talkers – the essence of /i/ cannot be identified by any known algorithm. But the biological mechanism available to infants picks out the /i/-ness of a vowel despite who says it. It recognizes phonetic units that remain invariant or constant despite the acoustic differences of gender, colds and the like. The combined findings of CP and vowel categorization constitute strong evidence that infants are evolutionarily prepared for language acquisition.

Effects of Experience: Stored Representations and Formation of the Brain's Perceptual Maps

Infants are innately prepared to hear the sounds of a universal language. Adults' perception of speech is more restricted and culture-bound, which suggests an odd or reverse sort of learning. One of us, P.K. Kuhl, was graphically reminded of this. She was visiting a speech laboratory in Japan, preparing to test Japanese infants' perception of the American English /r/ and /l/ sounds. As the stimuli began to play out of the loudspeaker, her seven Japanese colleagues (1 professor, 3 graduate students and 3 undergraduate students) gathered in the sound-proof booth. Kuhl listened as crystal clear versions of /ra/ and /la/ played from the loudspeaker, pleased that the computer disk had survived the trip and that the experiment was ready to run. She looked at her Japanese colleagues as they quizzically looked at each other.

"Which is it?" one finally queried. Not a single one of the Japanese adults could identify whether the sound coming out of the loudspeaker was /ra/ or /la/, nor even identify when the sound changed from one to the other. This was true even though all of them understood a certain amount of English, and could communicate with Kuhl. It was a powerful reminder that the effects of language experience leave a mark on our perceptual abilities.

A similar example is that of American English listeners who have great difficulty hearing the difference between the Spanish /b/ and /p/, sounds that are perceived as belonging to the same phonetic category (/b/) in American English but are easily distinguished by Spanish listeners (Abramson and Lisker 1970). These examples show how the "language-general" pattern of phonetic perception we possessed as infants has become "language-specific." When, how and why does this happen?

Werker and her colleagues showed that by the end of the first year of life there is a change in infants' perception of foreign-language phonetic contrasts (Werker and Tees 1984; Werker and Lalonde 1988; Werker and Pegg 1992). At this age, infants demonstrated a failure to discriminate foreign contrasts that they earlier showed an ability to discriminate. It was suggested that it might be mediated by the acquisition of word meaning (Werker 1991). It was thought that by 12 months, infants had begun to learn which sounds made a difference in their language and that they had began to ignore the phonetic variations that did not make a difference in word meaning.

However, more recent results from Kuhl's laboratory show that infants' perception of speech is altered by language exposure much earlier in life, which radically altered our view of the mechanism underlying this change. The new findings show that by 6 months, exposure to language has already altered infants' perception of speech (Kuhl, Williams, Lacerda, Stevens and Lindblom 1992). This new finding suggests that the change in infants' perception of speech does not depend on the acquisition of word meaning. What is the nature of this change and how is it brought about?

Phonetic Prototypes

Recent work in Kuhl's laboratory has produced an effect that helps explain how language experience alters speech perception and production. The effect shows that language experience alters the perceived distances between speech stimuli – that it, in effect, "warps" the perceptual space underlying speech.

The effect, termed the *perceptual magnet effect*, was uncovered in experiments using phonetic "prototypes," the best or most representative instances of a phonetic category (Kuhl 1991a; Kuhl et al. 1992; Kuhl 1993a, 1993b, 1993c, 1994; Iverson and Kuhl 1995, in press). Experiments on visual prototypes were orignially done by Rosch, who defined them as "good instances" of categories, instances that are representative of the category as a whole (Rosch 1975, 1978; Posner and Keele 1968). It has been demonstrated that the prototypes of categories are special – they are easier to classify, easier to remember, and often preferred over other members of a category (Mervis and Rosch 1981; Rosch 1975, 1977).

Initial studies in Kuhl's laboratory on phonetic prototypes were undertaken with adults to establish whether listeners perceived that the members of speech categories differed in quality (Kuhl 1991a). Three discoveries were made: (a) listeners are very good at identifying phonetic prototypes, sounds that were the best instances of the category; (b) phonetic prototypes are language specific in adults; and (c) phonetic prototypes have a unique function in perception, acting as "magnets" for other sounds in the category.

First, studies revealed that adult listeners were very good at identifying best instances or prototypes of the consonants and vowels of their native language (Davis and Kuhl 1992, 1993; Grieser and Kuhl 1989; Iverson and Kuhl 1995, in press; Kuhl 1991a, 1992a). Listeners' goodness ratings revealed "hot spots," places in acoustic space where ratings for a particular category were very high. As one moved away from that location, the ratings consistently dropped. Moreover, these ratings were language specific. American listeners had hot spots in places the Swedes did not and vice versa (Kuhl 1992b). This was true even for the same phonetic unit. For example, the /i/ judged best by the Swedes was located in a different place than the /i/ judged best by the Americans. The data suggested that the adults of different languages mapped the vowel space very differently, with varying numbers and locations of vowel hot spots.

A second finding revealed the psychological effect of the prototype. Prototypes acted as "perceptual magnets" for other sounds in the phonetic category. When listeners heard a prototype of a phonetic category and were asked to compare the prototype to similar sounds that surrounded it in an acoustic space (Figure 4 A), the prototype displayed an attractor effect on the sounds (Figure 4 B) (Kuhl 1991a). The prototype perceptually pulled other members of the category towards it. Poor instances from the same category (non-prototypes) did not function in this way.

How does the magnet effect work? Studies using multidimensional scaling (MDS) techniques reveal that the magnet effect distorts the perceptual space underlying a phonetic category (Iverson and Kuhl 1995, in press; Kuhl and Iverson 1995). Specifically, MDS was used

A.

B.

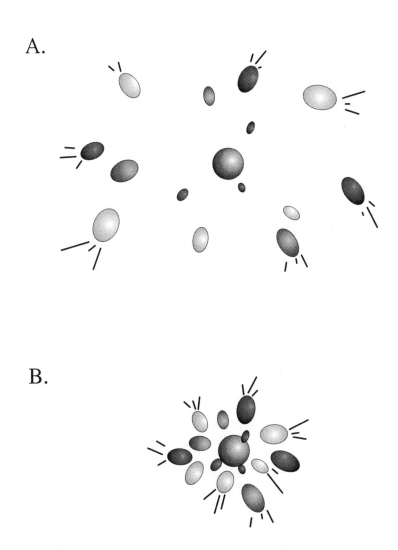

Figure 4: The perceptual magnet effect: When a variety of sounds in a category surround the category prototype (A), they are perceptually drawn towards the prototype. The prototype appears to function like a magnet for other stimuli in the category. From P.K. Kuhl (1993b), Infant speech perception: A window on psycholinguistic development. *International Journal of Psycholinguistics* 9: 33–56.

to assess potential *contraction* and *expansion* of the perceptual space underlying vowels.

Subjects were tested with vowel stimuli spaced at equal physical distances in vowel space. Listeners first identified the stimuli as either the /i/ in the word "he" or /e/ in the word "hey." They then rated the category goodness of each vowel on a scale from 1 (poor) to 7 (excellent). Finally, they listened to all pairs of the 13 stimuli and judged whether the tokens in each pair were the same or different. If a pair of sounds were very different, the subject's reaction time (RT) was quite short; if the pair of sounds was very similar, the RT was relatively long. Subjects' responses were analyzed using multidimensional scaling techniques (Kruskal 1964) which organize RTs in a spatial array so that pairs of stimuli with long RTs (high similarity) are placed close together, while tokens with short RTs (low similarity) are placed far apart.

The magnet effect predicts a tight clustering in space in the region of the best instances (prototypes), and separation in space for stimuli that approach the boundary between categories. The results supported this hypothesis (Figure 5). Although the actual physical acoustic differences between stimuli were equal, the perceived distance was clearly *reduced* near the prototype, and *expanded* in the region of the boundary between categories. The results suggested that language experience *warped* physical space to produce a perceptual space in which perceived distances were altered. Good stimuli act like perceptual magnets by drawing tokens toward them in perceptual space. Near the boundary between two categories, the perceptual space appears to be stretched. This results in the creation of a "perceptual map" that specifies the perceptual distances and thus the relationships among stimuli. The map helps define speech categories by creating a cluster in the centre of the category and gaps at the boundaries between categories.

Development of Prototype Magnet Effects

The perceptual magnet effect was shown to be powerful for adults. Would infants demonstrate the perceptual magnet effect?

Kuhl (1991a) demonstrated the magnet effect early in life, by 6 months, prior to the time that infants uttered or understood their first words. The next question was the degree to which the magnet effect was the product of linguistic experience. Would all 6-month-old infants, regardless of language experience, exhibit the effect for the same hot spots in vowel space? Or would the effect differ in infants being reared in different language environments? If the hot spots were the same for young infants irrespective of language experience, one could argue that it constituted part of infants' innate biological endowment for language. On the other hand, the hot spots could differ in infants

Acoustic Spacing of Tokens

Best /i/ Tokens

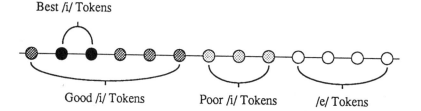

Good /i/ Tokens   Poor /i/ Tokens   /e/ Tokens

Perceptual Spacing of Tokens (One Dimensional MDS Solutions)

2500 millisecond Interstimulus Interval

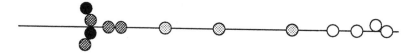

Figure 5: Acoustic and perceptual spacings of vowels. Vowel tokens are equidistant from one another in acoustic space; however, in perceptual space, distance is distorted. Perceptual space is shrunk in the region of the best instances of /i/ and stretched in the region of the poorest instances. From P. Iverson and P.K. Kuhl (1994), Mapping the perceptual magnet effect for speech using signal detection theory and multidimensional scaling. *Journal of the Acoustical Society of America* 97: 553–62.

being reared in different language environments. By 6 months of age, infants have heard a considerable amount of native-language input, and this might alter perception.

The two alternatives were tested by conducting a cross-language experiment involving English and Swedish and using vowel prototypes from both languages (Kuhl et al. 1992). Swedish was an ideal language to test the hypothesis. Infants in Sweden hear naturally occuring speech that includes three different high-front vowels, none of which is identical to American English /i/. The Swedish vowel we chose to test was the front rounded /y/, a vowel that is not produced by American adults and is thus never heard by American babies. The Swedish /y/ prototype vowel and its 32 variants were synthesized using the same techniques used to create the American English /i/ and its variants. The entire laboratory and the research team travelled to Stockholm, Sweden.

This ensured that all aspects of the tests in the two countries were identical except the language experience of the infants who were tested.

The results clearly showed that the perceptual magnet effect in 6-month-old infants was affected by exposure to a particular language. American infants demonstrated the perceptual magnet effect for the American English /i/; they treated the Swedish /y/ as a non-prototype. Swedish infants showed the opposite pattern. They demonstrated the perceptual magnet effect for the Swedish /y/ and treated the American English /i/ as a nonprototype. The data indicate a strong interaction between language environment of the infant and the sound tested. No other effects were significant. The results demonstrated an effect of language experience that was measurable by 6 months of age, clearly demonstrating that infants' exposure to ambient language alters their perception of language. This is the earliest age at which experience has been found to affect phonetic perception.

Language Experience and the Formation of Memory Representations for Speech

Kuhl (1991a, 1992a, 1993a, 1993c, 1994) argued that infants listening to language form representations of speech, creating some type of memory for the sounds of their native language. The kind of learning and memory described here is not conscious learning of specific facts or events. It could not be described as explicit, "declarative" memory (Sherry and Schacter 1987; Squire 1987; Tulving 1983, 1985). The kind of learning and memory demonstrated by infants who learn from listening to ambient language is unconscious, automatic and not due to extrinsic reinforcement; it is probably best thought of as non-declarative memory of some (as yet undefined) type. Although information about the nature of declarative memory and the brain mechanisms that control it is rapidly increasing (Squire 1987), much less is known about non-declarative memory. Such memory is likely to be species-typical and relatively permanent. It might be implicated in the type of permanent changes involved in producing an indelible "accent" or in hearing foreign-language contrasts.

If memory representations are being created as infants listen to speech, two issues will need to be addressed in future studies. Both have to do with the amount of detail preserved in speech representations: (a) do speech representations consist of individual exemplars or abstract summaries? and (b) how are the effects of speech context reflected in the representations?

Considering the first issue, early theorists assumed that because representative instances (prototypes) of categories were associated with special effects, this meant that people mentally calculated and stored some abstract version that characterized the category as a whole (Posner and Keele 1968). It was thought that perhaps an average of all the experienced exemplars was derived. An alternative, "exemplar-based" model of categorization has recently gained support (Estes 1993; Hintzman 1986; Medin and Barsalou 1987; Nosofsky 1987). According to this model, classification and the effects of good stimuli on perception can be accounted for by the storage and retrieval of individual exemplars. Exemplar theories maintain that newly encountered items act as retrieval cues to access stored individual exemplars from a category. Since the most representative (prototypic) stimuli are similar to a large number of individual exemplars, they are more likely to be accessed quickly. Thus the exemplar model offers an alternative explanation for the results of studies showing superior or more efficient recognition of prototypic items from a category.

As Estes (1993) and others have pointed out, both models account for prototype effects. In the case of speech it is not yet clear what form the underlying representation of phonetic categories might take. The magnet effect is compatible with either type of representation. Speech category information might be stored in terms of an abstract summary or as individual instances (see Kuhl 1993b, 1993c for further discussion). We underscore an additional point: there is nothing that precludes people from having access to both kinds of memory systems – one that stores information about individual exemplars and also a system that stores general category information that is derived from individual exemplars (see, e.g., Knowlton and Squire 1993).

Another issue with regard to representation is the effect of context. There are data to suggest that the location of best instances of the category shifts with changes in variables such as the rate of speech (Miller and Volaitis 1989; Volaitis and Miller 1992; Miller 1994). Similarly, we would expect that the location of the best instance of /i/ would shift with the gender of the speaker. What we do not yet know is whether a good instance produced by a male talker has an effect on perception of instances spoken by a female talker. Is the magnet's attractor effect restricted to variants that share basic parameters (such as the gender of the speaker) with the tested stimulus, or does it extend to tokens in which these basic parameters have been changed? If the representation is talker-neutral, as suggested by infants' perception of constancy for the speech of different talkers, one would expect the magnet's attractor effect to generalize.

Memory Representations for Speech Are Polymodal

The discussion thus far has concerned auditory perception. However, we do not think that speech representations are unimodal, nor do we think that they are confined to perception. Our hypothesis is that speech representations – prototypes and the magnet effects they cause – are *polymodally mapped*, that is, they are defined in such a way that multiple sensory and motor systems have access to them. Data in support of this view come from both perception and production studies.

Perception

It was classically thought that the speech we perceived was based solely on the auditory information that reached our ears. This belief has been deeply shaken by data showing that speech perception is an intermodal phenomenon in which vision plays a role in determining what a subject reports hearing. Visual information contributes to speech perception even in the absence of a hearing impairment and even when the auditory signal is perfectly intelligible. In fact, it appears that when it is available, visual information cannot be ignored by the listener; it is automatically taken into account.

One of the most compelling examples of the polymodal nature of speech are auditory-visual "illusions" that result when discrepant information is sent to two separate modalities. Subjects report perceiving a syllable that is halfway between the one sent to the auditory and the visual system (McGurk and MacDonald 1976; Green and Kuhl 1989, 1991; Green, Kuhl, Meltzoff and Stevens 1991; Kuhl et al. 1994; Massaro 1987a, b; Summerfield 1979). One such illusion can be demonstrated when auditory information for /b/ is combined with visual information for /g/. Perceivers report the phenomenal impression of /d/ despite the fact that this information was not delivered to either sense modality.

The effect is robust and mandatory, even when a situation is created in which the discrepant information is derived from two clearly different talkers. We created a situation in which there was an obvious discrepancy between the gender of the talker presenting the information in the two modalities (Green et al. 1991). A male face was combined visually with the voice of a female talker, and vice versa. We took pains to choose our speakers such that the gender incompatibility was highly salient. A very male-looking football player's face was paired with a high and feminine-sounding female voice, and vice versa. There was no mistaking the gender mismatch.

The results showed that even though the gender discrepancy was readily apparent to viewers, they nonetheless integrated the auditory and visual information, reporting that they perceived the illusory consonant /d/. The effect was as pervasive in the gender-discrepancy situation as it was when the gender of the talker remained constant. The results show that even in situations in which the two inputs could not have derived from a common biological source, the integration of the information from the two modalities is not disrupted. Observers knew that the two inputs did not go together; yet they were compelled to integrate them. This demonstrates how thoroughly speech is poly-modally specified.

Even very young infants appear to represent speech polymodally. Infants reveal their knowledge in two situations: when watching and listening to another person speak, and when attempting to imitate a sound they hear another produce. We demonstrated that 18- to 20-week-old infants recognize auditory-visual connections, akin to what we as adults do when we lipread (Kuhl and Meltzoff 1982, 1984; Kuhl, Williams and Meltzoff 1991). In the experiment, infants viewed two filmed faces, side by side, of a woman pronouncing two vowels silently, the vowel /a/ and the vowel /i/ (Figure 6). The faces pronouncing the

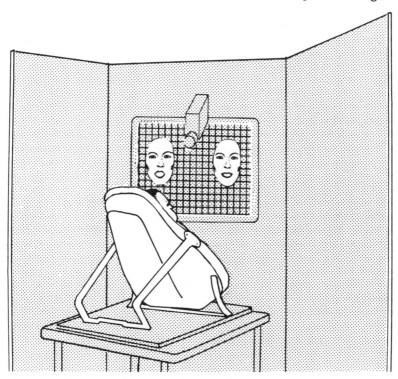

Figure 6: Technique used to test infant cross-modal (auditory-visual) speech perception. Infants watched two faces, side-by-side, producing two different vowels, /a/ and /i/. At the same time they listened to a single vowel (either /a/ or /i/) presented from a loudspeaker located midway between the two faces. The results demonstrated that 18- to 20-week-old infants looked longer at the face that matched the vowel they heard. From P.K. Kuhl and A.N. Meltzoff (1982), The bimodal perception of speech in infancy. *Science* 218: 1138–41.

two vowels opened and closed in perfect synchrony; one mouthed the vowel /a/ and the other the vowel /i/. While viewing the two faces, infants heard one of the two vowels (either /a/ or /i/), played from a loudspeaker located midway between the two faces. The sound was played in synchrony with the two facial movements. The results of the test showed that infants who heard the vowel /a/ looked longer at the face pronouncing /a/, while the infants who heard the vowel /i/ looked longer at the face pronouncing /i/. The only way infants could do this is by recognizing the correspondence between the auditory and visual speech information – there were no temporal or spatial clues telling the infant which face uttered the sound. The experiment shows that by 4 months, infants appear to know that an /a/ sound "goes with" a face mouthing /a/, while an /i/ vowel "goes with" a face mouthing /i/. Infants' cross-modal speech perception abilities indicate that they are beginning to recognize the relationship between sound and articulatory movement, at least when they observe another person speak. (See also MacKain, Studdert-Kennedy, Spieker and Stern 1983; Walton and Bower 1993.)

Production

Can infants relate sound to movement in their own speech? Studies on vocal imitation offer evidence that infants hearing an auditory signal know what to do with their own articulators to produce the sounds themselves. In a recent experiment, infants' vocalizations in response to speech were recorded at three ages – at 12, 16 and 20 weeks (Kuhl and Meltzoff, in press). Infants listened to a woman producing one of three vowels, /a/, /i/, or /u/ . Infants' vocalizations were analyzed perceptually by having them phonetically transcribed, and analyzed instrumentally using computerized spectrographic techniques.

Two findings are noteworthy. First, there was developmental change in infants' vowel productions. Figure 7 displays the vowels of 12-, 16- and 20-week-old infants in an acoustic space. In each graph, infants' vowel utterances are classified according to a transcription provided by a phonetically trained listener. The closed circles enclose 90% or more of the utterances in each category. As shown, utterances in each of the three categories formed clusters in acoustic space. More importantly, the areas of vowel space occupied by infants' /a/, /i/, and /u/ vowels become progressively more *separated* between 12 and 20 weeks of age. Infant vowel categories were more tightly clustered at 20 weeks than at 12 weeks. What causes the increased separation of vowel categories over this relatively short (8-week) period? We suggest that infants listening to their ambient language have begun to form *memory representations* of vowels; these representations serve as "targets" that infants

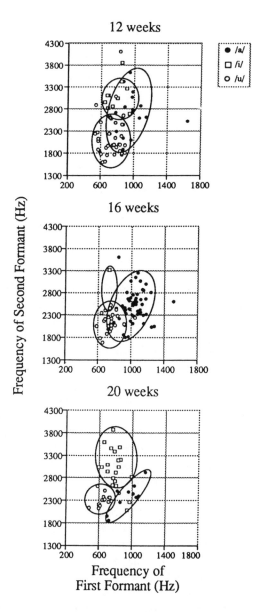

Figure 7: The location of /a/, /i/, and /u/ vowels produced by 12-, 16- and 20-week-old infants. The curves were drawn by visual inspection to enclose 90% or more of the infants' utterances. Across age, infants' vowel productions show tighter clustering in vowel space. From P.K. Kuhl and A.N. Meltzoff (in press), Infant vocalizations in response to speech: Vocal imitation and developmental change. *Journal of the Acoustical Society of America.*

try to match. Our view is that the memory representations resulting from infants' exporsure to ambient language influences not only their perception of speech but their subsequent productions as well.

A second result of the study demonstrated that infants' vowel productions can be influenced by short-term exposure to sound. Infants' vowel productions were influenced by what they heard. Infants produced more /a/-like utterances when exposed to /a/ than when exposed to /i/ or /u/; similarly, they produced more /i/-like utterances when exposed to /i/ than when exposed to /a/ or /u/; finally, they produced more /u/-like utterances when exposed to /u/ than when exposed to /a/ or /i/. In short, infants vocally imitated the gross spectral quality of the stimulus they heard.

The surprising thing was that the total amount of exposure that infants received was only 15 minutes (5-min. exposure to a specific vowel for each of three days). If 15 minutes of laboratory exposure to a vowel is sufficient to influence infants' vocalizations, then listening to the ambient language for 12 weeks certainly provides sufficient exposure to induce change. There is some evidence from the results of babbling studies conducted on infants from different cultures that 1-year-olds in different cultures have begun to be influenced by native-language input (de Boysson-Bardies, Sagart and Durand 1984; de Boysson-Bardies, Halle, Sagart and Durand 1989). The new experimental data demonstrate that even short-term laboratory exposure is sufficient to alter infants' vocal productions.

How do 12-week-old infants know how to move their articulators in a way that achieves a specific auditory target? Some primitive tendency for human speech to drive infants' vocal productions may exist that is analogous to the innate tendency for visually perceived body movements to drive corresponding motor acts, as manifest in newborn gestural imitation (Meltzoff and Moore 1977, 1983, 1992, 1994). Meltzoff and Moore have shown that in the absence of sound, infants imitate movements that involve the speech articulators, such as mouth opening and tongue protrusion (Meltzoff and Moore 1977). The youngest infant tested in this work was 42 minutes old. This is truly an innate ability, one documented in the first *hour* of postnatal life (Meltzoff and Moore 1983). We do not know if an innate mapping from auditory to articulatory events exists, but it is not out of the question, given Meltzoff and Moore's findings of visual-motor mappings of mouth movements used in speech.

Even if primitive connections exist initially, they must be rapidly expanded to create the repertoire that infants possess just a short time later. This rapid expansion is gained, we believe, through experience as infants engage in cooing and sound play. Infant cooing, which begins at about 4 weeks of age, allows extensive exploration of the nascent auditory-articulatory map during which (self-produced) auditory events are related to the motor movements that caused them. Presumably, infants' accuracy in producing vowels improves as infants relate the acoustic consequences of their own articulatory acts to the acoustic targets they heard. This account implies that infants not only have to be able to hear the sounds produced by others, but that they need to hear the results of their own attempts to speak in order to make progress. Both hearing the sound patterns of ambient language (auditory exteroception) and being able to hear one's own attempts at speech (auditory proprioception) are critical determinants of vocal development.

Social Context: Motherese and the Effects of Language Input

The cross-language perception results, coupled with the developmental change in vocal production, suggest that as infants listen to early speech their perception-motor system is being altered. Infants are bathed in language from the time they are born, and this early language experience affects them. What do we know about the nature of early linguistic input?

We know that the prosodic characteristics of "motherese" are unique: it has a higher pitch, a slower tempo and exaggerated intonation contours (Fernald and Simon 1984). We also know that this speaking style is near universal in the speech of caretakers around the world when addressing infants (Grieser and Kuhl 1988). Motherese is socially pleasing and attention-getting, and parents from almost all cultures use it when speaking to their infants. Research has also shown that infants prefer to listen to motherese over speech that is directed towards another adult (Fernald 1985; Fernald and Kuhl 1987). Motherese attracts infants' attention. Are the phonetic units contained in motherese somehow special?

Motherese is "vowel-drenched," and the vowels contained in motherese tend to be prolonged due to its slower tempo. A recent study in Kuhl's laboratory examined the phonetic content of motherese. Women were recorded speaking naturally to their 2-month-old infants and to an adult. They were told to use three words containing the vowel /i/ in both conversations: "bead," "keys," and "sheep." The three words were edited out of these dialogues and rated by adults using the 7-point goodness rating scale. The study revealed that the vowels contained in motherese were perceived as better instances than the same vowels spoken by the same women when addressing an adult. The vowels of motherese may thus be ideal signals for learning.

Are the higher pitch and expanded intonation contours typical of motherese *necessary* for learning? Our guess is that they are not. The context in which language is presented to the child – both the auditory characteristics of motherese and its visual aspects (greatly exaggerated facial expressions) – grab infant attention and fix it on the talking caretaker. This might maximize learning but exaggerated pitch and intonation are probably not necessary for language learning. It would be useful to examine whether interaction with another human being is necessary for this kind of learning to occur. Infants have been shown innately to react to other humans (Meltzoff and Moore 1983, 1993, 1995), and learning often occurs in interpersonal encounters. A person may be a biological signal that triggers the kind of learning we have described. Nonetheless, we would be interested in knowing whether infants can learn language information in the absence of a person. Would, for example, an infant's perception of speech be altered by playing Berlitz language tapes via a device hung on the infant's crib.

Evolution: Are Language Precursors Uniquely Human?

Language in human infants, even at the level of phonetics, has been shown to have multiple determinants: innate perceptual predispositions; magnet effects that alter perceptual space; a cognitive system that forms memory representations accessible to multiple modalities and (possibly) social interaction among people. Is this entire set of abilities uniquely human? Are any aspects of this composite common to humans and other animals? Modern studies of speech perception reveal that some of the speech effects found in human infants can be replicated by a monkey (see Kuhl 1991b for summary). Others appear to be uniquely human. The relevant studies have been done with three different phenomena – CP, speech prototypes and auditory-vocal mapping – and the points of convergence and divergence between monkeys and humans is of considerable interest.

Tests of CP were conducted by Kuhl and colleagues on animals whose auditory systems are very similar to humans', such as chinchillas and monkeys (Kuhl and Padden 1982, 1983; Kuhl and Miller 1975). The results showed that animals responded as though they heard a sudden change in the speech stimuli at the exact location where human adults perceived a shift from one phonetic category to another.

These findings on animals influenced our theories of infants. It showed that the innate CP effects in human infants are not, in themselves, evidence compelling the postulation of a speech module. Evidently, CP can be accomplished in the absence of a speech module, because animals also show the same CP effects as human newborns. Kuhl theorized that CP in infants – the perception of "basic cuts" – was attributable to a *general auditory processing mechanism* rather than a special language module, and that it was very deeply embedded in our phylogenetic history (Kuhl and Miller 1975, 1978; Kuhl 1988). On this view, the perception of basic cuts in auditory signals, which would have been available in early hominids, was exploited in the evolution of the sound system used in language (Kuhl 1987, 1991b). It may have helped in determining which oral sounds were good candidates for language to use.

In contrast to CP, humans and animals strongly diverge in tests examining the prototype's magnet effect (Kuhl 1991a). Monkeys displayed no magnet effect; they equated variants to the prototype and the non-prototype to the same degree. Whether or not animals would learn speech prototypes if they were repeatedly exposed to speech in a social setting is an interesting question. We doubt that the kind of learning that we have described for speech would take place in monkeys. It would be even less likely to take place if we placed a tape recorder playing the sounds of language inside the monkey's cage. The kind of learning that we are describing may well require a social setting and interaction among conspecifics. (Monkeys would perhaps exhibit magnet effects for the perception of their own calls.) We thus offer the hypothesis that the formation of perceptual representations based on experience is innately guided and species-specific. Human infants may have to interact with other persons who are perceived as "like me" (Meltzoff and Gopnik 1993; Meltzoff and Moore 1995) before this kind of learning is triggered.

Is the cross-modal representation of speech information species-specific? Non-human primates may lack the cross-modal connections between the auditory-vocal channel necessary for both auditory-visual speech perception and for vocal imitation. *Homo sapiens* is the only mammal that displays vocal learning, the tendency to acquire the species-typical vocal repertoire by hearing the vocalizations of adults and mimicking them. Humans share this ability with a few avian species, the songbirds (Marler 1976; Konishi 1989), who learn their species-specific songs if they are exposed to them during a sensitive period early in life (Nottebohm 1975). In the case of birds there are data showing that learning is enhanced in the presence of a visual instance of the species. In fact, the presence of a conspecific bird allows a young bird to learn some of the notes of an alien species. This suggests how intricately woven the mechanisms of learning may be with social (hormonal?) aspects.

A Theory of Early Speech Development

The diverse research described here has been integrated into a model of the development of speech perception called the *Native Language Magnet* (NLM) theory (Kuhl 1992a, 1993a, 1993b, 1994). The theory encompasses the initial state as well as the changes brought about by experience with language. It explains how infants' developing speech representations alter both speech perception and speech production.

NLM theory holds that what is "given by nature" is the ability to partition the sound stream into gross categories separated by natural boundaries. As illustrated in Figure 8, these boundaries are what is tested in studies of CP. Tests of CP have shown that infants are sensitive to the acoustic cues that underlie phonetic distinctions (both consonants and vowels) in language. Infants' abilities to partition the acoustic stream serves to *initially structure* phonetic perception.

The boundary effects associated with CP are also displayed by non-human animals. Thus, perceptual boundaries are not due to an innate module that evolved for language. Infants' abilities to hear the relevant differences between phonetic units is innate, but is based on a long phylogenetic history and attributable to general auditory processing mechanisms. These general auditory processing abilities are neither language-specific nor species-specific.

By 6 months, infants have something more than the innate "basic cuts" for phonetic perception. By 6 months, infants show *language-specific* magnet effects, due to memory representations of the sound patterns of the ambient language. The development of magnet effects is illustrated in Figure 9. Here magnet effects are schematically presented for infants being raised in Sweden, America and Japan. Both the number and location of vowel sounds differ across the three languages. The graphs are not meant to precisely mark the locations of vowel magnets

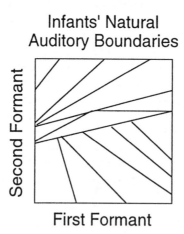

Infants' Natural Auditory Boundaries

Second Formant

First Formant

Figure 8: At birth, infants perceptually partition the acoustic space underlying phonetic distinctions in a language-universal way. They are capable of discriminating all phonetically relevant differences in the world's languages. From P.K. Kuhl (1994), Learning and representation in speech and language, *Current Opinion in Neurobiology* 4: 812–22.

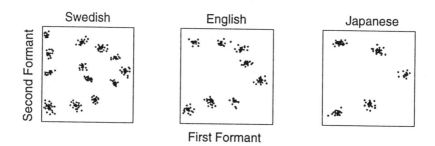

Figure 9: By 6 months of age, infants reared in different linguistic environments show an effect of language experience. They exhibit language-specific magnet effects that result from listening to the ambient language. From P.K. Kuhl (1994), Learning and representation in speech and language, *Current Opinion in Neurobiology* 4: 812–22.

but to convey in conceptual terms that linguistic experience in the three different cultures has resulted in magnet effects (memory representations with magnet-like properties) that differ in number and location for infants growing up listening to the three different languages.

Magnet effects are the result of infants' stored representations of language input. These representations are derived from infants' analysis of the distributional properties of speech produced by native speakers of the language, mostly but not exclusively in interaction with them. Infants' analysis of ambient language results in learning of the properties of the native language; as a result, infants commit a particular language's regularities to memory. Infants' initial perceptual boundaries assist this process: boundaries set limits on the area that infants' representations must organize. Because of this, infants do not form representations that encompass the entire vowel space; instead, infants' representations organize input that falls within a bounded area of the vowel space. The innate partitioning (Figure 8) thus constrains and helps organize language input to the child.

Effects of Speech Representations on Speech Perception

What effects do infants' stored representations (shown in Figure 9) have on speech perception? According to NLM, of speech stored in memory representations are responsible for the magnet effect observed in experiments. However, infants' stored representations go beyond this and affect the perception of foreign-language sounds as well. The warping of acoustic space causes certain perceptual distinctions to be minimized (those near the magnet attractors) while others are maximized (those near the boundaries between two magnets). The result is that some of the boundaries that innately divided the space "disappear" as the perceptual space is reconfigured to incorporate a language's particular magnet placement. This is schematically illustrated in the diagrams of Figure 10. Magnet effects functionally erase certain boundaries – those relevant to foreign but not native languages.[1]

NLM thus offers an explanation for two related findings: (a) infants' loss of discrimination of foreign-language contrasts they once had (Werker 1991), and (b) adult reactions to foreign sounds. According to NLM, the developing magnet pulls sounds that were once discriminable towards a single magnet, making them no longer discriminable. The prediction is that magnet effects occur first, before the failure to discriminate; they developmentally precede and underlie the changes in infants' perception of foreign-language contrasts. They thus offer a *mechanism* that explains the change in phonetic perception that Werker observed. The magnet effect also helps account for the results of studies on the perception of sounds from a foreign language by adults. These studies suggest that phonetic units from a foreign language that are similar to a category in the adult's own native language are particularly difficult to perceive as different from the native-language sound; sounds not similar to a native-language category are relatively easy to discriminate (Best 1993; Best, McRoberts and Sithole 1988). The theory accounts for this because the prototype of, for example, the Japanese category is similar to both /r/ and /l/; its magnet effect makes the two sounds difficult for native-speaking Japanese people to discriminate. The prediction from this theory is that the difficulty posed by a given foreign-language unit will depend on its proximity to a native-language magnet. The nearer it is to a magnet, the more it will be pulled toward the native-language category, making it indistinguishable from the native-language sound. One way to visualize the effects of native-language magnet effects on foreign-language sounds is to imagine that native-language representations serve as filters for in-

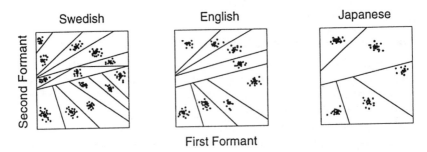

Figure 10: After language-specific magnet effects appear, certain phonetic boundaries are functionally "erased." From P.K. Kuhl (1994), Learning and representation in speech and language, *Current Opinion in Neurobiology* 4: 812–22.

coming sounds; the sounds of a second language have to be "pulled through" the filters formed by the first.

Effects of Speech Representations on Production

Human infants learn speech by listening to ambient language and attempting to produce sound patterns that match what they hear. The specific inventory of phonetic units, words and prosodic features employed by a particular language are learned largely through imitation (broadly construed). By 2 years of age, infants have begun to "sound like" a native speaker of their language.

The theory developed here attributes infants' learning of the speech patterns to the memory representations formed in early infancy by listening to ambient language. The speech patterns stored in memory serve as "targets" that infants try to match. The data gathered in our study of infant imitation (Kuhl and Meltzoff, in press) provided evidence of long-term change in infants' vocal repertoires, changes that occurred over the 8-week period (from 12 to 20 weeks) during which infants' vocalizations were measured (Figure 7), as well as evidence of short-term change in infants' vocalizations, changes that occurred with 15 minutes of laboratory exposure. These findings strongly suggest that infants' acquisition and production of speech is highly influenced by the auditory information that surrounds them. Speech representations learned in early infancy drive infants' early production of speech and account for the fact that adult speakers produce speech with an "accent." Hearing a specific language early in life puts an indelible mark on one's speech.

Two streams of research – that linguistic exposure alters infants' perception of speech (Kuhl et al. 1992) and linguistic exposure alters infants' production of speech (Kuhl and Meltzoff, in press) – can thus be unified by the suggestion that memory representations of speech underlie both findings. The emerging view suggests that the tighter clustering observed in infant vowel production and the tighter clustering among vowels in infant perception are both attributable to a common underlying mechanism – the formation of memory representations that derive initially from perception of the ambient input and then act as targets for motor output (Figure 11). The speech representational system is thus deeply and thoroughly polymodal. Early experience affects both sensory perception and motor learning.

Summary and Conclusions

We have described a three-step theory of speech development (Native Language Magnet theory or NLM), which embraces nativism, evolution and learning in the development of speech.

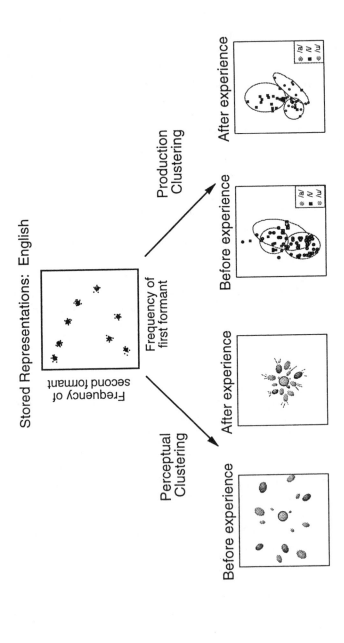

Figure 11: Infants' stored representations affect both speech perception, producing the perceptual clustering evidenced by the magnet effect, as well as speech production, producing the increased clustering seen in infants' vocalizations. From P.K. Kuhl (1994), Learning and representation in speech and language. *Current Opinion in Neurobiology* 4: 812–22.

Native Language Magnet Theory

Phase 1: Infants are born with innate boundaries that partition the incoming speech stream into phonetically relevant categories. Innate perceptual abilities undergird language learning. Auditory boundaries deeply embedded in our phylogenetic history strongly influenced the original selection of sounds used in the world's languages. Infants' abilities are thus derived from a mechanism that is innate and attributable to a general auditory processing mechanism (not a language module per se).

Phase 2: Exposure to ambient language results in speech representations, stored memories of the sound patterns that reflect the distributional properties of the infant's native language. Infants' stored representations of speech have unique psychological properties and indicate a special kind of learning. Regarding the psychological properties, two facts stand out. First, stored representations produce perceptual magnet effects: members of the category are clustered in perceptual space. Thus we say that perceptual magnets *warp* the underlying space. Second, stored representations are polymodal, coding not only the auditory properties of language but its visual and motor aspects as well. Stored representations thus contain information from a variety of modalitites. Regarding learning, the kind of learning described here is not the typical stimulus-response learning with external reinforcement that psychologists often describe. It is unconscious, automatic, long-lasting and extremely difficult to undo. This kind of learning is likely to be species-specific and highly constrained.

Phase 3: Perceptual space is reconfigured such that certain innate perceptual boundaries have been functionally erased. The theory is recursive in the sense that the output of phase 2 reaches back and reorganizes the innately given framework. A space characterized by simple boundaries has been replaced by a dynamically warped space dominated by magnets.

What NLM Theory Accounts For

The Native Language Magnet theory accounts for a wide variety of facts in the perception and production of speech by infants and adults. Some of these are the following.

(a) The loss of discrimination that was innately present. Infants' language-general speech perception abilities change to ones that are language-specific. By the end of the first year, infants fail to discriminate contrasts that they once demonstrated the ability to discriminate. According to the theory, this change is due to the development of speech representations and their corresponding magnet effects.

(b) Speech production converges on target sounds of the native language. Infants' language-general speech production capabilities change to ones that are language-specific. According to the theory, the production system is guided by infants' speech representations. Infants babble, and in doing so they provide themselves with the opportunity to compare the auditory results of their own productions to the representations stored in memory. This sound play also enriches the sensory-motor map specifying the relationship between mouth movements and sound. The map helps infants correct their motor movements to converge on the intended target, which is specified in the memory representation.

(c) Second-language learning is difficult for adults. Memory representations for speech are formed early during a period in which we are particularly sensitive to language experience. These representations and the magnet effects they cause can be thought of as forming a set of filters through which all subsequent language input passes. The set of filters established when we learn our primary language subsequently interferes with the ability to acquire a second language. This is because the filters required to process the second language do not match those that characterize the first.

(d) "Accent." Speakers of different languages, and even speakers of the same language who speak different dialects, exhibit an "accent," a speaking pattern that identifies them as coming from a particular language group. Accents involve motor patterns that are unconsciously learned. Accents indelibly mark our speech even after we acquire a new language, providing evidence of interference between the production pattern of one's primary language and the production pattern of a new language.

(e) Early learning is long-lasting and difficult to alter. The effects on speech perception and speech production are long-lasting and difficult to change. The acquisition of a second language past puberty is more difficult than at an earlier age. This is also true for the elimination of an accent. Our native language indelibly marks us through the formation of representations that "distort" future inputs but are not easily changed by them. Once acquired, the altered magnet-induced perceptual map and the magnet-driven production patterns that characterize our native language resist change.

(f) Polymodal effects: Visual speech perception is mandatory. If infants' stored representations of speech have encoded both the auditory and visual aspects of speech, then one would expect that when visual information accompanies speech, observers would be compelled to take

that information into account. This result has been confirmed in numerous experiments on auditory-visual speech perception in adults. The fact that infants of only 18 weeks demonstrate an ability to relate auditory speech to its visual concomitants further supports the view that the representations are polymodal in nature right from the earliest phases of life.

Final Thoughts

Our research shows that infants' innate abilities initially structure language growth. In that sense we are nativists. However, these innate abilities do not solely determine language. The three-step model we described shows how linguistic experience yields representations that recursively alter the innately provided system in a profound and long-lasting way.

The type of learning we described does not correspond to Skinner's conditioning and extrinsic reinforcement. Nor is the restructuring well captured by the notion that "learning" is simple triggering nor by the idea that "learning" is the deletion or subtraction of information that was innately present. It is true that perceptual boundaries are innately determined and then deleted (in a sense), but the deletion of boundaries would not, by itself, produce the phonology of a particular language. The critical information for a mature phonology is not where the boundaries are located. The critical information for phonology is where in phonetic space a particular language locates its category centres and the distribution of members around those centres. Particular languages utilize only some of the bounded spaces and place category prototypes in different locations within bounded spaces. The functional erasure of boundaries is thus a secondary process caused by the formation of phonetic category centers, hot spots in space that vary as a function of ambient language input. It is the formation of category centres and the perceptual similarity space that surrounds them that needs to be understood in seeking the developmental roots of a particular language's phonology.

The learning we have described in speech development – unconscious, automatic and long lasting – is species-typical and probably species-specific. The learning itself may have two biological constraints. It may require social interaction with other humans – the recognition of other humans itself being innately specified (Meltzoff and Moore 1995). For this reason, infants' perception may not be altered by playing Berlitz language tapes. A further constraint is provided by a neural system prepared to receive input at a particular time in ontogenesis, described by Greenough as an "experience-expectant" neural process (Greenough and Alcantara 1993; Greenough and Black 1992).

Greenough argues that neural systems are prepared for experience by an overproduction of synaptic connections that are subsequently pruned to achieve a more efficient neural organization. Synaptic overproduction occurs for cases in which a specific kind of experience is highly reliable in the environment of the organism. Language input is a reliable feature of infants' early postnatal growth. Thus, evolution, nativism and experience all meet in the human infant. The indelible mark of early speech or language learning may be traceable to a biological preparation for receiving language input from other humans during the first years of life.

Acknowledgment

Preparation of this chapter was supported by grants from NIH (HD-22514, HD-18286, and DC 00520).

Note

1 Work on adults suggests that the boundaries do not literally disappear; with-training it is possible to increase performance on the discrimination of foreign-language contrasts in adults (e.g., MacKain, Best and Strange 1981; Logan, Lively and Pisoni 1991). Thus the alterations that occur do not involve changes at a sensory level, but ones at a higher level involving memory and/or attention.

References

Abramson, A.S., and L. Lisker (1970). Discriminability along the voicing continuum: Cross-language tests. In *Proceedings of the Sixth International Congress of Phonetic Sciences Prague 1967*, 569–73. Prague: Academia

Best, C.T. (1993). Emergence of language-specific constraints in perception of non-native speech: A window on early phonological development. In B. de Boysson-Bardies, S. de Schonen, P. Jusczyk, P. McNeilage and J. Morton (eds.), *Developmental Neurocognition: Speech and Face Processing in the First Year of Life*, 289–304. Dordrecht: Kluwer

Best, C.T., G.W. McRoberts and N.M. Sithole (1988). Examination of perceptual reorganization for nonnative speech contrasts: Zulu click discrimination by English-speaking adults and infants. *Journal of Experimental Psychology: Human Perception and Performance* 14: 345–60

Davis, K., and P.K. Kuhl (1992). Best exemplars of English velar stops: A first report. In J.J. Ohala, T.M. Nearey, B.L. Derwing, M.M. Hodge and G.E. Wiebe (eds.), *Proceedings of the International Conference on Spoken Language Processing*, (495–98). Edmonton, AB: University of Alberta

——— (1993). Acoustic correlates of phonetic prototypes: Velar stops. *Journal of the Acoustical Society of America* 93: 2392 de Boysson-Bardies, B., P. Halle, L. Sagart and C. Durand (1989). A crosslinguistic investigation of vowel formants in babbling. *Journal of Child Language* 16: 1–17

de Boysson-Bardies, B., L. Sagart and C. Durand (1984). Discernible differences in the babbling of infants according to target language. *Journal of Child Language* 11: 1–15

Eimas, P.D., E.R. Siqueland, P. Jusczyk and J. Vigorito (1971). Speech perception in infants. *Science* 171: 303–6

Estes, W.K. (1993). Concepts, categories, and psychological science. *Psychological Science* 4: 143–53

Fernald, A. (1985). Four-month-old infants prefer to listen to motherese. *Infant Behavior and Development* 8: 181–95

Fernald, A., and P. Kuhl (1987). Acoustic determinants of infant preference for Motherese speech. *Infant Behavior and Development* 10: 279–93

Fernald, A., and T. Simon (1984). Expanded intonation contours in mothers' speech to newborns. *Developmental Psychology* 20: 104–13

Fodor, J.A. (1983). *The Modularity of Mind: An Essay on Faculty Psychology.* Cambridge, MA: MIT Press

Green, K.P., and P.K. Kuhl (1989). The role of visual information in the processing of place and manner features in speech perception. *Perception and Psychophysics* 45: 34–42

———— (1991). Integral processing of visual place and auditory voicing information during phonetic perception. *Journal of Experimental Psychology: Human Perception and Performance* 17: 278–88

Green, K.P., P.K. Kuhl, A.N. Meltzoff and E.B. Stevens (1991). Integrating speech information across talkers, gender, and sensory modality: Female faces and male voices in the McGurk effect. *Perception and Psychophysics* 50: 524–36

Greenough, W.T., and A.A. Alcantara (1993). The roles of experience in different developmental information stage processes. In B. de Boysson-Bardies, S. de Schonen, P. Juscyzk, P. McNeilage, and J. Morton (eds.), *Developmental Neurocognition: Speech and Face Processing in the First Year of Life,* 3–16. Dordrecht: Kluwer

Greenough, W.T., and J.E. Black (1992). Induction of brain structure by experience: Substrates for cognitive development. In M. Gunnar and C. Nelson (eds.), *The Minnesota Symposia on Child Psychology, Vol. 24: Developmental Behavioral Neuroscience,* 155–200. Hillsdale, NJ: Erlbaum

Grieser, D.L., and P.K. Kuhl (1988). Maternal speech to infants in a tonal language: Support for universal prosodic features in motherese. *Developmental Psychology* 24: 14–20

———— (1989). Categorization of speech by infants: Support for speech-sound prototypes. *Developmental Psychology* 25: 577–88

Hintzman, D.L. (1986). "Schema abstraction" in a multiple-trace memory model. *Psychological Review* 93: 411–28

Iverson, P., and P.K. Kuhl (1995). Mapping the perceptual magnet effect for speech using signal detection theory and multidimensional scaling. *Journal of the Acoustical Society of America* 97: 553–62

—— (in press). Influences of phonetic identification and category goodness on American listeners' perception of /r/ and /l/. *Journal of the Acoustical Society of America.*

Knowlton, B.J., and L.R. Squire (1993). The learning of categories: Parallel brain systems for item memory and category knowledge. *Science* 262: 1747–49

Konishi, M. (1989). Birdsong for neurobiologists. *Neuron* 3: 541–49

Kruskal, J.B. (1964). Multidimensional scaling by optimizing goodness of fit to a nonmetric hypothesis. *Psychometrika* 29: 1–27

Kuhl, P.K. (1979). Speech perception in early infancy: Perceptual constancy for spectrally dissimilar vowel categories. *Journal of the Acoustical Society of America* 66: 1668–79

—— (1987). The special-mechanisms debate in speech research: Categorization tests on animals and infants. In S. Harnad (ed.), *Categorical Perception: The Groundwork of Cognition*, 355–86. New York: Cambridge University Press

—— (1988). Auditory perception and the evolution of speech. *Human Evolution* 3: 19–43

—— (1991a). Human adults and human infants show a "perceptual magnet effect" for the prototypes of speech categories, monkeys do not. *Perception and Psychophysics* 50: 93–107

—— (1991b). Perception, cognition, and the ontogenetic and phylogenetic emergence of human speech. In S.E. Brauth, W.S. Hall, and R.J. Dooling (eds.), *Plasticity of Development*, 73–106. Cambridge, MA: MIT Press

—— (1992a). Infants' perception and representation of speech: Development of a new theory. In J.J. Ohala, T.M. Nearey, B.L. Derwing, M.M. Hodge and G.E. Wiebe (eds.), *Proceedings of the International Conference on Spoken Language Processing*, 449–56. Edmonton, AB: University of Alberta

—— (1992b). Psychoacoustics and speech perception: Internal standards, perceptual anchors, and prototypes. In L.A. Werner and E.W. Rubel (eds.), *Developmental Psychoacoustics*, 293–332. Washington, DC: American Psychological Association

—— (1993a). Innate predispositions and the effects of experience in speech perception: The Native Language Magnet theory. In B. de Boysson-Bardies, S. de Schonen, P. Jusczyk, P. McNeilage, and J. Morton (eds.), *Developmental Neurocognition: Speech and Face Processing in the First Year of Life*, 259–74. Dordrecht: Kluwer

—— (1993b). Infant speech perception: A window on psycholinguistic development. *International Journal of Psycholinguistics* 9: 33–56

———— (1993c). Early linguistic experience and phonetic perception: Implications for theories of developmental speech perception. *Journal of Phonetics* 21: 125–39

———— (1994). Learning and representation in speech and language. *Current Opinion in Neurobiology* 4: 812–22

Kuhl, P.K., and P. Iverson (1995). Linguistic experience and the "perceptual magnet effect." In W. Strange (ed.), *Speech Perception and Linguistic Experience: Issues in Cross-Language Research*. Timonium, MD: York Press

Kuhl, P.K., and A.N. Meltzoff (1982). The bimodal perception of speech in infancy. *Science* 218: 1138–41

———— (1984). The intermodal representation of speech in infants. *Infant Behavior and Development* 7: 361–81

———— (in press). Infant vocalizations in response to speech: Vocal imitation and developmental change. *Journal of the Acoustical Society of America*

Kuhl, P.K., and J.D. Miller (1975). Speech perception by the chinchilla: Voiced-voiceless distinction in alveolar plosive consonants. *Science* 190: 69–72

———— (1978). Speech perception by the chinchilla: Identification functions for synthetic VOT stimuli. *Journal of the Acoustical Society of America* 63: 905–17

Kuhl, P.K., and D.M. Padden (1982). Enhanced discriminability at the phonetic boundaries for the voicing feature in macaques. *Perception and Psychophysics* 32: 542–50

———— (1983). Enhanced discriminability at the phonetic boundaries for the place feature in macaques. *Journal of the Acoustical Society of America* 73: 1003–10

Kuhl, P.K., M. Tsuzaki, Y. Tohkura and A.N. Meltzoff (1994). Human processing of auditory-visual information in speech perception: Potential for multimodal human-machine interfaces. In *Proceedings of the International Conference on Spoken Language Processing*, 539–42. Tokyo: Acoustical Society of Japan

Kuhl, P.K., K.A. Williams, F. Lacerda, K.N. Stevens and B. Lindblom (1992). Linguistic experience alters phonetic perception in infants by 6 months of age. *Science* 255: 606–8

Kuhl, P. K., K.A. Williams and A.N. Meltzoff (1991). Cross-modal speech perception in adults and infants using nonspeech auditory stimuli. *Journal of Experimental Psychology: Human Perception and Performance* 17: 829–40

Lasky, R.E., A. Syrdal-Lasky and R.E. Klein (1975). VOT discrimination by four to six and a half month old infants from Spanish environments. *Journal of Experimental Child Psychology* 20: 215–25

Liberman, A.M., F.S. Cooper, D.P. Shankweiler and M. Studdert-Kennedy (1967). Perception of the speech code. *Psychological Review* 74: 431–61

Logan, J.S., S.E. Lively and D.B. Pisoni (1991). Training Japanese listeners to identify English /r/ and /l/: A first report. *Journal of the Acoustical Society of America* 89: 874–86

MacKain, K.S., C.T. Best and W. Strange (1981). Categorical perception of English /r/ and /l/ by Japanese bilinguals. *Applied Psycholinguistics* 2: 369–90

MacKain, K., M. Studdert-Kennedy, S. Spieker and D. Stern (1983). Infant intermodal speech perception is a left-hemisphere function. *Science* 219: 1347–49

Marean, G.C., L.A. Werner and P.K. Kuhl (1992). Vowel categorization by very young infants. *Developmental Psychology* 28: 396–405

Marler, P. (1976). Sensory templates in species-specific behavior. In J.C. Fentress (ed.), *Simpler Networks and Behavior*, 314–29. Sunderland, MA: Sinauer

Massaro, D.W. (1987a). Psychophysics versus specialized processes in speech perception: An alternative perspective. In M.E.H. Schouten (ed.), *The Psychophysics of Speech Perception*, 46–65. Boston: Nijhoff

——— (1987b). *Speech Perception by Ear and Eye: A Paradigm for Psychological Inquiry.* Hillsdale, NJ: Erlbaum

McGurk, H., and J. MacDonald (1976). Hearing lips and seeing voices. *Nature* 264: 746–48

Medin, D.L., and L.W. Barsalou (1987). Categorization processes and categorical perception. In S. Harnad (ed.), *Categorical Perception: The Groundwork of Cognition*, 455–90. New York: Cambridge University Press

Meltzoff, A.N. (1990). Towards a developmental cognitive science: The implications of cross-modal matching and imitation for the development of representation and memory in infancy. In A. Diamond (ed.), *The Development and Neural Bases of Higher Cognitive Functions: Annals of the New York Academy of Sciences* 608: 1–31

Meltzoff, A., and A. Gopnik (1993). The role of imitation in understanding persons and developing a theory of mind. In S. Baron-Cohen, H. Tager-Flusberg and D.J. Cohen (eds.), *Understanding Other Minds: Perspectives from Autism*, 335–66. New York: Oxford University Press

Meltzoff, A.N., and M.K. Moore (1977). Imitation of facial and manual gestures by human neonates. *Science* 198: 75–78

——— (1983). Newborn infants imitate adult facial gestures. *Child Development* 54: 702–9

——— (1992). Early imitation within a functional framework: The importance of person identity, movement, and development. *Infant Behavior and Development* 15: 479–505

——— (1993). Why faces are special to infants: On connecting the attraction of faces and infants' ability for imitation and cross-modal processing. In B. de Boysson-Bardies, S. de Schonen, P. Jusczyk, P. McNeilage and J. Morton (eds.), *Developmental Neurocognition: Speech and Face Processing in the First Year of Life*, 211–25. Dordrecht: Kluwer

——— (1994). Imitation, memory, and the representation of persons. *Infant Behavior and Development* 17: 83–99

———— (1995). Infants' understanding of people and things: From body imitation to fold psychology. In J. Bermúdez, A.J. Marcel and N. Eilan (eds.), *The Body and the Self*, 43–69. Cambridge, MA: MIT Press

Mervis, C.B., and E. Rosch (1981). Categorization of natural objects. *Annual Review of Psychology* 32: 89–115

Miller, J.L. (1994). On the internal structure of phonetic categories: A progress report. *Cognition* 50: 271–85

Miller, J.L., and L.E. Volaitis (1989). Effect of speaking rate on the perceptual structure of a phonetic category. *Perception and Psychophysics* 46: 505–12

Miyawaki, K., W. Strange, R. Verbrugge, A.M. Liberman, J.J. Jenkins and O. Fujimura (1975). An effect of linguistic experience: The discrimination of [r] and [l] by native speakers of Japanese and English. *Perception and Psychophysics* 18: 331–40

Nosofsky, R. (1987). Attention and learning processes in the identification and categorization of integral stimuli. *Journal of Experimental Psychology: Learning, Memory and Cognition* 15: 87–108

Nottebohm, F. (1975). A zoologist's view of some language phenomena with particular emphasis on vocal learning. In E.H. Lenneberg and E. Lenneberg (eds.), *Foundations of Language Development*, Vol. 1, 61–103. San Francisco: Academic Press

Posner, M.I., and S.W. Keele (1968). On the genesis of abstract ideas. *Journal of Experimental Psychology* 77: 353–63

Rosch, E. (1975). Cognitive reference points. *Cognitive Psychology* 7: 532–47

———— (1978). Principles of categorization. In E. Rosch and B. Lloyd (eds.), *Cognition and Categorization*, 27–48. Hillsdale, NJ: Erlbaum

Rosch, E.H. (1977). Human categorization. In N. Warren (ed.), *Studies in Cross-Cultural Psychology*, Vol. 1, 1–49. San Francisco: Academic Press

Sherry, D.F., and D.L. Schacter (1987). The evolution of multiple memory systems. *Psychological Review* 94: 439–54

Squire, L.R. (1987). *Memory and Brain*. New York: Oxford University Press

Streeter, L.A. (1976). Language perception of 2-month-old infants shows effects of both innate mechanisms and experience. *Nature* 259: 39–41

Summerfield, Q. (1979). Use of visual information for phonetic perception. *Phonetica* 36: 314–31

Tulving, E. (1983). *Elements of Episodic Memory.* Oxford: Clarendon Press

———— (1985). Memory and consciousness. *Canadian Psychology* 26: 1–12

Volaitis, L.E., and J.L. Miller (1992). Phonetic prototypes: Influence of place of articulation and speaking rate on the internal structure of voicing categories. *Journal of the Acoustical Society of America* 92: 723–35

Walton, G.E., and T.G.R. Bower (1993). Amodal representation of speech in infants. *Infant Behavior and Development* 16: 233–43

Walton, G.E., A.G. Shoup-Pecenka and T.G.R. Bower (1991). Speech categorization in infants. *Journal of the Acoustical Society of America* 90: 2296

Werker, J. (1991). The ontogeny of speech perception. In I.G. Mattingly and M. Studdert-Kennedy (eds.), *Modularity and the Motor Theory of Speech Perception*, 91–109. Hillsdale, NJ: Erlbaum

Werker, J.F., and C.E. Lalonde (1988). Cross-language speech perception: Initial capabilities and developmental change. *Developmental Psychology* 24: 672–83

Werker, J.F., and J.E. Pegg (1992). Infant speech perception and phonological acquisition. In C.A. Ferguson, L. Menn, and C. Stoel-Gammon (eds.), *Phonological Development: Models, Research, Implications*, 285–311. Timonium: York

Werker, J.F., and R.C. Tees (1984). Cross-language speech perception: Evidence for perceptual reorganization during the first year of life. *Infant Behavior and Development* 7: 49–63

3

In the Beginning: On the Genetic and Environmental Factors That Make Early Language Acquisition Possible

Laura Ann Petitto

1. Introduction

My journey towards understanding the biological foundations of human language has crossed a diverse path, involving (a) comparative analyses of two different species – apes and humans; (b) comparative analyses of languages in two different modalities – signed and spoken; and (c) comparative analyses of the structure, grammar and acquisition of different signed languages. In trying to understand the biological foundations of a capacity, it is first necessary to determine the extent to which the capacity is species-specific. Hence, while still a college undergraduate, I moved into a large mansion on the Hudson Palisades in New York with an infant, West-African male chimpanzee, named "Nim Chimpsky." This animal was part of a research project at Columbia University in which I attempted to raise the chimp like a child and to teach him signed language. Our research question concerned whether aspects of human language were species-specific or whether human language was entirely learnable (and/or teachable) from environmental input (Terrace, Petitto, Sanders and Bever 1979).

Although there is much controversy surrounding the ape language research, what has remained surprisingly uncontroversial about all of the ape language studies to date is this: all chimpanzees fail to master key aspects of human language structure, even when you bypass their inability to produce speech sounds by exposing them to other types of linguistic input, for example, natural signed languages. In other words, despite the chimpanzees' general communicative and cognitive abilities, their linguistic abilities do not equal humans ability with language, whether signed or spoken. This fact suggested to me the hypothesis that humans possessed something at birth in addition to the mechanisms for producing and perceiving speech sounds per se. Indeed, whatever this elusive "something" was, I knew that attempts to understand it would provide the key to what distinguishes human language and thought from the communication of other animals.

2. Research Questions

Since working with Nim, my research has been motivated by basic questions in Cognitive Science and Cognitive Neuroscience concerning the neural architecture underlying language acquisition in the developing brain. I ask two general questions of the infant and of the environment: (1) Are infants born with any innate mechanisms that aid them in the task of acquiring language? If so, are any of these mechanisms specifically sensitive to the unique organizational properties found only in natural language, or are general perceptual mechanisms sufficient for discerning the regularities of linguistic structure? (2) Are some aspects of the environmental input more critical than others in order to begin and to maintain the language acquisition process?

Most contemporary answers to the above questions have been based on the fundamental presupposition that the infant's emerging linguistic abilities are determined by the mechanisms underlying the production and perception of speech per se and/or mechanisms of general auditory perception. Given that only languages utilizing the speech modality are studied (i.e., spoken languages), it is in principle, *a priori*, impossible to find data that would do anything but support this hypothesis. Only by examining languages in another modality (i.e., signed languages) can we more fully determine the relative contribution of motor production and perception constraints – versus other factors (e.g., abstract regularities of linguistic structure) – to the time course and nature of early human language acquisition.

In my laboratory, I compare hearing and deaf infants' acquisition of spoken and signed languages. Because spoken and signed languages utilize different modalities (acoustic versus visual), and because the motor control of spoken and signed language articulators are subserved by different neural substrates in the brain, comparative analyses of these languages provide key insights into the specific neural architecture that determines early human language acquisition. Indeed, the existence of these languages permits us to tease apart which aspects of language acquisition reflect *modality-specific* properties of the language transmission and reception modality, and which aspects reflect *modality-free* properties of language representation in the developing brain.

Here I summarize two unique sets of findings about human language acquisition that have resulted from over a decade of research in my laboratory involving comparative analyses of very young children's acquisition of spoken and signed languages. One index of whether a capacity is under biological control is whether it develops along a specific time course. Thus, in the first set of findings, I address the issue of the timing of linguistic milestones in early language acquisition as well as the critical environmental input factors that may (or may not) determine them.

Another index of whether a capacity is under biological control is whether (and, if yes, how) it is expressed in the face of fundamental change to the organism (the change may be either environmental and/or morphological). For example, in the case of language, I examine acquisition in the absence of sound, and acquisition in the face of radical morphological change to the language articulators and receptive mechanisms at the moment of birth. Thus, in the second set of findings, I ask whether infants are born with any innate mechanisms that aid them in the task of acquiring language by examining the presence or absence of structural homologies in the very early linguistic productions of sign- and speech-exposed infants. In the final pages of this chapter, I articulate a theory that best explains these facts of very early language acquisition, and I consider the impact of the present work on our understanding of the phylogeny of language in our species.

3. Research Findings

3.1. Timing Milestones: Identical Time Course in Speech and Sign Acquisition

3.1.1. *Hearing children acquiring a spoken language and deaf children acquiring a signed language from birth.* To investigate whether certain aspects of the environmental input are more critical than others in early language acquisition, I conducted comparative analyses of monolingual hearing children acquiring spoken languages (English or French) and monolingual deaf children acquiring signed languages (American Sign Language, ASL, or Langue des Signes Québécoise, LSQ), ages 8 months through 4 years. (ASL and LSQ are distinct, naturally evolved signed languages. Neither ASL nor LSQ are based on the majority spoken languages used around them, English or French, respectively, and LSQ is grammatically distinct from the signed language used in France.)

The most striking finding is that deaf and hearing children acquire signed and spoken languages (respectively) in virtually identical ways, despite dramatic differences in the modalities. Deaf children acquiring signed languages from birth do so without any modification, loss or delay to the timing, sequence, content and maturational course associated with reaching all linguistic milestones observed in spoken language (Petitto 1984, 1986, 1987a, 1988, 1992; Petitto and Marentette 1990). Beginning at birth and continuing through age 5 and beyond, speaking and signing children exhibit the identical stages of language acquisition, including the "syllabic babbling stage" (7 to 10 months approximately) as well as other developments in babbling, including variegated babbling (ages 10 to 12 months) and jargon babbling (ages 12 months and beyond), "first word stage" (11 to 18 months approximately), "first two-word stage" (18 to 22 months approximately), and systematic morphological and syntactic developments (for example, "over-regularizations," negation, question formation and so forth, 22 to 36 months approximately and beyond). Signing and speaking children also exhibit remarkably similar semantic, pragmatic, discourse as well as conceptual complexity. Indeed, analyses of signing children's social and conversational patterns of language use over time and the types of things that signing children "talk" about over time (i.e., the semantic and conceptual content, categories and referential scope of their "talk") have demonstrated unequivocally that their language acquisition follows the identical path as is observed in age-matched hearing children acquiring spoken language (Charron and Petitto 1991; Petitto 1992; Petitto and Charron 1988).

The present findings are very surprising.[1] Despite modality differences, deaf and hearing children acquiring signed and spoken languages (respectively) do so in highly similar ways, and they do so on an identical time course. The findings cast doubt on the hypothesis that the ability to hear and produce speech, per se, determines the time course and content of human language acquisition.

3.1.2. Hearing children acquiring both a spoken and a signed language from birth. To further determine whether speech was critical to language acquisition, a study of hearing children in "bilingual" and "bimodal" homes was conducted (their home environment provided both ASL and spoken English, or, LSQ and spoken French), ages 7 months through 24 months. For example, in these homes, one parent was deaf and used a signed language (e.g., ASL) and the other parent was hearing and spoke (e.g., English; the same holds for homes where both LSQ and spoken French were used). Thus, in these homes, each child was exposed to both a signed language and a spoken language from birth. The results revealed that these children achieved all linguistic milestones in both modalities at the same time (Petitto, Costopoulos and Stevens, in preparation).

The parallels observed in the children's achievement of signed and spoken language milestones cannot be overemphasized. In Petitto, Costopoulos and Stevens (in preparation), the children in all 4 families studied (2 families used ASL and English, and 2 used LSQ and French) achieved vocal and manual babbling, first words and first signs, first two words and first two signs, and so forth, either on the same day or within one or two days of each other. Not only was the overall time course and content of their acquisition similar to that which has been observed in monolingual hearing and deaf children, but the children's patterns of language acquisition exhibited the same time course and content as is seen in other bilingual hearing children acquiring two spoken languages (e.g., spoken French and spoken English: Genesee 1987; Petitto and Marentette 1990; Petitto, Costopoulos and Stevens, in preparation).

These findings are inconsistent with the hypothesis that speech, per se, is critical to language acquisition. They challenge the related hypothesis that speech is uniquely suited to the human brain's maturational needs in language ontogeny, and they raise questions about our views of language phylogeny. If speech, per se, were neurologically privileged in ontogeny, bilingual and bimodal hearing children might be expected to attempt to glean every morsel of speech that they could get from their environment. Faced implicitly with a choice between speech and sign, the very young hearing infant in this context might be expected to turn away from the sign input, favouring instead the speech input, and thereby acquire signs later. This did not happen. Further, *some* vestige of the apparent phylogenetic preference for speech should have been seen in these infants – especially when faced with both types of input. That it was not observed raises questions about many of the presuppositions underlying theories of language phylogeny as well as its neurological roots in ontogeny, which will be discussed further below.

3.1.3. Hearing children with no speech input from birth. I recently began close investigations of a fascinating group of children. Children of the following sort have never before been studied; moreover, the findings from this first-time study have already proven to be theoretically powerful.

Like the children mentioned previously, these children are hearing. Like the hearing children above, they are acquiring two entirely different languages from birth. However, they differ from the bilingual, bimodal hearing children above in an important way. First, unlike the hearing children above, these hearing children are not being exposed to spoken language! In these families, both of the parents are profoundly deaf and both have made the radical decision not to expose their children to spoken language. To be clear, both deaf parents have chosen to expose their hearing children to language in only one modality from birth – specifically, to signs only (rather than to signs and speech). Second, each deaf parent uses a *different* signed language from the other parent. That is, in these families, one deaf parent uses ASL exclusively with the hearing child, and the other deaf parent uses LSQ exclusively with the hearing child. Thus, the hearing children in this study are in a bilingual, *unimodal* (sign-only) environment, whereby they are acquiring two different signed languages from birth (but no spoken language).

A second group of hearing children is also under investigation. These hearing children are also not being exposed to spoken language. They, too, have profoundly deaf parents, but both parents use the same signed language (i.e., both parents use ASL, or, both parents use LSQ). Thus, these hearing children are in a monolingual, unimodal (sign-only) environment, whereby they are acquiring one signed language from birth (but no spoken language).

Why is this population so critical? These children are so interesting because they can hear but they are not being exposed to speech. As such, the children constitute an experiment in nature. Under other circumstances, it would not be possible to intentionally withhold spoken language from a normally hearing child. Thus, by investigating this population, it is possible to answer key questions about the mechanisms that underlie human language acquisition in an entirely novel way. If speech and sound are critical to the human language acquisition process, then these speech-deprived hearing children should demonstrate fundamentally atypical acquisition of signed language. This would be especially true if, for example, several prevailing views about very early language ontogeny are correct. In particular, numerous researchers have claimed that the motoric mechanisms for the production of speech, *determine* the time course, sequence and linguistic and semantic content of early language acquisition (e.g., Locke 1983; Mac-Neilage and Davis 1990; MacNeilage, Studdert-Kennedy and Lind-blom 1985; Studdert-Kennedy 1991; Van der Stelt and Koopmans-van Bienum 1986; more below). On this view, without the guiding force of the development of speech production (and speech perception), the acquisition of signed language in these hearing children should exhibit timing and sequencing anomalies in addition to other peculiarities of a semantic and conceptual nature. Indeed, it could be argued that the bilingual, bimodal hearing children reported in section 3.1.2 above had similar patterns of spoken and signed language acquisition because sign was somehow yoked to speech. The present data address this important hypothesis.

The results revealed that the speech-deprived but sign-exposed hearing children achieved every linguistic milestone in signed language on the identical time course as has been observed for hearing children acquiring spoken language (as well as deaf children acquiring signed language – that is, manual babbling, first signs, first two-sign combinations and so forth). The things that these hearing children signed about (their semantic content, categories, referential scope), the way that the children used signed language (its pragmatic and discourse structure) and the morphological and syntactic complexity of their signed utterances all mirrored that which is seen in children acquiring spoken language. Moreover, the hearing children acquiring two signed languages (but no speech) demonstrated the same overall linguistic developments as bilingual hearing children acquiring two spoken languages. For example, in the first-word stage they avoided the use of signs in each language that stood for the same lexical item (for example, if they produced the sign "cup" in ASL, they would avoid the use of the sign "cup" in LSQ; and there were other intriguing patterns of sign language "mixing"; see Petitto, Costopoulos, and Stevens, in preparation).

The above findings are surprising because normal language acquisition occurred in hearing children (i) without the use of auditory and speech perception mechanisms and (ii) without the use of the motoric mechanisms for the production of speech. Recall that most all accounts of early language acquisition root the infant's emerging linguistic abilities in the mechanisms for the production and perception of speech, per se, and/or mechanisms of general auditory perception.

Thus, the results of these studies provide dramatic support for the claim that speech and sound are not critical to the language acquisition process. Again, the children can hear but they are receiving no spoken language input – only sign. Moreover, our findings here fail to support the hypothesis that language acquisition proceeded normally in the bilingual, bimodal (speech- and sign-exposed) hearing children above, because the acquisition of sign was somehow yoked to the acquisition of speech. We see here that hearing children with no spoken language input nonetheless demonstrated entirely normal patterns of language acquisition, albeit in signed language.

3.1.4. *Summary of timing milestone studies.* We have seen that signed and spoken languages are acquired in virtually identical ways, despite the fact that the brain-based neural substrates are different for both (i) the motor control of speech and sign and (ii) the perception of speech and sign. The above findings, therefore, fundamentally challenge the hypothesis that speech and sound, per se, are critical to the process of language acquisition. The findings also provide support for the hypothesis that language is under maturational control and that unitary timing constraints determine the acquisition of all linguistic milestones, be they spoken or signed (cf. Lenneberg 1967).

Having established that the overall time course, sequence and content of signed and spoken language acquisition are highly similar, questions remain about just how deep the similarities are in acquisition at the specific, structural level. I will now review a series of studies that addresses this issue in an attempt to shed new light on whether (and/or which) innate mechanisms aid very early language acquisition.

3.2. Innate Mechanisms in Early Language Acquisition: Insights from Structural Homologies in Babbling across Different Modalities

3.2.1. *Why Babbling?* A hallmark of human development is the regular onset of vocal babbling well before infants are able to utter recognizable words (Lenneberg 1967). One period of babbling, beginning around age 7 to 10 months, has been referred to as "syllabic vocal babbling." Syllabic vocal babbling is characterized by the infant's (a) use of a reduced subset of possible sounds (phonetic units) found in spoken languages (Locke 1983), (b) syllabic organization (well-formed consonant-vowel clusters: Oller and Eilers 1988) and, crucially, (c) use without apparent meaning or reference (Elbers 1982).

Why has infant babbling received so much scientific attention? In trying to understand the biological roots of human language, researchers have naturally sought to find its "beginning." The regular onset of babbling, as well as its systematic stages in the young infant (despite variation in rearing environments), have lead researchers to conclude that babbling is under maturational control and fundamentally linked to later language development. As such, infant babbling has been universally regarded as representing the "beginning" of human language acquisition (albeit, language production), and it has been the focus of intensive study and theorizing for many decades.

The very existence of babbling and its characteristic stages have been used by researchers to answer one of the most passionately sought after questions in human language ontogeny: How does language acquisition begin? To answer this question, researchers have used their findings about the nature of babbling to advance theories about the infant's brain at the onset of language acquisition. In particular, analyses of babbling have been used to support proposals regarding the underlying neural substrates that may determine (and drive) the maturational time course, sequence and referential content of all of early language acquisition.

As for the answer to the crucial question, the prevailing view about the origins of babbling, and, hence, the beginning of language acquisition in our species, has been that its very syllabic structure is *determined* by the development of the anatomy of the vocal tract and the neuroanatomical and neurophysiological mechanisms subserving the motor control of speech production (Locke 1983; MacNeilage and Davis 1990; MacNeilage, Studdert-Kennedy and Lindblom 1985; Studdert-Kennedy

1991; Van der Stelt and Koopmans-van Bienum 1986). The behaviour has been further used to argue that the human language capacity has a *unique link* to innate mechanisms for producing speech in ontogeny (Liberman and Mattingly 1985, 1989). Crucially, it has also been used to argue that human language has been shaped by properties of speech in phylogeny (Lieberman 1984).

3.2.2. Manual babbling in infants exposed to signed languages from birth. In the course of conducting research on deaf infants' transition from pre-linguistic gesturing to first signs, I first discovered a class of manual behaviours that contained linguistically relevant units, was produced in entirely meaningless ways and was wholly distinct from all other manual activity during the "transition period" (9 to 12 months; Petitto 1984). Further analyses revealed that this class of manual activity constituted genuine instances of *manual babbling* (Petitto 1986, 1987a, 1987b).

An additional study was undertaken to understand better the underlying basis of this extraordinary behaviour. Physical and articulatory analyses (as in acoustic and phonetic analyses of sound) were conducted of all manual activity produced by ASL deaf and English hearing infants, ages 10, 12 and 14 months. The presence of hearing controls in this study was crucial, because it was necessary to determine whether the manual activity observed in deaf infants exposed to signed languages was similar or dissimilar to that which is observed in all infants, even those who are not exposed to signed languages. The findings, reported in Petitto and Marentette (1991), revealed unambiguously a discrete class of linguistically relevant, meaningless manual activity in ASL deaf infants that was structurally identical to the meaningless vocal babbling observed in hearing infants. Crucially, its structure was wholly distinct from all (hearing and deaf) infants' rhythmic manual motor activity as observed by Thelen (1991), Thelen and Ulrich (1991) and others. Further, its structure was wholly distinct from all (hearing and deaf) infants' communicative gestures (Petitto 1988, 1992). Most surprising of all, manual babbling possessed *syllabic organization*. It alone possessed signed-phonetic units and combinations of units that were structurally identical to the phonetic and syllabic organization known only to human language (signed or spoken). The findings raised the following question: Given that the same phonetic and syllabic babbling units are observed to occur across two radically different modalities, where does the common syllabic structure come from?

To understand this question better, a new study was conducted, using innovative technology in an entirely novel way (see Petitto, Ostry, Sergio and Levy, in preparation). Here analyses were conducted of all hearing and deaf infants' rhythmic, non-linguistic hand movements

(Thelen 1991). This manual activity was then compared to sign-exposed infants' rhythmic, opening-closing hand movements – movements that form the nucleus of the signed (and the spoken) syllable (indeed, this behaviour constituted the rhythmic nucleus of the manual activity identified as "syllabic manual babbling"; recall, also, that manual babbling forms were further constrained by the use of restricted sign-phonetic units that were used without apparent reference or meaning).

One goal of this new study was to address an alternative hypothesis from the one that I offer. The alternative hypothesis is as follows: manual babbling does not share syllabic organization with vocal babbling, but is, instead, more similar to all hearing and deaf infants' rhythmic motor activity. A further goal was to identify any universals of syllabic structure in the signed and spoken modalities, should they exist.[2] To conduct this study the powerful OPTOTRACK Computer Visual-Graphic Analysis System was used. The precise physical properties of all infants' manual activity were measured by placing tiny Light-Emitting Diodes (LEDs) on infants' hands and feet. The LEDs transmitted light impulses to cameras that, in turn, sent signals into the OP-TOTRACK system. This information was then fed into computer software that we designed to provide information analogous to the spectrographic representation of speech, but adapted here for the *spectrographic representation of sign*. Thus, for the first time, we were able to obtain recordings of the timing, rate, path movement, velocity and analyses analogous to fundamental frequency (f_o) for all infant hand activity, and to obtain sophisticated, 3-D graphic displays of each. This permitted us to empirically evaluate rhythmic, non-linguistic activity versus rhythmic, linguistic manual activity in infants in a way that (i) has never before been analyzed, and (ii) would be impossible to obtain through the analysis of videotapes alone. This system permitted us to perform the critical analyses of the study, including comparative analyses of the various classes of infant manual activity, deaf (and hearing control) adult-to-adult signing content and "sign prosody, and deaf (and hearing control) adult-to-infant signing content and "sign prosody" (see Petitto, Ostry, Sergio and Levy, in preparation).

Preliminary results reveal the following. (i) Systematic differences have been observed in the rhythmic timing, velocity and spectral frequencies of sign-exposed infants' manual babbling versus all infants' rhythmic hand activity (be they hearing or deaf). (2) Systematic similarities have been observed in the *timing* contours of infants' manual and vocal babbling. (3) Converging structures observed in infant and adult-to-infant signing and speaking productions suggest that all humans at birth may possess peak sensitivity to a rudimentary "timing envelope" – a rhythmic timing bundle in natural language prosody of about 1.2 seconds, which is currently under intensive further investigation (see Petitto, Ostry, Sergio and Levy, in preparation, for a comprehensive discussion of the formal differences between syllabic manual babbling versus other rhythmic manual activities in infants). In addition, early handedness differences may distinguish manual babbling and linguistic productions from other motoric manual activity (Marentette, Girouard and Petitto 1990).

Homologous structural organization was observed in manual and vocal babbling, even though the neural substrates for manual articulation differ from the neural substrates for the articulation of speech. The above research confirms the hypothesis that speech is not critical to the production of babbling or to early language acquisition. This research fails to confirm the alternative hypothesis introduced above; manual babbling was found to be fundamentally different from hearing and deaf infants' other rhythmic motor activity.

Such studies have provided new insights into the relative contribution of the body's motor production constraints on the structure of the syllable in human language (be it spoken or signed), and they have provided a key window into the elementary units of perceptual sensitivity that may underlie very early language acquisition in our species. The implications of the studies above are returned to below, when I propose a theory of early language ontogeny.

3.2.3. Cross-linguistic analyses of manual babbling in infants acquiring ASL and LSQ. Cross-linguistic data have been collected on the entire range of manual activity of ASL and LSQ infants (ages 8 to 20 months; Petitto, in preparation, a). Like vocal babbling, these deaf infants first produced common sign-phonetic units – units that were not drawn from the particular sign-phonetic inventories of either ASL or LSQ. To be clear, infants exposed to signed languages from birth do not manually babble in any particular signed language. However, as is reported for vocal babbling (de Boyssen-Bardies and Vihman 1991), language-specific phonetic units are observed in these infants' manual babbling after or around 12 months. Thus, manual babbling occurs in more than one signed language, and the effects of experience with the target language observed in hearing infants are also observed in deaf infants.

3.2.4. Hearing infants and manual babbling. Surprisingly, bilingual and bimodal hearing infants exposed to signed and spoken languages produced two kinds of babbling – manual and vocal – and did so within the same developmental time period (Petitto, Costopoulos and Stevens, in preparation). Analyses of data from 8 infants (4 ASL and English; 4 LSQ and French) reveal that these infants demonstrate the

same "stages" of babbling in both modalities. The infants also demonstrate intriguing parallels in the overall types of phonological processes that they exhibit, regardless of the modality. Crucially, modality-
specific differences regarding the specific phonological permutations
that are possible and/or impossible in the respective modalities have
also been observed, which are currently under investigation (Petitto,
in preparation, b).

Taken together, the above findings indicate that babbling in early language ontogeny is not restricted to speech. Such cross-modal convergent findings point to the existence of a robust period of human language ontogeny during which infants produce the raw "form" of
language, which may ultimately help them identify the inventory of
units, and permissible combination of units, in their target language
(cf. Jusczyk 1986). These findings also suggest that the syllable may be
a natural unit of language distinctions (Bertoncini, Bijeljac-Babic,
Blumstein and Mehler 1987; Bertoncini and Mehler 1979; Moon, Bever
and Fifer 1992). My ongoing work is providing new insights into the
origin of universal patterns in all infant babbling, as well as modality-
specific differences. As such, these studies are providing a window into
the relative contribution of (i) raw phonological constraints (i.e., linguistic, structural) versus (ii) motor production constraints in early
phonological development.

4. The Genetic Foundations of Language

The key issue for students of early brain development is not the fact
that signed and spoken languages are acquired similarly, but to determine *why* this is so. How is it possible that languages in two radically
different modalities can be acquired on a similar time course? Where
does the capacity to produce common linguistic structures come from,
given that the neural substrates controlling the production of signed
and spoken language differ?

Crucially, how is it possible that the modality of language transmission and reception can be changed at birth – from speech to sign, or vice
versa – without any delay or alteration to the nature and course of human language acquisition? How can the brain tolerate this radical
change in the morphology of its expressive and receptive mechanisms
for language, and what is the genetic basis for such stunning equipotentiality? Why are we justified in proposing that aspects of language
acquisition are under genetic control in the face of such profound environmental influences (in particular, the ability to acquire language in
one or the other modality, depending upon the specific environmental
input)? Indeed, what do the present findings tell us about the role of
genetics in language acquisition?

The present findings demonstrate that the brain at birth cannot be working under rigid genetic instruction to produce and receive language via the auditory, speech modality, per se. If this were the case, both the maturational time course and the nature of signed and spoken language acquisition should be different. By contrast, using a wide variety of techniques and subject populations, I have discovered that the acquisition of signed and spoken language is fundamentally similar.

The present findings suggest that the neural substrates that support the brain's capacity for language can be potentiated in multiple ways in the face of varying environmental pressures. The fact that the brain can tolerate variation in language transmission and reception, depending upon different environmental inputs, and still achieve the target behaviour, provides support for there being a strong *amodal* genetic component underlying language acquisition, rather than the reverse. That is, the genetic foundations of language are not at the level of modality, but at the level of abstract features of *language patterning*.

At birth, there appears to be a genetically determined sensitivity to specific aspects of language patterning – that is, a nascent sensitivity to specific aspects of the raw form or structure of language in the input (specified below). Crucially, there are multiple genetic pathways by which language acquisition can occur. Indeed, recent findings in molecular biology have demonstrated that a key feature of many genomes is that there is a large degree of genetic material that is duplicated. There are multiple pathways by which a human trait can be expressed (Tautz 1992; Wilkins 1993). As such, a growing number of biologists are abandoning simplistic arguments for a single gene locus of traits in favour of a multigenic loci of traits. In this multigenic view, metabolic and cellular networks provide a context for genetic expression (cf. Strohman 1994).

When the multigenic or epigenetic perspective is applied to the present findings, it can be seen that the acquisition of language is most probably achieved through the interaction of many genes and, therefore, it has the potential to be realized in different forms. While there is clearly a genetic component to language and the ability to acquire it, the particular realization of a given genetic component is subject to the modulation and expansion of both (1) other gene products in the brain and (2) environmental input. Thus, the human brain has the capacity to forge neurological connections for speech and for signing, because the articulators for both meet the necessary conditions for the expression and reception of natural language. Both types of articulators can be (i) perceived, (ii) segmented and (iii) produced (and both are inalienable parts of the human body). The maturation of the neurological circuitry of the brain occurs on a particular timetable that can be seen through indices such as babbling, first words, first two-word combinations and the like.

Like the expression of other biological traits under genetic control, what we have witnessed here is a flexibility with regard to the modality of language transmission and/or reception, but a rigidity with regard to the underlying linguistic patterns or structures that are realized. Above I have articulated how it is possible for a capacity to be both under genetic control and still capable of morphological change. That is, I have addressed the issue of genetic flexibility in the face of environmental vagaries.

So what is genetically rigid or fixed? Here I suggest that a sensitivity to aspects of the specific distributional patterns found only in natural language is genetically determined and present at birth. We saw telltale indices of what these elementary structures may be when we observed the linguistic forms that were pushed out onto the hands and pushed out onto the tongue in early language ontogeny, especially manual and vocal babbling. Below I describe the particular mechanism by which genes and environment interact in early language acquisition. I propose that humans are born with a neural substrate that has peak threshold saliency to particular input patterns over others that are relevant to the structure of natural language.

5. A Theory of Early Language Ontogeny

5.1. The Infant: A Pattern or Structure-Recognition Mechanism

Signing infants' and speaking infants' ability to produce common structures (timing milestones and babbling studies) suggests that a common mechanism may be operating across signed and spoken language input. All infants may be born with a sensitivity to units of a particular size with particular distributional patterns in the input regarding aspects of the form or structure of language per se, irrespective of the modality of the input. The hypothesis being advanced here is that this sensitivity reflects the existence of structural constraints at birth – a "structure-recognition mechanism" – by which particular distributional patterns in the input have peak threshold saliency over others. It is further hypothesized that the structure-recognition mechanism is specifically tuned to the unique stimulus characteristics of the input that correspond to two aspects of linguistically organized input – not modality – including (a) input structures that correspond to the rhythmic, timing and stress patterns common to natural language prosody and (b) input structures that correspond to the maximally contrasting, rhythmically alternating patterns common to the level of the syllable in natural language.

5.1.1. The biological plausibility of a mechanism sensitive to particular input patterns over others. Infants' sensitivity to aspects of language structure at birth may be possible due to a structure-sensitive mechanism similar to that which has been postulated for the recognition of faces (Gross 1992; Horn and Johnson 1989; Johnson and Morton 1991). For example, currently it is held there is no single "feature detector" neuron per se, for the detection of faces in the brain, but "patterned ensembles" of neurons (area IT in primates) that are selectively sensitive to particular spatial configurational patterns in the input and not others; and, the particular configurational patterns happen to correspond to just those frequency values that are found in faces (Gross 1992). Similarly, the infant's nascent sensitivity to aspects of language structure may reflect the presence of a neural substrate that is uniquely sensitive to the stimulus values specified in prosodic and syllabic structure. Specifically, the substrate may contain tuned neurons for contrasts and combination-sensitive neurons (Sussman 1984, 1989) which would make possible the infant's initial sensitivity to aspects of input that contain these particular values. Note that I am not proposing that the substrate, should it exist, has a particular language's structure written into it at birth. But it is a mechanism ready to differentially process input signals consisting of the language-specific values specified above (i.e., the rhythmical and temporal variables and maximally contrasting units that are unique to human language prosodic and sub-lexical organization). The nascent sensitivity to these patterns can serve as the foundation upon which knowledge of language is subsequently built.

5.1.2. The role of parental input. Without a doubt, parents' specifically linguistic and general affective interactions with their infants provide enormous clues to language structure. Parents impart structural information using multiple modalities (voice and intonation changes, facial expressions and lip movements etc.; Fernald et al. 1989), which is why it is probably best that the infant's sensitivity to structure is not tied to one modality. However, it would appear that we still need to posit some mechanism by which the infant is made capable of *attending to* particular input structures that will ultimately be relevant to their target language. In other words, there still must be some mechanism that provides the infant with the ability to perceive – in the first place – the adult's voice and/or face cues that are carrying information relevant to early language ontogeny. For example, adult prosodic cues can mark: (a) rhythmic, timing and stress variation that can regulate infant attention important for adult-infant "shared-regard," hence early reference; (b) conversational and interactional alternating patterns important for achieving rudimentary discourse conventions; (c) phrase structure information critical to the acquisition of syntax (e.g., clausal, phrasal and word boundaries) and (d) phonetic segment information and its combinatorial possibilities in the target language and so forth (no specific ordering of importance is intended here, as prosodic variables can convey multiple types of information simultaneously). Indeed, by merely attributing to infants the innate sensitivity to the two features of natural language structure just described (prosodic and sub-lexical or syllabic), we provide them with the initial means to begin the language acquisition process well in advance of their having knowledge of the target language's grammar and its meanings. This is so because all of the information carried in prosody listed above (reference cues, conversational conventions, phrase structure, phonetic segments and so forth) are, in principle, derivable from giving the infant sensitivity to these two levels of natural language phonology. Thus, the infant's sensitivity to particular aspects of the input over others – posited here to be a "structure recognition mechanism" present at birth – may provide the infant with the ability (i) to attend to, (ii) to lay down in memory and, crucially, (iii) to establish a motor production loop with particular aspects of the abundant input that is bombarding its senses.

5.2. Critical Factors of the Environment

The specific modality of the environmental input is not critical either to begin or to maintain human language acquisition. Speech, per se, is not critical to the human language acquisition process. It is the structure of the input that is the key, essential factor both to begin and to maintain the human language acquisition process. To be clear, linguistically structured input – and not modality – is the critical factor required to begin and maintain very early language acquisition.

5.3. Within Infant Interactions: Structure, Motor and General Perceptual Constraints

When perceptual input enters, be it visual or auditory, it may shunt around the brain hitting its special processors (e.g., vision, the "structure-recognition mechanism" that I refer to above, or the way that the immune system uses both a rigid genetic program and environmental input to produce an immune response). The structure-recognition mechanism will be engaged if incoming perceptual information contains the specific structures above, thereby permitting (i) tacit decomposition of the input (which ultimately provides the infant with knowledge of the phonetic units and/or possible combinations; cf. Jusczyk

1986) and (ii) links with motor production that constrain the production of such structures. Because information about the input modality is preserved (Damasio, Damasio, Tranel and Brandt 1990; Maurer 1993; Meltzoff 1990), an infant can begin to produce babbling units in sign, if exposed to sign, babbling units in speech, if exposed to speech, and babbling units in speech and sign, if exposed to both modalities. Thus, language ontogeny begins through the complex interaction of three mechanisms: (1) general perceptual mechanism, (2) constraints on motor production and crucially, (3) specific structural constraints that are especially tuned to particular aspects of linguistic input. (For a discussion of why general perceptual, general motor, and/or general motor and general perceptual mechanisms alone are insufficient to account for early human language acquisition see Petitto 1993).

5.4. Predictions of the Theory

The above processes can and do occur across multiple modalities. Language acquisition is not restricted to speech. The prediction here is that as long as the input contains the appropriate patterns (or structures) relevant to natural language, input containing this structure should be acquired on the same time course, irrespective of the modality of the input. The findings from the above studies demonstrated this pattern.

6. Language Phylogeny

The very existence of (non-invented) naturally evolved signed languages, as well as the apparent effortless way in which they are acquired in ontogeny, present us with the following phylogenetic puzzle. If most of our species presently speaks – presumably due to phylogenetic processes – where does the ontogenetic capacity to acquire signed languages come from? To be sure, it is not advisable to go from behavourial facts of language ontogeny to theories of language phylogeny. Nonetheless, I provide preliminary speculations here because current hypotheses about language phylogeny have ignored the facts of signed language acquisition. For example, the fact that there is an equipotentiality of the signed and spoken modalities to receive and produce language in ontogeny has been clearly established but it is routinely ignored. Although it is desirable that accounts of language ontogeny be compatible with hypotheses about language phylogeny, it is utterly essential that hypotheses about language phylogeny be wholly consistent with the facts of language ontogeny. Here I provide extremely preliminary speculations about language phylogeny that, at the very least, are consistent with the facts from early signed and spoken language acquisition.

6.1. Why Is There Not a Preference for Speech in Language Ontogeny? What Characteristics of Language Have Been Selected for?

It has been argued that the mechanisms for producing speech were selected for first, and then came language (i.e., "syntax"; see Lieberman 1984, 1991). A clear implication, then, is that our brains are neurologically "wired" for speech per se which, in turn, makes human language acquisition possible. On this view, when large numbers of deaf people coalesced in a stable way to form communities of signers, these signed languages were developed within the already existing signalling system geared for speech. Thus, according to this view, it is not surprising that speech and signed languages share common linguistic structures.

There are at least three important problems with this type of hypothesis. First, this account does not explain *how* such common structures are possible in signed and spoken language acquisition, given that the neural substrates underlying the motor control of the speech and sign articulatory apparatus are distinct. Second, the clear prediction consistent with this hypothesis is that speech should be far better fitted to language structure, expression and reception than signed languages. However, all psycholinguistic and neurolinguistic studies to date on the structure, grammars and acquisition of signed languages indicate that this is not the case. Third, a further prediction here is that bilingual and/or bimodal children should show some preference for speech, which is not observed.

In an alternative view, the evolution of language has not occurred exclusively in terms of the mechanisms for the motor production of speech per se (as is asserted above). In this view, some form of symbolic capacity may have existed prior to, and/or at the same time as, the ability to express it was evolving. Internal factors, for example, deriving from an awareness of self and/or consciousness, the symbol, as in X "stands for" Y and so forth, could have exerted pressure on the means for expressing its contents.

The hands and the tongue provided the brain with two optimal candidates for language expression and reception. Both satisfy the criteria for serving as the articulators for natural language; both can be (1) produced, (2) segmented and (3) perceived. Because of certain signalling advantages common to sound (its speed and rate of transmission and reception; use of speech frees up the hands for other activities and so forth), speech was preferred. Whatever the elusive advantage is, it provided speech with an edge, and, hence, most of us speak.

Crucially, it does not follow from the fact that most of us speak that speech per se was exclusively selected for in the phylogeny of language. Because speech proved more useful than sign it has been tempting to conclude that speech has been selected for. However, the present data are inconsistent with this hypothesis. The fact that all of us have the capacity to sign in ontogeny is telling in this regard. Why *is* there no preference observed for speech in ontogeny? One reason may be that selection has occurred for "Language" – that is, aspects of its abstract structure and semantic and/or conceptual underpinnings – but it has not yet fully selected for the expressive modality, although it has come very close regarding existing speech perception and production mechanisms.[3] Another reason, one that I favour, is that to solve the problem of differentiating between speech-linguistic versus speech-non-linguistic information being received and expressed in the same auditory modality, the brain was pushed to some other level of language abstraction.[4] Perhaps an abstract structure-recognition mechanism evolved due to the problem of separating out linguistic speech from non-linguistic sounds – a mechanism that does not itself have motor specifications in it, although it is linked with them. A spinoff of the existence of this structure-recognition mechanism would be that humans could generate alternative pathways for perceiving and producing language because they already have a structure-recognition mechanism that is not tied to a particular modality. This may be how it is possible that signed languages exist. And, this may be why we see no preference for speech over signed input in language ontogeny, because (i) both demonstrate the requisite structures of natural language; (ii) both can be just as easily acquired and used and (iii) both can be just as easily used as a vehicle for the representation and expression of thought.

It may be that certain pressures – for example, the need to separate linguistic speech from non-linguistic vocalizations (as well as speech input from non-linguistic auditory input) – rendered a solution to these pressures by pulling away from a strictly *speech-motor representation* of language to a new, more abstract *structure-motor* representation.

7. Summary and Conclusions

In this chapter, I have tried to articulate a plausible theory of language acquisition, taking into account what is currently known about genetically endowed systems, as well as the facts of early epigenesis. When the neural substrates underlying language acquisition are seen as having a great deal of redundancy built into them, then the system is protected against both environmental and physiological changes that could potentially occur. It is not the case that if the preferred pathway is unavailable, then another pathway will kick in. Rather, other pathways will develop if one set of genetic or environmental inputs is not present. This view predicts that there will be no delay in the acquisition of language if the hearing pathway is unavailable, or if speech input is not presented to the hearing pathway. Having multiple genes and pathways available for the expression of fundamental capacities in an organism is common in biology. In this important way, the human language capacity is entirely consistent with the way other biological systems work, and I have articulated precisely which components of our capacity for language may be under genetic control.

I have argued here for the existence of a structure-recognition mechanism in newborns that is uniquely sensitive to particular aspects of natural language structure in the input (i.e., prosodic and sub-lexical or syllabic aspects), not to modality. I outlined how this mechanism crucially works in conjunction with general motor production and general perceptual constraints in early language ontogeny. I advanced the hypothesis that speech input per se is not critical to early language ontogeny. Instead, linguistically relevant structures encoded within the input are key. I further demonstrated that there is an equipotentiality of the modalities (spoken or signed) to receive and produce natural language from birth. As long as the input contains the specific distributional patterns of natural language structure, infants will begin to acquire it, irrespective of the modality of the input. Further, I have suggested ways in which the course of early signed language acquisition, as well as the very existence of human signed languages, can be suggestive regarding our understanding of human language phylogeny. These conclusions have radical implications for how we construe the genetic foundations of language, and suggest new ways of theorizing about the genetic and environmental factors that together create the neurological foundations of language.

Acknowledgments

I am indebted to Kevin N. Dunbar for his insightful comments on drafts of this chapter. I thank the researchers (students and staff) who assisted in the studies discussed within, and, crucially, the deaf and hearing families who so lovingly gave their time and support to these studies. I also thank the following for funding this research: Natural Science and Engineering Council of Canada, the MacDonnell-Pew Centre Grant in Cognitive Neuroscience and the McGill-IBM Cooperative Project.

Notes

1 Previously, researchers posited that signed languages should be acquired in a *different* way than spoken languages. To be sure, several researchers have claimed that there is a "sign advantage" (Meier and Newport 1991). That is, deaf children exposed to signed languages are said to produce their first signs prior to the time when hearing children produce their first words. These researchers have further posited that signed languages are acquired earlier than spoken languages.

   Most of the claims regarding the earlier onset of first signs over first words stem from one group of researchers (e.g., Bonvillian, Orlansky and Novack 1983; Bonvillian Orlansky, Novack and Folven 1983; Folven and Bonvillian 1991). The subjects in their studies were reported to have produced their "first sign" at a mean age of 8.2 months (a date that differs from hearing children's first words, which occur at approximately 11 months). However, in their studies, "first signs" were *not* required to be used referentially (that is, they were not required to be used in any meaningful way). Instead, if the children's productions contained "recognizable" adult phonetic forms, they were attributed sign (= lexical) status, even if the productions were not used "referentially." Equally damaging is the fact that the primary data used to make the "first sign" attributions were not based on actual samples of the young children signing. Instead, the attributions were based on analyses of the mothers' productions, and, worse, on her memory of what her child had produced. However, like speaking mothers, signing mothers tend not to recall the actual form of the way children sign things, only what its communicative intent and content was (see Petitto 1992; see also Brown and Hanlon 1970). Given that the criteria established by Bonvillian et al. for the children's "first signs" did not have to have referential status, and given their reliance on data from the mother rather than from the child, it is not surprising that they attributed sign status to productions that were not lexical. What they actually measured is clear from the spoken language acquisition literature and from my own work: in spoken language, we see that hearing infants around ages 7 to 10 begin production of "syllabic babbling," whereupon they produce vocal sounds containing recognizable adult phonetic forms without any referential content, forms that are not used in any meaningful way. Thus, it would appear that Bonvillian et al. have mislabelled genuine instances of manual babbling in signing infants as being "first signs" (recall that their date for the age of first signs is 8.2 months – which is right in the middle of infants' manual babbling stage). To complicate matters further, Meier and Newport (1991) then based their theoretical arguments in support of the existence of a "sign advantage" largely on the claims of Bonvillian et al.

2 As is common and productive in scientific discourse, there is dissenting discussion about the sign-syllable. However, it has focused largely on whether "Hold" is analyzed as being part of the syllabic stem, along with "Movement," or whether it occurs with Movement due to a phonological process (e.g., Brentari 1989, 1990). Crucially, however, despite technical arguments of linguistic theory, there is no debate over the existence of syllabic organization within signed languages (for articles on the phonological, and/or syllabic, structure of signed language see also Coulter 1986; Liddell and Johnson 1989; Perlmutter 1989, 1991; Sandler 1986; Stokoe 1960).

3 I thank Kevin Dunbar for first suggesting this possibility to me.

4 I thank Leda Cosmides who first made this connection after I had argued that there appeared to be a common, higher level of abstraction that characterizes the observed commonalities between signed and spoken language structure.

References

Bertoncini, J., R.V. Bijeljac-Babic, S.E. Blumstein and J. Mehler (1987). Discrimination in neonates of very short CVs. *Journal of the Acoustic Society of America* 82: 31–37

Bertoncini, J., and J. Mehler (1979). Syllables as units in infant speech perception. *Infant Behavior and Development* 4: 247–60

Bonvillian, J., M.D. Orlansky and L.L. Novack (1983). Developmental milestones: Sign language acquisition and motor development. *Child Development* 54:1435–45

Bonvillian, J., M.D. Orlansky, L.L. Novack and R.J. Folven (1983). Early sign language acquisition and cognitive development. In D. Rogers and J.A. Sloboda (eds.), *The Acquisition of Symbolic Skills*, 201–14. New York: Plenum Press

Brentari, D. (1989). Licensing in ASL handshape change. Unpublished Ph.D. dissertation, Department of Linguistics, University of Chicago

———— (1990). Harmonic phonology in ASL. Unpublished dissertation, Department of Linguistics, University of Chicago

Brown, R., and C. Hanlon (1970). Derivational complexity and order of acquisition in child speech. In J.R. Hayes (ed.), *Cognition and the Development of Language*. New York: Wiley

Charron, F., and L.A. Petitto (1991). Les premiers signes acquis par des enfants sourds en langue des signes québécoise (LSQ): Comparaison avec les premiers mots. *Revue Québécoise de Linguistique Théorique et Appliquée* 10 (1): 71–122

Coulter, G. (1986). ASL consonants, syllables, and stress: Implications for universals of prosodic structure. Unpublished paper, Department of Psychology, University of Illinois, Urbana-Champaign

Damasio, A.R., H. Damasio, D. Tranel and J.P. Brandt. (1990). Neural regionalization of knowledge access: Preliminary evidence. *Cold Spring Harbor Symposia on Quantitative Biology, Volume LV*, 1039–47. Cold Spring Harbor, NY: Cold Spring Harbor Laboratory Press

de Boysson-Bardies, B., and M. Vihman (1991). Adaptation to language: Evidence from babbling and first words in four languages. *Language* 67: 297–319

Elbers, L. (1982). Operating principles in repetitive babbling: A cognitive continuity approach. *Cognition* 12 (1): 45–63

Fernald, A., T. Taeschner, J. Dunn, M. Papousek, B. de Boysson-Bardies and I. Fukui (1989). A cross-language study of prosodic modifications in mothers' and fathers' speech to preverbal infants. *Journal of Child Language* 16: 477–501

Folven, R.J., and J. Bonvillian (1991). The transition from nonreferential to referential language in children acquiring American Sign Language. *Developmental Psychology* 27 (5): 806–16

Genesee, F. (1987). *Learning through Two Languages*. Cambridge, MA: Newbury House

Gross, C.G. (1992). Representation of visual stimuli in inferior temporal cortex. *Philosophical Transactions of the Royal Society of London, B* 335 (1273): 3–10

Horn, G., and M. Johnson (1989). Memory systems in the chick: Dissociations and neuronal analysis. *Neuropsychologia* 27 (1): 1–22

Johnson, M., and J. Morton (1991) *Biology and Cognitive Development*. Oxford: Blackwell

Jusczyk, P.W. (1986). Toward a model of the development of speech perception. In J.S. Perkell and D.H. Klatt (eds.) *Invariance and Variability in Speech Processes*, 199–299. Hillsdale, NJ: Erlbaum

Lenneberg, E. (1967). *Biological Foundations of Language*. New York: Wiley

Liberman, A.M., and I.G. Mattingly (1989). A specialization for speech perception. *Science* 243 (4890): 489–94

——— (1985). The motor theory of speech perception revised. *Cognition* 21 (1): 1–36

Liddell, S., and R. Johnson (1989). American Sign Language: The phonological base. *Sign Language Studies* 64: 195–278

Lieberman, P. (1984). *The Biology and Evolution of Language*. Cambridge, MA: Harvard University Press

——— (1991). *Uniquely Human: The Evolution of Speech, Thought, and Selfless Behavior*. Cambridge, MA: MIT Press

Locke, J. (1983). *Phonological Acquisition and Change*. New York: Academic Press

MacNeilage, P.F., and B. Davis (1990). Acquisition of speech production: Frames, then content. In M. Jeannerod (ed.), *Attention and Performance XII: Motor Representation and Control*, 453–76. Hillsdale, NJ: Erlbaum

MacNeilage, P.F., M.G. Studdert-Kennedy and B. Lindblom (1985). Planning and production of speech: An overview. In J. Lauter (ed.), *Proceedings of the Conference of Planning and Production of Speech by Normally Hearing and Deaf People*. American Speech and Hearing Association Reports. Washington, DC: American Speech and Hearing Association

Marentette, P., P. Girouard and L.A. Petitto (Apr. 19–22, 1990). "Hand preference as evidence for laterality of language in the early stages of sign language acquisition." Seventh International Conference on Infant Studies, Montréal, Québec, Canada; and Technical Report No. 4, *McGill Working Papers in Cognitive Science*. Montréal: Centre for Cognitive Science, McGill University

Maurer, D. (1993). Neonatal synesthesia: Implications for the processing of speech and faces. In B. de Boysson-Bardies, S. de Schonen, P. Jusczyk, P. MacNeilage and J. Morton (eds.) *Changes in Speech and Face Processing in Infancy: A Glimpse at Developmental Mechanisms of Cognition*, 109–24. Dordrecht: Kluwer

Meier, R., and E. Newport (1991). Out of the hands of babes: On a possible sign advantage in language acquisition. *Language* 66: 1–23

Meltzoff, A. (1990). The implications of cross-modal matching and imitation for the development of representation and memory in infancy. *Annals of the New York Academy of Science* 608: 1–37

Moon, C., T.G. Bever and W.P. Fifer. (1992). Canonical and non-canonical syllable discrimination by two-day-old infants. *Journal of Child Language* 19: 1–17

Oller, D.K., and R.E. Eilers. (1988). The role of audition in infant babbling. *Child Development* 59 (2), 441–49

Perlmutter, D. (1989). A moraic theory of American Sign Language syllable structure. Unpublished paper. Department of Linguistics, University of California, San Diego

———— (1991). Sonority and syllable structure in American Sign Language. Unpublished paper. Department of Linguistics, University of California, San Diego

Petitto, L.A. (1984). From Gesture to Symbol: The Relationship between Form and Meaning in the Acquisition of Personal Pronouns in American Sign Language. Unpublished Ph.D. dissertation. Harvard University.

———— (1986). *From Gesture to Symbol: The Relationship between Form and Meaning in the Acquisition of Personal Pronouns in American Sign Language.* Bloomington, IN: Indiana University Linguistics Club Press

———— (1987a). On the autonomy of language and gesture: Evidence from the acquisition of personal pronouns in American Sign Language. *Cognition* 27 (1): 1–52

———— (1987b). Theoretical and methodological issues in the study of sign language babbling: Preliminary evidence from American Sign Language (ASL) and Langue des Signes Québécoise (LSQ). Fourth International Symposium on Sign Language Research, Lappeenranta, Finland, July 15–19

———— (1988). "Language" in the pre-linguistic child. In F. Kessel (ed.), *Developmental of Language and Language Researchers: Essays in Honor of Roger Brown*, 187–221. Hillsdale, NJ: Erlbaum

———— (1992). Modularity and constraints in early lexical acquisition: Evidence from children's first words/signs and gestures. In M. Gunnar and M. Maratsos (eds.), *Modularity and Constraints in Language and Cognition: The Minnesota Symposia on Child Psychology*, 25–58. Hillsdale, NJ: Erlbaum

———— (1993). On the ontogenetic requirements for early language acquisition. In B. de Boysson-Bardies, S. de Schonen, P. Jusczyk, P. MacNeilage and J. Morton (eds.), *Developmental Neurocognition: Speech and Face Processing in the First Year of Life*, 365–83. Dordrecht: Kluwer

———— (in preparation, a). Cross-linguistic analyses of manual babbling in two signed languages: American Sign Language and Langue des Signes Québécoise

———— (in preparation, b). Babbling with the hands and the tongue: Cross-linguistic, cross-modal studies of hearing infants' babbling in two modalities

Petitto, L.A., and F. Charron (1988). The acquisition of semantic categories in two sign languages. Theoretical Issues in Sign Language Research, II, Gallaudet University, Washington, DC, May 18–21

Petitto, L.A., and P. Marentette (1990). The timing of linguistic milestones in sign language acquisition: Are first signs acquired earlier than first words?

Fifteenth Annual Boston University Conference on Language Development, October 19–21

——— (1991). Babbling in the manual mode: Evidence for the ontogeny of language. *Science* 251: 1483–96

Petitto, L.A., N. Costopoulos and L. Stevens (in preparation). The identity of linguistic milestones in signed and spoken languages: Evidence for a unitary timing mechanism in the ontogeny of language.

Petitto, L.A., D. Ostry, L. Sergio, B. Levy (in preparation). Linguistic versus non-linguistic manual activity in signing and non-signing infants under one year: The motoric underpinnings.

Sandler, W. (1986). The spreading hand autosegment of American Sign Language: A new approach to sequential segments and autosegments in ASL. *Sign Language Studies* 50: 1–28

Strohman, R. (1994). Epigenesis: The missing beat in biotechnology? *Bio/Technology* 12: 156–64

Stokoe, W. (1960). Sign language structure: An outline of the visual communication system of the American deaf. *Studies in Linguistics, Occasional Papers*, Vol. 8. Buffalo, NY: University of Buffalo Press

Studdert-Kennedy, M.G. (1991). A note on linguistic nativism. In R.R. Hoffman and D.S. Palermo (eds.), *Cognition and the Symbolic Processes: Applied and Ecological Perspectives*, 38–58. Hillsdale, NJ: Erlbaum

Sussman, H. (1984). A neuronal model for syllable representation. *Texas Linguistic Forum* 24: 93–127

——— (1989). Neural coding of relational invariance in speech: Human language analogs to the Barn Owl. *Psychological Review* 96 (4): 631–42

Tautz, D. (1992). Redundancies, development and the flow of information. *BioEssays* 14: 263–66

Terrace, H.S., L.A. Petitto, R.J. Sanders and T.G. Bever (1979). Can an ape create a sentence? *Science* 202: 891–902

Thelen, E. (1991). Motor aspects of emergent speech: A dynamic approach. In N.A. Krasnegor, D.M. Rumbaugh, R.L. Schiefelbush, M. Studdert-Kennedy (eds.), *Biological and Behavioral Determinants of Language Development*, 339–62. Hillsdale, NJ: Erlbaum

Thelen, E., and B.D. Ulrich (1991). Hidden Skills. *Monographs of the Society for Research in Child Development* 56 (1): 1–106

Van der Stelt, J.M., and F.J. Koopmans-van Bienum (1986). The onset of babbling related to gross motor development. In B. Lindbloom and R. Zetterstrom (eds.), *Precursors of Early Speech*, 163-73. New York: Stockton

Wilkins, A.S. (1993). *Genetic Analysis of Animal Development*, 2nd ed. New York: Wiley-Liss

4

Exploring Innateness through Cultural and Linguistic Variation

Martha B. Crago, Shanley E.M. Allen
and Wendy P. Hough-Eyamie

Introduction

This chapter reports on three separate but interwoven studies that documented varying aspects of language acquisition as it occurs in the Inuit population of two communities in northern Quebec, whose inhabitants speak Inuktitut on a routine basis. Issues concerning the innate and variable properties of language will be addressed with culturally based ethnographic language socialization data, linguistically based acquisition data and elements from a case study of an Inuk child with language impairment.

Certain specific properties of both the Inuktitut language and Inuit cultural patterns of socialization, when contrasted with other cultures and languages, allow some degree of delineation of innate from socially constructed properties of language. The examination of cross-cultural and cross-linguistic commonalities helps to define some of the core features of both language input and language acquisition. Cross-cultural and cross-linguistic variations, on the other hand, can serve as evidence for certain of the innate properties of the human child's mind by demonstrating both the extent and the limitations of variation. Finally, developmental language impairment represents a variation in the organism, creating a skew in the process of normal development and thereby providing another source of information concerning the mutable and immutable aspects of language. Evidence of this disorder in a polysynthetic language contributes to defining the core characteristics of both the language and the disorder. It is the contention of this chapter, then, that certain core qualities of language, its instantiation in the human mind and its acquisition by the growing child can be explored by teasing apart the universal from the specific – and the impaired from the unimpaired. The Inuktitut language and Inuit cultural patterns of language socialization both have several properties that when compared with other languages and cultures are extremely informative in this process.

Inuktitut Language and Inuit Culture

Inuktitut

The Inuktitut language, a member of the Eskimo Aleut family, encompasses several mutually intelligible dialects and is spoken by the 23,000 Inuit of northern Canada. It exhibits a high degree of polysynthesis with prolific verbal and nominal inflections. This means that a nominal or verbal root is followed by from zero to eight morphemes corresponding to the Indo-European independent verbs, auxiliaries, deverbals, denominals, adverbials, adjectivals and so on; then an obligatory inflectional affix; and finally optional enclitics. The following example shows how nominal elements may include a variety of modifiers suffixed to the root:

    (1) *Quttukallakutaatsiaraapimmut.*
        qut-juq-kallaq-kutaaq-tsiaq-apik-mut
        be.funny-NOM-DIM-tall-nice-handsome-ALL.sg
        Be a nice tall handsome cute funny person.[1]

Verbal elements typically show a greater degree of polysynthesis, as in this example:

    (2) *Annuraarsimalukatsitipaujaaluumijuq.*
        annuraaq-sima-lukat-siti-paujaaluk-u-mi-juq
        clothe-PERF-unusually-well-very-be-also-PAR.3sS
        She also often dresses up very unusually.

Inuktitut also has an ergative case-marking system, SOXV word order and ellipsis of both subject and object.

Inuit Culture

Present-day Inuit culture in Northern Quebec is based on the Thule culture, in which caribou and seal hunting were the mainstays of the economy and people lived a nomadic and seasonally based existence in snow houses and tents, travelling by dogsled and kayak. Today, families live in modern houses with telephones and television, and travel by airplanes, skidoos and motor boats. Their children go to school while many adult family members work for cash wages. Despite this, a number of aspects of family structure and activities of daily living are still rooted in traditional patterns. Many children are raised in extended multigenerational family networks where custom adoption and fictive kinship are important elements of family structure (Crago 1988). Traditional subsistence activities associated with hunting and gathering are still routine parts of family life. It is evident that forces of cultural and linguistic assimilation are strong, with the risk that much of what is documented here may change or disappear.

The Children and Families

The families and children involved in the three studies come from Kangirsuk and Quaqtaq, two small communities on Ungava Bay, located some 1,200 kilometres northeast of Montreal. First settled in the 1960s, these communities had, by the late 1980s, populations of just over 200 and 300 permanent residents, only 8 to 12 of whom were non-Inuit. In the communities of Kangirsuk and Quaqtaq, all verbal transactions between Inuit take place in Inuktitut. This includes the language addressed to children and spoken by them.

Data in this chapter are taken from three different studies: a language socialization study, an acquisitional study and a study of a language-impaired child, each with its own cohort of children. The language socialization study involved four monolingual Inuit children aged 1;0 to 1;9 at the outset who were selected at random from the general population. Videotapes and observations of a full range of naturalistic family activities were made every three months for a year. In addition, mothers of all the children taped and a random sample of other mothers, representing about a third of the women in one community, were interviewed at length about their concepts of language input and acquisition.

The acquisitional study involved a second cohort of four monolingual children aged 2;0 to 2;10 at the outset. Approximately four hours of data from each of the four children in this additional cohort were collected every month for nine months by videotaping naturalistic spontaneous speech used by the children with their families and friends.

Data from the language-impaired child are part of an ongoing study of a larger group of developmentally language-impaired Inuktitut speakers. This particular girl was 5;4 when we videotaped her at play with a friend. She is a member of a large extended family network of over 60 individuals in which there are five other developmentally language-impaired individuals. The impaired child's utterances have been matched by mean length of utterance (MLU) to a 2-year-old boy from the language acquisition study and by age to her playmate.

All Inuktitut language data were entered on the computer following the CHAT transcription conventions from the CHILDES project, and subsequent analyses were conducted using the CLAN programs (MacWhinney and Snow 1990). Transcriptions and translations were done by Inuit research assistants.

Elements of Language Socialization

Approximately a decade ago, Bruner (1981; 1983) introduced the idea that a LASS (Language Acquisition Support System) was the perfect accompaniment to a LAD (Language Acquisition Device). Ninio and Bruner (1978) demonstrated some of the elements of this system that they referred to as "scaffolding" and "fine-tuning" (Bruner 1981, 167). However, a number of cross-cultural studies spanning the last 10 years have indicated that scaffolding and fine-tuning need not take the form that Bruner delineated in his studies of white middle-class British and American children and mothers. The present research demonstrates that while Inuit caregivers provide a sociopragmatic framework for their children during their language-learning years, it is not the same as that evidenced in anglocentric studies of the white middle class. Furthermore, the different patterns of input and interaction are undergirded by each culture's own complex nexus of values, family structures and sociocultural activities.

To illustrate this, some points of comparison in Bruner's Vygotskian data (1981) and the Inuit data that we have gathered merit discussion. Scaffolding and fine-tuning in Bruner's model of the LASS includes the frequent pairing of child and mother as conversational partners within a dyadic framework. Many of these conversations take place within a series of "nanocosms" or mini-discourse routines (Bruner 1985, 27). In the early stages of language acquisition, these include embedding phonologically constant forms into ritualized what and where games. According to Ninio and Bruner (1978), at two to three years old, bookreading also becomes a scaffold for question-and-answer routines with a set of interactional properties that revolve around shared attention, querying, labelling and feedback. In general, Bruner's version of the LASS involves a mother and child engaged in a performance-based verbal interactional model. Parental labelling, expansions of the child's utterances and queries for labels play a principal role in the language input to children. These particular properties of dyadic interaction, then, form the basis of the system that Bruner considers quintessential to the activation of a language-acquisition device.

The Inuit pattern of environmental support for language learning is strikingly different (Crago 1988). Inuit children are raised even today, for the most part, in multi-aged, multiparty talking environments. At a young age, children are oriented toward a great deal of interaction with their age-similar peers. One- and 2-year-olds in the language socialization study played daily with cousins or near-age brothers, sisters and friends. Peer talk among the 1- to 3-year-olds involved pretend play with and without toy props and talk that accompanied physical play.

The input to children from their peers did not involve the fine-tuning depicted by Bruner. There was some minimal register adjustment and occasional corrections of one child by a slightly older child, but peer language surrounding children in this age range involved, in large part, the not yet phonologically constant units of early language, some early combinatorial units, some ungrammatical constructions, some grammatical constructions and a limited lexicon. It did not involve the repetitive mini-dialogues consisting of alternating queries and labels that Bruner described.

On the other hand, Inuit children are frequently cared for by sibling teenagers or, in certain families, by young mothers. Interactions with these partners often included extensive repetition routines that centred around instructing the 1- to 2-year-old child how to engage in greeting routines by modelling directly after the competent member. These routines resembled in some ways Bruner's nanocosms with fine-tuned scaffolding steering the child to appropriate production. They did not, however, scaffold the child's language by the use of question-and-answer routines or by expansions of the child's utterances (Crago and Eriks-Brophy, 1993). Furthermore, these repetition routines were very limited in the particular linguistic structures that they addressed.

Of perhaps even greater interest was the communicative interaction of young children with their older (40 years old and more) traditional mothers. These women considered their role to be different than that of the sibling caregivers. One older mother expressed this difference as follows: "If the child has siblings, she is taught more to talk by them; when they look after their younger siblings they talk to them. The mother talks less to the baby than the one who is taking care of the baby for her. The mother teaches the child to talk less than the person who is looking after the baby."

Yet, now that sibling caregivers are in school all day, these older mothers have become more constant companions of their young children. Older mothers are represented in large numbers in the population due to the practice of custom adoption. These women engaged in about a third as much conversation with their children as younger mothers did (Hough-Eyamie 1993). When their infants babbled, these older mothers sometimes repeated the sounds or the intonation contour of the babble but they did not interpret the sound string as meaningful communication. These women only occasionally labelled objects for their children, rarely expanded their children's utterances or made semantically contingent remarks. They asked their children almost no test questions to which they, the mothers, knew the answer. The older mothers would sometimes address the child using strings of nonsense syllables synthesized into their speech as a form of affectionate talk. Affectionate talk sounded harsh and loud to the non-Inuit researchers who sometimes mistook it for anger. A large proportion of utterances addressed to the child were directives in the imperative form. Furthermore, these mothers frequently co-constructed communication in silence with their children. Disciplinary negotiation, instructional activities, bedding, eating, dressing and bathing took place in silence. These mothers did not read their children books nor did they involve themselves in toy play, and they did not issue children invitations to produce language by saying, "Tell so and so about such and such." Their children were deliberately excluded from participating in adult conversation. In their role as spectators, the children, for their part, were eavesdroppers on considerable talk that was not addressed to them. In their homes there were often several adults, older siblings and visitors who conversed in the children's presence. The Bible was read aloud, while family members (including the 1- and 2-year-olds) listened. Older mothers sometimes conversed in the child's presence, about the child, to the sibling caregivers without addressing talk specifically to the child. In their interviews, all the women over 40 in one community said that the measure of whether children had learned language was by whether children understood what was being addressed to them. They typically expressed this idea in statements such as this: "When she is able to understand then if she is told to go and get the mitten and if she went and got it, and when she was told to bring it over to the person who sent her to get it and if she understood that, then, we can know she has learned language in that way today."

In these and other comments, the older women essentially described themselves as involved with their children in a largely comprehension-based model of learning language. Production aspects of language learning, then, occurred principally in the interactions of children with their peers and sibling caregivers or young mothers. These interactions conformed only in very small measure with the specific description of fine-tuning and scaffolding that Bruner provided. Interestingly enough, while the sociopragmatic use of language differed in the homes of the older mothers, the children's acquisitional stages were not necessarily any different from children in homes with younger mothers. In fact, some children of older parents were both reported and observed to have more well developed language and more extensive vocabularies (Allen and Crago 1992).

The Inuit example of caregiver input and interaction, taken together with evidence from other cultures (Ochs and Schieffelin 1984; Schieffelin

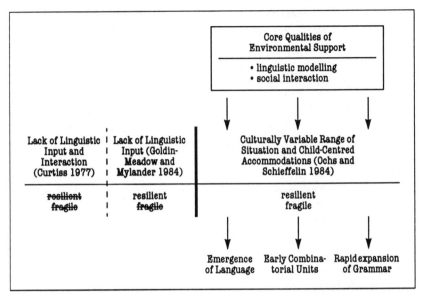

Figure 1: Cultural Variation between Caregiver and Child: Input and Interaction. Curtiss
(1977) claimed that lack of input affected both the resilient and fragile aspects of language acquisition in children. Goldin-Meadow and Mylander (1984) claimed that only
the fragile aspects of language acquisition were affected.

and Ochs 1986), then, shows that if there is a LASS it must be able to include a wide range of culturally variable, environmentally supportive
behaviours. Ochs and Schieffelin (1984) have described the principal dimension of this continuum in terms of child- and situation-centred ac-
commodations. It is equally clear that such a continuum of environmental support has a point of demarcation beyond which language is not
fully acquired (Curtiss 1977; Goldin-Meadow and Mylander 1984).
Across the range of cultural variation, a small number of core qualities
stand out as necessary (Rogoff 1990). These include, quite simply, the
presence of language used interactively but not necessarily in interaction with the child and the presence of an affectionate interactional relationship between the child and others. With such essential elements intact, both what Goldin-Meadow and Mylander (1984) have called the
resilient and fragile properties of language emerge according to some
very robustly set developmental milestones (see Figure 1). These milestones include the emergence of single words, the early combination of
units and the rapid expansion of the grammar. The robustness of these
milestones, in the face of the considerable variation of input, can be
taken as evidence that there are some substantially innate properties in
the child's brain and mind that can be activated, given a fundamental
core of environmental support.

Some Acquisitional Properties of Inuktitut

Similar to the cultural range of variation in input and interaction that exists, there is also a range of variation in the languages to which children are exposed. Inuktitut, with its high degree of polysynthesis, represents an interesting contrast with Indo-European languages. How does this difference manifest itself in the acquisition of Inuktitut by Inuit monolingual speakers?

The Emergence of Single Words

The youngest cohort of children, those from the language socialization study, all passed through a one-word (one-morpheme) stage between 9 and 14 months. Their vocabulary, consisting of many more nouns than verbs, focused mainly on animate beings (people and animals), food and the enactment of personal desires. These types of words are similar to those reported for English by Nelson (1973). Furthermore, when Inuit mothers were asked at what age children spoke in single units (morphemes or words), they reported the typical age to be about one year. Despite the fact that the interpretation of what constitutes first words has been shown to vary across cultures by Ochs and Schieffelin (1984), the basic age at which such single linguistic units have been reported to emerge is between 9 and 15 months (except in cases of developmental language impairment).

Early Combinations of Words and Morphemes

Inuit mothers reported that Inuktitut-speaking children typically begin putting two units (words or morphemes) together between 1;6 and 2;0. The early combination of two morphemes in Inuktitut is an interesting phenomenon. What is manifested as a two-word stage in other languages becomes, in part, a two-morpheme stage in a polysynthetic language such as Inuktitut. Data from the youngest cohort were analyzed for this early combinatorial stage by eliminating all transcripts in which the child was clearly at a one-word stage or clearly beyond the two-morpheme, two-word stage. The data were then divided into two groups. One group consisted of utterances with two morphemes and one word, and the other of two morphemes and two words (see Tables 1 and 2 for samples of these groups).

The utterances in the two-morphemes, one-word category were divided into two groups, those with two lexical units and those that involved inflections. In a total of the four children's 110 two-morpheme, one-word utterances, 63% were inflected. These findings concur with data from Fortescue's (1985) study of a single speaker of Greenlandic Eskimo. However, they are strikingly at variance with Roger Brown's (1973) and Martin Braine's (1976) English data that show children at

Lexical Combinations	
ataata-ai	father-greetings
apaapa-una	food-this.one
qimmiq-apik	dog-cute
nanuq-aluk	polar.bear-big
qajaq-tuq	soup-eat
Inflected Combinations	
immi-guk	drink-you/it!
qai-git	come-you!
aammu-juq	sleep-he
qiu-vunga	be.cold-I
apaa-kka	clothes-my

Table 1: Sample Data: Two Morphemes, One Word

aani imii-	Annie drink
maani aapu-	here gone
iqaluk uuvaa-	fish bleed
anaana atai-	mom go.out
auka ruuta	no Rhoda
tiituq- anaana	drink.tea mom
una paapi	this.one baby
maani siaru	here later
una uvanga	this.one mine
ataata apaapa	dad food

Table 2: Sample Data: Two Morphemes, Two Words

this early combinatorial stage to be producing almost exclusively open class words (uninflected nouns, verbs and adjectives). Closed class words, including inflections, on the other hand, are usually missing in English at this stage and, when present, they are not reported to show the same productivity as they did with the Inuit children.

It appears that the polysynthetic nature of Inuktitut is influencing this particular stage of language acquisition. At the same time that these findings may be taken as evidence for language-specific varia-tion, it is important to note the universality of the two-unit combinato-rial stage and its age of emergence. This particular stage leaves open a variety of possible interpretations as to the nature of why children are constrained to two units. Is it a syntactic morphological constraint on word-building or a more cognitive constraint on concepts to be ex-pressed or a manifestation of a processing constraint or a reflection of limitations of speech motor control? The Inuktitut example suggests that the syntactic morphological skills at this age are less constrained than English data might have indicated.

Rapid Grammatical Expansion

The next major milestone in these core aspects of language develop-ment is the rapid expansion of the grammar. In our sample, there is a child who, a few scant months after being at the two-unit combinatorial stage, is in his early twos using very complex utterances, such as the following:

Age 2;0

(3) *Tursuuniituruluinikkua.*
tursuuk-ni-it-juq-guluk-it-ikku-a
porch-LOC.pl-be-NOM-pitiful-ABS.pl-that.one-ABS.pl
Those pitiful ones are on the porch.

(4) *Ataatamut takujautsaruarmat.*
ataata-mut taku-jau-tsaruaq-mat
father-ALL.sg see-PASS-really-might-CSV.3sS
It really might be seen by father.

Age 2;5

(5) *Quaqtalialaartunga uuminga takulaartunga.*
Quaqtaq-liaq-laaq-junga u-minga taku-laaq-junga
Quaqtaq-go.to-FUT-PAR.1sS this.one-MOD.sg see-FUT-PAR.1sS
When I go to Quaqtaq I'll see this one.

(6) *Kinaumuna pigilangalirtanga?*
kina-up-u-na pi-gi-langa-liq-janga
who-ERG.sg-this.one-ABS.sg thing-have.as-FUT-PRES-PAR.3sS.3sO
Who will have this one?

Age 2;9

(7) *Nunakkuujuuraalunga aluuraaluu atjitaartuvinialu.*
nunakkuujuuq-aluk-nga aluu-aluk-up atji-taaq-juq-viniq-aluk
truck-EMPH-ABS.3Ssg white.person-EMPH-ERG.sg same-
    acquire-NOM-former-EMPH
He got a truck like the white person's.

(8) *Nilattataukainnaqita anaana kinakkunut?*
nilak-taq-jau-kainnaq-vita anaana kina-kkut-nut
ice-fetch-PASS-PAST-INT.1pS mother who-and.group-ALL.sg
Who were we brought ice by, Mom?

Although these examples are somewhat precocious compared to the
language of certain other children in the sample, there is nevertheless
evidence across a variety of cultures and languages, including Inuktitut,
that grammar expands in a dramatic fashion between the ages of 2 and
3 years (Slobin 1985b, 1992a). Again, there is a margin of individual variation, but the phenomenon is, indeed, robust. As Pinker (this volume)
has pointed out, without the existence of some basically innate linguistic
structures, it seems impossible for this kind of expansion to take place
in the manner and time space that it does. However, the precise nature
and timetable of the grammatical expansion is language-specific. The
acquisition of the passive in Inuktitut is an interesting example of rapid
grammatical expansion occurring in a fashion that is quite different
from what has been documented for Indo-European languages.

Passives

Studies of passive structure have provided key information for both
linguistic theory and language acquisition because of the role that this
structure plays in demonstrating the existence of underlying subject
and object and in developing the notion of constituent movement. The
passive has been claimed to be a complex structure which is acquired
reasonably late, by about 4;0 in English, 5;0 in German and 8;0 in Hebrew (de Villiers and de Villiers 1985; Mills 1985; Berman 1985). Borer
and Wexler (1987) used such evidence to confirm their Maturational
Hypothesis. This hypothesis claims that ordering in acquisition is due
to certain grammatical principles that mature in a similar fashion to
certain biological functions such as secondary sex characteristics. According to this theory, linguistic structures such as the passive are
learned at a later age when the relevant linguistic principle matures
within the child. Furthermore, the phenomenon cannot be explained
by learning or triggering. The principle governing Argument (A) chain
formation implicated in Noun Phrase (NP) movement used in passives
is considered to be a late-maturing linguistic principle.

The acquisition of passive in Inuktitut presents an interesting test case for this theory. Inuktitut, like a number of other languages, has two passives: verbal and adjectival. Unlike English, these two forms of the passive in Inuktitut are not homophonous. Both the verbal and adjectival passives are formed syntactically. Verbal passives in Inuktitut and English, in fact, exhibit essentially the same linguistic characteristics, as seen below.

(9) *Jaaniup niqi nirijanga.*
     Jaani-up niqi-Ø niri-janga
     Johnny-ERG.sg food-ABS.sg eat-PAR.3sS.3sO
     Johnny is eating the food.

(10) *Niqi Jaanimut nirijaujuq.*
     niqi-Ø Jaani-mut niri-jau-juq
     food-ABS.sg Johnny-ALL.sg eat-PASS-PAR.3sS
     The food was eaten by Johnny.

Children in the language-acquisition cohort used passives at a very early age with a strikingly high frequency (Allen, in press; Allen and Crago, in press). The high frequency of passives in Inuktitut is particularly evident in contrast with English data. In English, only 12 passives occur in 113 hours of tape taken before age 3;1 (Demuth 1990) whereas Inuit children in the same age range produced 45 passives in 15.3 hours of tape. The number of passives per hour for Inuktitut was 2.8 for children (aged 2;0 to 3;6) in comparison to 0.4 passives per hour for English speaking children (Pinker, Lebeaux and Frost 1987). Furthermore, the use of passives by the Inuit children could be demonstrated to be productive. Inuit children, for example, formed novel utterances by putting passive morphology on verbs to achieve meanings not typical in adult language. They also demonstrated appropriate alternation between passive and active forms using the same verb. Finally, Inuit children demonstrated their productive use of the passive by self-correction.

Thus the acquisition of passive in Inuktitut is not in conformance with the conclusions and theory based on passive acquisition in Indo-European languages, but rather supports findings from other non-Indo-European languages (Demuth 1990; Pye and Quixtan Poz 1988) and lends support to Pinker's (1984) Continuity Hypothesis. This hypothesis states that all grammatical principles are available to the child at birth and remain constant throughout development. The variation in the timing of acquisition is due to language-specific factors. For instance, the use of the passive is high in the speech of Inuit adults. However, this high frequency, as well as the children's high frequency of usage, could be due to an avoidance strategy related to the complex inflectional system of Inuktitut. Verbal inflection on a transitive structure must agree with both subject and object, which, given 9 possible verbal modalities, 4 persons and 3 numbers, yields in the vicinity of 900 possible choices of inflection. The verbal inflection on a passive only needs to agree with subject and not object, decreasing the number of inflections to be mastered from approximately 900 to approximately 100. The high frequency of passives also reflects the highly polysynthetic nature of Inuktitut in which NP movement and head movement are used in a large number of structures. These same types of movement that are used to produce passive are also responsible for causatives, desideratives and antipassives. Such structures are being used by 2- and 3-year-old Inuktitut speakers whereas they do not normally occur in the speech of the English-speaking children of the same age.

If it is assumed that an innate capacity for grammatical structure is instantiated in the biological make-up of the individual child, the specific and variable aspects of particular languages, then, influence the exact manner in which this structure gets filled in.

Specific Language Impairment

Developmental language impairment demonstrates how linguistic structure does not function in accordance with normal acquisition. Data from a 5-year-old language-impaired child who is a member of a large extended family, five of whom are reported to have language impairment, provided evidence for the type of linguistic deficits that can result from this disorder. The child in question has hearing within normal limits. Despite a difficult start in an adopted family with whom she did not remain, this child is now reported by her family members and her Inuk school teacher to be normal cognitively and emotionally. The following examples of her deficits are taken from 200 utterances of this child's spontaneous speech.

The impaired members of this child's extended family were identified as impaired by their mothers, who indicated that the first evidence for abnormality was the children's late onset of language, with first words emerging well after the third year. The use of this milestone as an identifying factor in a culture that has not traditionally consulted normative charts lends credence to the robustness of this milestone as a pivot point in normal language development.

Unfortunately there is no information on how this child performed at the two-unit combinatorial stage, but the expansion of her grammar is interesting. Indeed expansion did take place but there is, for instance, no evidence for use of the passive structure in the language-impaired girl's utterances. This is quite different from the children matching her in MLU and in age, both of whom had several exemplars of productive passive use (Crago and Allen, in press).

Two other features of this child's grammar are particularly intriguing. She makes an error that the normal Inuit children in our sample never demonstrated at any stage in their acquisition of Inuktitut. Examples (11a), (12a) and (13a) below show how the language-impaired child violates a basically synthetic aspect of Inuktitut (note that "sit down" in (11a) is an English word which this subject is using in place of the Inuktitut verb root *ingi-*). The paired examples (11b), (12b) and (13b) show what would have been expected of an unimpaired child:

(11a) *Maunga ahm sitdownnnguami ivvit imaittumi.*
      ma-unga ahm sitdown-nnguaq-MI ivvit imaittumik
      here-ALL um sitdown-pretend-MI you one.like.this
      Here uhhm pretend to sit down you one like this.

(11b) *Maunga inginnguarit.*
      ma-unga ingi-nnguaq-git
      here-ALL sit-pretend-IMP.2sS
      Sit down here.

Or: *Maani itsivannguarit.*
      ma-ani itsivaq-nnguaq-git
      here-LOC sit-pretend-IMP.2sS
      Sit down here.

(12a) *Maani ivvit.*
      ma-ani ivvit
      here-LOC you
      Be here.

(12b) *Maaniigit.*
      ma-ani-it-git
      here-LOC-be-IMP.2sS
      Be here.

(13a) *Asuu upittumii taku ivvi uumaa aani.*
      asuu imaittumik taku ivvit uuma aani
      okay one.like.this see you this.one xxx
      Okay like this see you this one xxx.

(13b) *Asuu imaittumik uumunga takujauvutit.*
      asuu imaittumik uu-munga taku-jau-vutit
      okay one.like.this this.one-ALL see-PASS-IND.2sS
      Okay one like this was seen by this one.

This particular tendency to use *ivvit* rather than a verbal inflection was striking to our Inuit colleagues since, in their experience, this structural abnormality did not occur in normally developing children's language and because it bore a remarkable similarity to certain utterances that Inuit report being used by and to Inuktitut second-language speakers. The following utterances, taken from conversations between older Inuit men and white men, indicate how monolingual Inuit men presumably altered their own language to help speakers of a non-polysynthetic language, mimicking the kind of errors that English and French speakers make when attempting to speak Inuktitut. Sentences (14a), (15a) and (16a) are what our Inuit colleagues report that Inuit men said to non-Inuit men whereas sentences (14b), (15b) and (16c) are what Inuit speakers would say to each other:

(14a) *Ivvit maani auka.*
　　　ivvit ma-ani auka
　　　you here-LOC no
　　　You weren't here.

(14b) *Tamaaniiqqaunginavit.*
　　　Ta-ma-ani-it-qqau-nngit-gavit
　　　PRE-here-LOC-be-PAST-not-CSV.2sS
　　　You weren't here.

(15a) *Ivvit taku siaru.*
　　　ivvit taku siaru
　　　you see later
　　　You'll see later.

(15b) *Siaru takuniarqutit.*
　　　Siaru taku-niaq-vutit
　　　later see-FUT-you
　　　You'll see later.

(16a) *Uvanga taku una.*
　　　uvanga taku una
　　　me see this.one
　　　I see this one.

(16b) *Takujara.*
　　　taku-jara
　　　see-PAR.1sS.3sO
　　　I see it.

Example (17a) is reported to be taken from the speech of a white priest when learning to speak Inuktitut. A native speaker would have been expected to say (17b).

(17a) *Qquumat maani piujuq.*
qquuq-mmat ma-ani piu-juq
probably-CSV.3sS here-LOC be.good-PAR.3sS
It will probably be nice here.

(17b) *Maani piujuuqquumat.*
ma-ani piu-juq-u-qquuq-mmat
here-LOC be.good-that.which-be-probably-CSV.3sS
It will probably be nice here.

Slobin (1985b) has claimed that it is a universal operating principle in the acquisition of language to show a preference for analytic over synthetic expressions. Since only second-language and language-impaired learners of Inuktitut showed this analytic tendency, it may be that the polysynthetic nature of Inuktitut serves to reduce, if not eliminate, the analytic tendency that is exhibited in other languages. This, then, implies that this analytic tendency is not a universal phenomenon.

Another form of error is made by the language-impaired child. It involves form-class agreement. In the 200 utterances, there are 3 examples of nominal inflection used on a verbal element. -mi, -mit, -mik are three nominal endings that are often pronounced as /mi/ in present-day spoken Inuktitut. In the following examples (18a, 19a and 20a), the language-impaired girl puts the ending -mi on a verbal root. As in the previous examples, the correct version of these utterances appears in (19b) and (20b). This type of error does not occur in any of the normally developing children's language. (Note that utterance [18a] has no clear meaning other than as a composition of its parts, so there is no grammatical counterpart [18b].)

(18a) *Situramilli imaittumi?*
situraq-MI-li imaittumik
slide.down.slope-MI-and one.like.this
Sliding one like this?

(19a) *Maunga ahm sitdownnnguami ivvit imaittumi.*
ma-unga ahm sitdown-nnguaq-MI ivvit imaittumik
here-ALL um sitdown-pretend-MI you one.like.this
Here um pretend to sit down you one like this.

(19b) *Maunga inginnguarit.*
ma-unga ingi-nnguaq-git
here-ALL sit-pretend-IMP.2sS
Sit down here.

Or: *Maani itsivannguarit.*
ma-ani itsivaq-nnguaq-git
here-LOC sit-pretend-IMP.2sS
Sit down here.

(20a) *Atii aullanguami imittumi.*
 atii aullaq-nnguaq-MI imaittumik
 okay leave-pretend-MI one.like.this
 Okay pretend to leave the one like this.

(20b) *Atii aullanguarluk imaittukut.*
 atii aullaq-nnguaq-luk imaittuq-kkut
 okay leave-pretend-IMP.2dS one.like.this-VIA.sg
 Okay let's pretend to leave through this thing.

If, in fact, this type of error can be considered to be a form-class error, then, it represents a strikingly different property from what has been reported for English SLI where form-class errors have been reported not to occur.

Furthermore, observational comparisons show that the impaired child's vocabulary is more restricted than her age match and her MLU match. In the examples above, she frequently uses the word *imaittumik* (thingamajig). In Inuktitut, the limitations of her lexicon could represent both a lack of lexical items and / or a lack of synthesizing skills with which to handle the morphological complexity necessary to construct certain lexical items.

This preliminary evidence about developmental language impairment in Inuktitut confirms the hypothesis that this disorder reflects an underlying deficit in the grammar. This is demonstrated by the fact that the irregularities in this child's language affect a number of aspects of her grammar that are not explained by alternative hypotheses (Gopnik et al., this volume). It also underlines the importance of studying language impairment cross-linguistically as well as the importance of using the impaired model to inform the normal model of language acquisition and the corollary, the importance of using the normal model to inform the impaired model.

Conclusions

In this chapter, Inuit examples have been used to highlight both the specific and the universal, the environmental and the innate, the mutable and the immutable aspects of language. Concerning the variable aspects, the Inuit culture shows how input to children varies, creating a wide range of sociopragmatic features of language used by and to children. Heath (1989) has used such cultural multiplicity to argue for the exceptional plasticity of the human organism. Furthermore, evidence from the acquisition of the passive in Inuktitut demonstrates how specific timetables, ordering and forms of grammatical properties in children's language vary across languages. Such cultural and linguistic variation shows the importance of avoiding Anglocentrism in the study of language learning (Slobin 1985; 1992a). Indeed Slobin (1992b) has pointed out that as more cross-linguistic evidence accumulates, his list of universal operating principles is shortening.

The extent of the variability, however, does not prove that there is nothing at the core. Given certain core features of environmental support and an intact organism, the basic milestones for language acquisition first articulated by Lenneberg (1967) appear to be exceptionally robust across cultures and languages. The robustness of these milestones does not deny that they are individually sculpted by the specifics of each culture and language. Nor, however, does the individual sculpting deny the sturdiness of the phenomena. The milestones only break down when the organism is impaired. In cases of impairment, the language milestones can be shown to dissociate from other developmental milestones such as those in the cognitive motor areas. The commonality of the language milestones across cultures and languages leads to the conclusion that there are certain fundamental innate characteristics to the human mind involved in the acquisition of language. In other words, variation cannot eclipse the fundamental properties that cut across cultures, languages and races. To conclude, the linguistic properties of the mind can be seen as fashioning the variable aspects of language into an elegant tapestry of multiplicity and at the same time rendering the common features of acquisition into a statement of equal mental capacity. Furthermore, the cross-linguistic study of the innate and socially constructed aspects of language can be profitably addressed by examining language acquisition at the level of linguistic structure, both in impairment and normal development.

Acknowledgments

We would like to thank all of our Inuit colleagues: Betsy Annahatak, Lizzie Ningiuruvik, Johnny Nowra, Vicki Ookpik, Elisapee Durocher, Billy Nowkawalk and Louisa Angutigirk. Our greatest thanks, of course, go to the children and their families who so kindly shared their language and homes with us. Funding for the three studies came from a Social Science and Humanities Research Council grant (#410–90–1744), Fonds pour la Formation de Chercheurs et L'Aide à la Recherche (#92–NC–0704) and the Kativik School Board Research Council. We are most appreciative of this support.

Note

1 The following abbreviations are used:

ABS = absolutive case	ALL = allative case
CSV = causative verbal modality	DIM = diminutive
ERG = ergative case	IMP = imperative verbal modality

IND = indicative verbal modality   INT = interrogative verbal modality
LOC = locative case   MOD = modalis case
NOM = nominalizer   PAR = participial verbal modality
    (equivalent to indicative in Inuktitut)
PERF = perfective   pl = plural
PRE = prefix   sg = singular
VIA = vialis case

For possessive nominal inflection:
3Ssg = third person possessor of singular possessed item

For verbal inflection:

1 = first person	2 = second person	3 = third person
s = singular	d = dual	p = plural
S = subject	O = object	

References

Allen, S.E.M. (in press). *Aspects of Argument Structure Acquisition in Inuktitut.* Amsterdam: John Benjamins

Allen, S.E.M., and M.B. Crago (1992). First language acquisition in Inuktitut. In M.-J. Dufour and F. Thérien (eds.), *Looking to the Future: Papers from the Seventh Inuit Studies Conference. Inuit Studies Occasional Papers* 4: 273–281

—— (in press). Early passive acquisition in Inuktitut. *Journal of Child Language*

Berman, R.A. (1985). The acquisition of Hebrew. In D.I. Slobin (ed.), *The Cross-Linguistic Study of Language Acquisition, Vol.1: The Data*, 255–371. Hillsdale, NJ: Lawrence Erlbaum

Borer, H., and K. Wexler (1987). The maturation of syntax. In T. Roeper and E. Williams (eds.), *Parameter Setting*, 123–72. Dordrecht: Reidel

Braine, M. (1976). Children's first word combinations. *Monographs of the Society for Research in Child Development*, 41. Chicago, IL: University of Chicago Press and Society for Research in Child Development

Brown, R. (1973). *A First Language: The Early Stages.* Cambridge, MA: Harvard University Press

Bruner, J. (1981). The social context of language acquisition. *Language and Communication* 1: 155–78

—— (1983). *Child's Talk.* New York: Academic Press

—— (1985). Vygotsky: A historical and conceptual perspective. In J.V. Wertsch (ed.), *Culture, Communication, and Cognition: Vygotskian Perspectives.* Cambridge: Cambridge University Press

Crago, M.B. (1988). Cultural Context in Communicative Interaction of Young Inuit Children. Unpublished doctoral thesis. Montréal: McGill University

—— (1992). Communicative interaction and second language acquisition: An Inuit example. *TESOL Quarterly* 26: 487–505

Crago, M.B., and S.E.M. Allen (in press). Building the case for impairment in linguistic representation. In M. Rice 9ed.), *Toward the genetics of Language.* Hillsdale, NJ: Lawrence Erlbaum

Crago, M.B., and A. Eriks-Brophy (1993). Culture, conversation, and interaction: Implications for intervention. In J. Duchan (ed.), *Pragmatics: From Theory to Practice,* 43–58. Englewood Cliffs, NJ: Prentice Hall

Curtiss, S. (1977). *Genie: A Psycholinguistic Study of a Modern-Day "Wild Child."* New York: Academic Press

Demuth, K. (1990). Subject, topic and Sesotho passive. *Journal of Child Language* 17: 67–84.

de Villiers, J.G., and P.A. de Villiers (1985). The acquisition of English. In D.I. Slobin (ed.), *The Cross-Linguistic Study of Language Acquisition, Vol.1: The Data,* 27–140. Hillsdale, NJ: Lawrence Erlbaum

Fortescue, M. (1985). Learning to speak Greenlandic: A case study of a two-year-old's morphology in a polysynthetic language. *First Language* 5: 101–114

Goldin-Meadow, S., and C. Mylander (1984). Gestural communication in deaf children: The effects and noneffects of parental input on early language development. *Monographs of the Society for Research in Child Development* 49: 1–151

Gopnik, Myrna, J. Dalalakis, S.E. Fukuda and S. Fukuda (This volume). Familial language impairment

Heath, S.B. (1989). The learner as a cultural member. In M.L. Rice and R.L. Schiefelbusch (eds.), *The Teachability of Language,* 333–50. Baltimore, MD: Paul H. Brookes

Hough-Eyamie, W.P. (1993). A Microanalytic Analysis of Caregiver-Child Interaction: An Inuit Example. Unpublished M.Sc. thesis. Montréal: McGill University

Lenneberg, E.H. (1967). *Biological Foundations of Language.* New York: Wiley

MacWhinney, B., and C. Snow (1990). The Child Language Data Exchange System: An update. *Journal of Child Language* 17: 457–72

Mills, A.E. (1985). The acquisition of German. In D.I. Slobin (ed.), *The Cross-Linguistic Study of Language Acquisition: The Data,* Vol.1, 141–254. Hillsdale, NJ: Lawrence Erlbaum

Nelson, K. (1973). Structure and strategy in learning to talk. *Monographs of the Society for Research in Child Development,* No. 38. Chicago, IL: University of Chicago Press and Society for Research in Child Development

Ninio, A., and J.S. Bruner (1978). The achievement and antecedents of labelling. *Journal of Child Language* 5: 1–16

Ochs, E., and B.B. Schieffelin (1984). Language acquisition and socialization: Three developmental stories and their implications. In R.A. Shweder and R.A. Levine (eds.), *Culture Theory: Essays on Mind, Self, and Emotion,* 276–322. New York: Cambridge University Press

Pinker, S. (1984). *Language Learnability and Language Development.* Cambridge, MA: Harvard University Press

Pinker, S. (This volume). Evolutionary Biology and the Evolution of Language

Pinker, S., D. Lebeaux and L.A. Frost (1987). Productivity and constraints in the acquisition of the passive. *Cognition* 26: 195–267

Pye, C., and P. Quixtan Poz (1988). Precocious passives and antipassives in Quiche Mayan. *Papers and Reports on Child Language Development* 27: 71–80

Rogoff, B. (1990). *Apprenticeship in Thinking: Cognitive Development in Social Context.* Oxford: Oxford University Press

Schieffelin, B.B., and E. Ochs (1986). *Language Socialization across Cultures.* Cambridge: Cambridge University Press

Slobin, D.I. (1985a). Crosslinguistic evidence for the language making capacity. In D.I. Slobin (ed.), *The Crosslinguistic Study of Language Acquisition,* Vol. 2, 1157–1256. Hillsdale, NJ: Lawrence Erlbaum

——— (1985b). *The Crosslinguistic Study of Language Acquisition: The Data,* Vol. 1. Hillsdale, NJ: Lawrence Erlbaum

——— (1992a). *The Crosslinguistic Study of Language Acquisition,* Vol. 3. Hillsdale, NJ: Lawrence Erlbaum

——— (1992b). Introduction. In D.I. Slobin (ed.), *The Crosslinguistic Study of Language Acquisition,* Vol. 3, 1–14. Hillsdale, NJ: Lawrence Erlbaum

5
Epidemiology of Specific Language Impairment

J. Bruce Tomblin

This chapter will be concerned with a form of developmental language disorder termed specific language impairment (SLI) which has challenged speech-language pathologists for decades and in recent years has become the subject of study by those interested the potential this condition provides for insight into the nature of language and language acquisition. Specifically, this paper will focus on what we can learn about this language-learning problem through the use of epidemiological methods, including genetic epidemiology. The basic issue to be considered pertains to the cause of SLI and in particular the evidence for a biological basis for this problem of language acquisition.

Definition of SLI

The dependent variable in epidemiological research is the diagnosis itself. Everything learned about a condition in epidemiology is dependent on the diagnostic standard used. Therefore, we need to begin by considering the diagnostic standards that have been employed in epidemiological research on SLI.

The notion of SLI has been derived from the earlier diagnostic term "childhood aphasia." Arthur Benton characterized childhood aphasia as "the relative specific failure of the normal growth of language functions ... the disability is called a 'specific' one because it cannot readily be ascribed to those factors which often provide the general setting in which failure of language development is usually observed, namely, deafness, mental deficiency, motor disability or severe personality disorder" (Benton 1964, 41).

Very simply, this definition states that aphasia exists when the child presents unexpected and unexplained poor achievement in language acquisition. Benton suggested that this seems to be a rather selective impairment involving language. In fact, Johnston (this volume) has provided considerable evidence that, as a group, children with SLI also perform poorly on certain non-language tasks as well. Thus, the extent to which this is truly an impairment that is specific to linguistic development is questionable. In recent years the term aphasia has been replaced by SLI and there has also been a trend to replace the exclusionary conditions with their positive versions. That is, SLI exists when the child has poor language achievement despite normal non-verbal IQ (above an IQ of 85), normal hearing, normal social development, normal emotional status and normal motor skills. As with most theoretical notions including clinical diagnostic categories, the standards for the diagnosis of SLI have changed over the years. The evolution in the diagnostic standards for SLI, however, has primarily involved changes in those standards having to do with the non-language attributes of this construct. The perspectives regarding the language features of SLI have remained rather constant during the past 20 years, and this view is that we can characterize the SLI child's language status relative to normal learners in terms of the rate at which the child acquires language.

This viewpoint, sometimes called the delay hypothesis, has been tested through a number of studies that have compared children with SLI with normal learners of different ages with respect to their grammar, semantics, pragmatics and phonology. For example, Morehead and Ingram (1973) concluded that with respect to phrase structure rules, transformational rule usage and inflectional usage, the SLI children were largely very similar to younger children matched on MLU. Not long after this study, Johnston and Schery (1976)reported similar results with respect to the pattern of grammatical morpheme development. Johnston and Schery did, however, find that the SLI children seemed to be more delayed with respect to the development of grammatical morphemes than would be expected based on their MLU. This observation has been confirmed by others since then (Leonard 1987). Thus, there are characteristic variations in the rates of acquisition across areas of language, but the differences between normal language and impaired language in each area can still be represented in terms of quantitative growth rates. Because of these results, the relevant property of language used in the diagnosis of SLI has been a set of indices reflecting the child's rate of development in various domains of language.

Thus far, I have provided some background concerning the manner in which SLI has been defined and the language-learning characteristics of those with SLI have been viewed. Now we can turn to what we know about the epidemiology of SLI and the insights this type of research provides us with respect to biological factors influencing SLI.

Epidemiology

Very simply, epidemiology is a medical research field concerned with the study of rates of occurrence of diseases and the factors associated with variations in these rates. Thus, diagnostic entities serve as the dependent variables in epidemiology. Rates of disease are characterized in the form of prevalence and incidence, and these serve as the dependent variable for epidemiology. The independent variables of epidemiology consist of those things that are associated with variations in disease rates, such as exposures to environmental toxins and contagions, as well as personal attributes such as blood pressure or practices such as exercise.

Epidemiological research, like astronomy, relies to a great extent on the observation of naturally occurring events. That is, the independent variables are not directly manipulated as would be done in an experimental method. As such, epidemiology does not usually provide a definitive proof of the cause of a condition but rather provides early evidence concerning possible causal theories, particularly for conditions which lack strong candidate theories of cause. In this respect, then, epidemiology may be a useful research approach for the study of developmental language impairments such as SLI. At the same time, we must recognize that epidemiological research does not stand outside theory. Good theories make for more insightful observations and improve the likelihood that interpretable insights will come from the research. No better example of this can be found than in our efforts to study SLI using epidemiological methods.

The Epidemiology of SLI

Epidemiology asks basic questions about the variations in the rate of the condition as a function of such things as who is affected and when are they affected. According to the null hypothesis within epidemiology, a given condition is randomly distributed across the population, and there is no variation in the rate of the disease as a function of where the person has lived, worked and so forth, nor is there any variation in the rate of the condition overtime. When there is evidence that the rate of the condition deviates from a random distribution as a function of some variable, hypotheses can be generated about the underlying cause. The epidemiological study of SLI is quite new, but despite this, we will find that there is evidence that SLI is associated with certain variables and thus the underlying etiology is beginning to emerge.

Age of Onset and Course of SLI

We can begin to gain some insight into the basic nature of SLI by learning about its course. One way of viewing SLI is as a form of developmental language impairment. Although such language impairments are rather heterogeneous, a commonality among these language impairments is that the children present signs of language-learning problems from the outset of language development. Thus, parents of children with SLI will report that their child was slow to begin talking, and usually these children do not present the characteristic explosion of language growth often observed in children between 18 and 24 months. This delay in the initiation and early development of language is persistent through the preschool and school years. Furthermore, there is now evidence that for many of these people with SLI, there will be residual signs of language difficulties in adulthood (Tomblin, Freese and Records 1992). The fact that signs of SLI can nearly always be observed during the child's second year suggests that whatever the etiology is, it must be something that is present early in the child's life and it must be some factor that produces rather enduring language difficulties.

Estimates of Prevalence of SLI

Recall that epidemiological studies often look for variations in the rate of a condition. Therefore it is useful initially to establish what the rate or prevalence of SLI is within the general population. There are few studies that provide insight into the general prevalence of SLI. Most studies that bear on this topic do not distinguish between SLI and other forms of developmental language impairment such as those associated with hearing impairment or mental retardation. Two studies, both performed in Britain, provide some evidence concerning the prevalence of SLI. Randell, Reynell and Curwen (1974) reported that 2 children (1.1%) out of a sample of 176 3-year-old children sampled from the London borough of Barnet presented language abilities 2 or more standard deviations below age expectation. Neither of these children was mentally retarded, hearing impaired or from non-English-speaking homes and so qualified as SLI. Stevenson and Richman (1976) reported on the prevalence of specific expressive language delay. This condition was defined as expressive language skills, measured in terms of language age equivalence scores, which were two-thirds or more the child's non-verbal mental age. That is, the children's growth rate in language was two-thirds that of their growth rate in non-language areas. Of the 705 3-year-olds studied, 1.4% presented specific expressive language delay. Unfortunately, this study did not include measures of language comprehension, and therefore impairments involving receptive language impairments were not included. Fundudis, Kolvin and Garside (1979) studied a cohort of 3,300 British children and estimated the prevalence of speech and language disorders in this group to be 4% at age 3 and 3% at age 7. Further, they reported that specific speech and language disorders at age 7 occurred at the rate of 2.5%. Finally, we have just begun a study that will sample 6,000 kindergarten children in Iowa and will determine the rate of SLI in this population. We have recently sampled

542 kindergarten children in eastern Iowa. Of these children, 2.5% of them were found to present SLI. SLI in this case was defined in terms of language skills at or below −1.2 standard deviations despite having normal hearing and normal non-verbal intelligence.

Given the fact that these studies have used different language measures and different diagnostic standards, the consistency of their results is remarkable. It appears that the prevalence of SLI is likely to be somewhere around 2% to 3% of the preschool and kindergarten population. This prevalence estimate provides a base line against which we can begin to look for factors that elevate or reduce the prevalence rate. Since signs of SLI are usually present by the time the child is 2 years old, we can narrow our search for explanatory factors to those things that could have an impact on the child prior to or during infancy.

Child's Sex

One of the most robust risk factors for many speech and language problems has to do with a person's sex. Clinicians have long noted the greater numbers of males in their case loads. Several studies have shown that SLI is more common in males than females. Stevenson and Richman (1976) reported that among the children with language impairment in their study there was a 2:1 ratio of males to females. When those children who were mentally retarded were eliminated, the ratio declined, but still favoured boys. Likewise, Fundudis, Kolvin and Garside (1979), and Silva (1980) reported a 2:1 ratio of males over females for their children with language impairment.

A common explanation for the elevated rates of SLI in males has been that males in general may have poorer verbal skills than females. Thus, as depicted in Figure 1, if we were to create two distributions having to do with language growth, one for each sex, and overlay them, we would see that a greater number of males would end up at the lower end of the distribution and thus be identified as language impaired.

In fact, however, the differences between males and females with respect to performance on receptive and expressive language measures have not been found to be very great. Siegel (1982) followed a group of pre-term and full-term children through the preschool years and administered the Reynell Scales to these children when they were 3 years old. She reported that the child's sex accounted for 1% and 2.5% of the variance of receptive and expressive language respectively. The 542 kindergarten children participating in our epidemiological study described earlier were administered a language-screening test. No significant differences were found between the boys and girls on this test.

The evidence strongly suggests that there is something about maleness that is associated with SLI, but is not associated with language

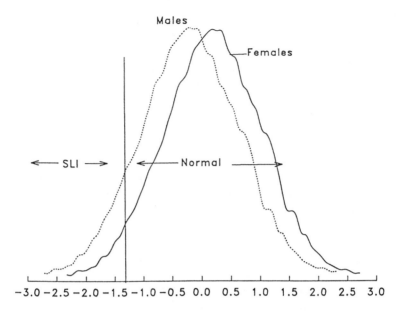

Figure 1: Hypothetical distributions of language ability for males and females in which males are poorer with respect to language than females. The vertical line represents the cut-off point below which individuals would be considered language impaired, thus producing a greater rate of language impairment in males.

development in general, and any explanatory theory will need to incorporate this property. In fact during the past decade, Geschwind and Behan (1982) and Galaburda, Sherman, Rosen, Aboitiz and Geschwind (1985) have proposed that exposure to testosterone during the late fetal period may produce cortical abnormalities in some children that predisposes them to speech, language and reading problems. This theory has yet to be tested with respect to SLI, but it stands as a good example of a theory that does account for the elevated rates of SLI in males.

Prenatal and Birth Events

Along with the recognition that males are more susceptible to SLI than females, many have assumed that SLI may be the product of some trauma or disease process during fetal development or during delivery. There are numerous ways in which the fetal development and birth of the child can be affected, and as we will see, the data regarding the association of many of these events with SLI are sparse.

Events during Pregnancy. The Collaborative Perinatal Project of the National Institute of Neurological and Communicative Disorders and Stroke (NINCDS) (Vetter, Fay and Winitz 1980) followed 30,000 children from birth to 3 years of age. This study found no association between the child's speech and language outcomes at age 3 and such things as the mother's status with respect to smoking, infectious diseases, toxemia or other pregnancy complications. There have been no other studies of such exposures and language impairment; however, as part of the epidemiological study mentioned earlier, we are gathering data that will bear on this issue.

Prematurity. A common birth complication is prematurity. There have been several studies following children born prematurely (Drillien, Thomson and Burgoyne 1982; Klein, Hack, Gallagher and Fanaroff 1985; Siegel 1982). The results of these studies show that infants born with birthweights between 1,500 and 2,500 grams have very good developmental outcomes in general. Further, there is little evidence that poor language skills are associated with children with birthweights between 1,200 and 1,500 grams. Few of these studies were concerned with SLI in particular; however, these studies did examine language development and they do not provide clear evidence of any form of language impairment in premature infants. Recently, Aram, Hack, Hawkins, Weissman and Borawski-Clark (1991) addressed SLI and prematurity and concluded that infants with very low birthweights (< 1500 g) did not present elevated rates of SLI when compared with full-term infants, although an elevation in general cognitive impairment was found for the low-birth-weight infants. Similar results were found by Menyuk, Liebergott, Schultz, Chesnick and Ferrier (1991). Recently, Byrne, Ellsworth, Bowering and Vincer (1993) followed 71 low-birth-weight infant through 24 months of age and found low rates of SLI at 12 months, but an elevated rate of expressive language delay at 24 months. The interpretation of these results is difficult, however, because their study did not contain a control group.

Obstetrical Medication. There are no studies concerned specifically with obstetrical practices and SLI. However, Friedman and Neff (1987) examined the relationships between labour and delivery variables and developmental outcomes for 58,000 children. In their study they found among the drugs administered to the mother during delivery that only one drug was associated with an increased rate of language delay at 3 years. This medication was oxytocin, which has been used to induce labour. Friedman and Neff cautioned, however, that the drug may not be the causal factor for this language delay because an synthetic analog of oxytocin – syntocinon – did not yield this outcome. They speculate that factors that lead to the induction of labour, such as high blood pressure in the mother, may instead be the culprit.

Asphyxia. Breathing difficulties have been the only other birth event examined with respect to language outcome. Creavey (1986) has reviewed research on the relationship between asphyxia at birth and later learning disorders in children. Creavey concluded that the effect of asphyxia was "all or nothing" and therefore it is unlikely to produce the subtle impairments found in children with learning disability (and by extension we can include children with SLI). One study, however, suggests that asphyxia might be associated with some instances of SLI. D'Souza, McCartney, Nolan and Taylor (1981) reported that one-third of the 24 children with histories of asphyxia in their study presented speech and language problems with no other handicaps. The sample size of this study is too small for us to conclude that asphyxia is a principal cause of SLI; however, this study requires that we consider this as a possibility at least for some children.

Despite the fact that children with subtle learning problems such as SLI have long been thought to have suffered some form of minimal brain injury during the perinatal period, there is no substantial support for this conclusion. Even in those children who have experienced troublesome births we find at best only a slightly elevated rate of SLI. Subtle traumatic events during fetal development or the birth process may contribute to SLI in some children; however, it does not appear that this is likely to be the explanation for many children with SLI.

Home and Family Characteristics. There is a large and rather extensive literature concerned with the relationships between various home and family variables and language outcomes. In general, there is some evidence that SLI is associated with those variables that constitute the notion of "lower socio-economic status" (SES). Interpretation of these studies is made difficult by the complex interactions that often exist among variables such as parental education, parental income, family size, richness of home environment, nature of language input, dialect, culturally related language differences, and so forth. Recently, I have reviewed many of these factors (Tomblin 1992) and I will not delve extensively into this topic here. There is some evidence that children with SLI are more often found in homes associated with lower incomes and parents with poorer educational levels. Tomblin, Hardy and Hein (1991) reported that it was the fathers' educational level that was associated with poorer language development rather than the mothers' educational level. Since the fathers were less likely to be the caregivers than the mothers, we must be cautious about drawing conclusions that implicate the language-rearing environment. In fact, there is considerable evidence that the language spoken to SLI children is not substantially different from that provided to normal language-learners

(Leonard 1987). Later, I will show that there is a strong familial pattern for SLI, and therefore we must at least consider the possibility that the causal relationship between SLI and the home environment is one in which parental language impairment, particularly of the fathers, leads to educational and economic limitations, and that this is why there is a concentration of SLI in the lower SES population. That is, SLI in the family may cause the social and economic conditions associated with low SES, rather than these factors causing SLI.

Epidemiological study of SLI is new. Because of this we cannot come to clear and convincing conclusions. It does seem that the primary factor that has been found to be associated with elevated rates of SLI is maleness. There are some suggestions that some children with SLI may have experienced undesirable birth events such as asphyxia, but at this time I am not aware of published replications of these results. During the past few years one important epidemiological finding has been identified and replicated. This is the observation mentioned earlier that SLI runs in families.

Genetic Epidemiology

Although most clinicians working with this population have often observed that more than one child in a family would present SLI, this clinical observation was not confirmed until recently. Using a mixture of direct assessment and/or historical reports, Neils and Aram (1986), Tallal, Ross and Curtiss (1989), Tomblin (1989), Lewis, Ekelman and Aram (1989), and Beitchman, Hood and Inglis (1992) have all reported that the immediate family members of SLI children had a heightened rate of language and language-related difficulties when compared to the immediate family members of probands who were typical language learners. Figure 2 summarizes the results of these studies. In each of these studies it was found that the rate of language impairment in the relatives of the SLI probands was higher than in the relatives of the non-SLI probands. Only one study (Whitehurst et al. 1991) has not found evidence of familiality, but there is some doubt as to whether these children had long-term language problems since the language-impaired (LI) group was performing at normal levels by 4 years.

These studies all used historical reports for their determination of a language impairment in the adult family members, and some also used this method with the siblings as well. Also, this historical report was usually obtained from the mother. It seems likely that in some instances family members who were language-impaired as children, but who were not presenting clear signs as adults, may have been reported as having normal language status. Thus these studies under-reported the rate of SLI. It is also possible the SLI families reported heightened rates

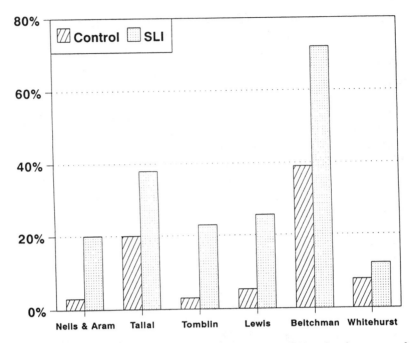

Figure 2: Rates of SLI among the immediate family members of SLI probands as reported in 6 separate studies.

of SLI over the control families because the parents of children with SLI were led by their child's diagnosis to review their background, as well as that of their family members. In contrast, the parents of the control probands would not have been led to think about their family history. Thus, it could be claimed that the increased rate of family history in the families with SLI probands was due to this reporting bias.

In order to overcome these problems with studies using historical reports, family studies of SLI that involve the direct assessment of all family members are needed. Gopnik and Crago (1991) have reported such data on one extended family. In this family, a particular difficulty with the use of morphological rules was found in 53% of the family members.

For the past two years we have been conducting a family study of SLI in which we have directly tested all the first-degree family members of SLI probands. We have also tested extended family members as well when the parents of the proband were found to be affected. At this point we have studied 42 families and examined 245 individuals. Figure 3 displays the rate of SLI in the family members tested. The overall rate of SLI in the first-degree family members was 22% (this does not include the proband). This suggests that the family members of SLI cases have more than 7 times the risk for SLI than the population in general.

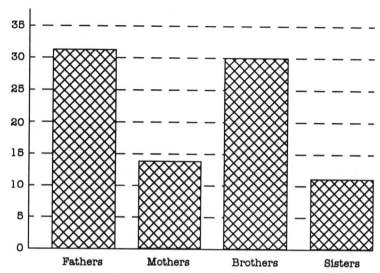

Figure 3: Rates of diagnosed SLI among the first degree family members of 42 SLI probands.

This rate of SLI in these families is very similar to the rates obtained in the prior studies using family history, and it clearly demonstrates that the familiality of SLI found in these studies is not the result of a reporting bias. In fact, our data show that historical reports of language impairment underestimate the rate of SLI in a family rather than over-estimate it. These data were obtained by asking each individual who was tested for SLI if he had language problems as a child. The responses to this question are contrasted with our diagnostic test results in Table 1. We learn from these data that most individuals who tested normal also reported no history of language problems; however, several of those who were tested as SLI reported no history of SLI.

Earlier I noted that there have been several studies showing that SLI is more common in males than females. With this in mind, we should not be too surprised to find that SLI occurred nearly twice as often in male relatives than female relatives in the families we studied. These

		Diagnostic Examination	
		Normal Language	SLI
Historical	Normal Language	153	26
Report	SLI	1	9

Table 1: The agreement between reports of SLI in family members of SLI probands compared with results of diagnostic examination.

results contrast with recent data concerning the rate of dyslexia in males and females. Several papers have recently reported a slightly elevated rate of dyslexia in males over females or no differential rate of dyslexia between males and females when the subjects were obtained through some form of research sampling other than clinical referral (DeFries 1989; Finucci and Childs 1981; Hallgren 1950; Shaywitz, Shaywitz, Fletcher and Escobar 1990; Vogler, DeFries and Decker 1985; Wadsworth, DeFries, Stevenson, Gilger and Pennington 1992). This has led some (Wadsworth et al. 1992) to conclude that the often reported elevated rate of dyslexia in males has been due to a referral bias. The family members in our study also represent a non-referred, sample and yet unlike the studies of dyslexia, we continue to find an increased rate of SLI in the males of this sample.

Association of SLI with Reading Problems among Family Members

While constructing pedigrees for each of our family members, we also obtained a historical report of reading and spelling problems. Out of the 226 family members and probands who had been examined for SLI, 57% showed no SLI or reading problems, 28% presented both SLI and a history of reading problems and 13% presented just SLI. These data show that reading impairment is quite common in families of SLI probands, and further that often SLI and reading impairment occur in the same person. We also see that reading impairment without signs of SLI is more common than SLI without a history of reading impairment. It seems that the presence of SLI will imply the presence of reading problems, but the presence of reading problems does not imply SLI.

We can hypothesize that SLI and reading impairment are strongly associated within families and therefore the factors that lead to the familiality of one are likely to also be contributing to the familiality of the other. The relationship between oral language problems and reading within children has been well documented recently (Aram and Hall 1989; Bishop and Adams 1990; Silva, Williams and McGee 1987; Stark and Tallal 1988). Of those children identified as SLI during late preschool years, 50% to 80% go on to have reading problems. These data now show that this association between reading problems and SLI extends to the relatives of the SLI proband. At this point we must begin to ask whether we should consider reading disorder and SLI as two separate conditions that co-occur in families, or if there is one condition that is expressed in sightly different forms. A very similar process is occurring in psychiatry with respect to Tourette Syndrome and Obsessive Compulsive Disorders (George, Trimble, Ring, Sallee and Robertson 1993; Pauls 1992). These conditions seem to run together in families, and some have proposed that they represent different variants of the same underlying etiology. This could also be true with reading impairment and SLI.

The research using family history data can be combined with those using direct diagnosis of family members. These combined data show that SLI has a strong familial character. Research questions must now turn toward the examination of which familial factors contribute to SLI. Specifically, we must ask to what extent genes as well as the environment contribute to SLI.

SLI among Twins

Studies of twins often provide evidence about the extent to which a familial trait is the product of genetic and/or environmental influences. Twins offer an excellent basis of experiment for genetic research because identical (monozygotic, MZ) twins share all of their genes, whereas fraternal (dizygotic, DZ) twins share, on average, only 50% of their genes. It is also believed that the two types of twinships do not differ with respect to their environment. As a result, if a condition is genetically influenced, we will expect to find that the MZ twins will be more similar (concordant) to each other with respect to the trait than will be the DZ twins because the MZ twins share more genes than do the DZ twins.

A few years ago, we performed a crude twin study as a pilot to see if a more extensive twin study was worthwhile. We sent a questionnaire to a large number of public school speech-language clinicians in Iowa asking if they had a member of a twinship in their caseload. If they did, we asked them to report the speech and language status of each twin, as well as the educational status, sex and type of twinship. We treated as SLI in this study those children who were identified as having a language impairment, but who were not identified as being mentally retarded or hearing impaired. Of the 82 twin pairs (56 MZ and 26 same-sex DZ) 38% of the DZ were concordant for SLI and 80% of the MZ twins were concordant. These results suggested that the concordance rate closely parallelled the rate of shared genes. As I noted earlier, this was a crude study, particularly because of the manner in which zygosity was determined. The data from this study, therefore, must be viewed with caution.

Lewis and Thompson (1992), however, used a better measure of zygosity and reported similar values of concordance for a group of twins with developmental phonological and language disorders. Their phenotype was based upon treatment histories, and the majority of the twins appeared to have phonological problems; however, many also had language problems. They reported a concordance for MZs of .86 and DZs of .48. Clearly, there is need for further replications of this work. Nevertheless, the data from these studies do provide a strong suggestion of a substantial genetic contribution to SLI. If this is true, we then need to pose questions about the nature of this genetic transmission among family members.

Potential Modes of Genetic Transmission for SLI

There are three general models of genetic transmission that serve as the principal hypotheses tested by genetic epidemiologists. Each of these models then have parameters within them that yield numerous subtypes. The simplest model is a single-gene system. It is this manner of genetic transmission that Mendel discovered, and as a result this mode of genetic transmission is often referred to as Mendelian. Traits or phenotypes that are produced by single genes are often found to be qualitative, in that variation is not continuous. The A, B and O blood types provide a good example of such a trait. In light of this, the phenotype for SLI should be a qualitative deviation in language development rather than a quantitative trait if it is Mendelian. Recently, Gopnik (1990) as well as Clahsen (1989) have argued that there is evidence of a qualitative difference in rule acquisition in SLI children and adults. Their description of the linguistic properties of SLI differs from the standard view that considers SLI as a quantitative trait having to do with differences in growth rate. If their account is correct, the SLI phenotype would be in accord with a single-gene model.

Contrasting with the single-gene model of transmission is the multifactorial model. This model assumes that there are several genes that influence the phenotype and that furthermore there are likely to be non-genetic, environmental influences. Multifactorial traits are expected to be expressed in a continuous fashion and to approximate the normal distribution: thus they are usually viewed as quantitative traits. Each genetic and environmental component adds or subtracts from the overall quantitative trait value and thus individual differences with respect to the multifactorial trait are the result of the summation of these components. In a multifactorial system of language acquisition, those individuals who possess several etiological components that lead to poor language-learning will have lower rates of language acquisition and thus a high susceptibility to SLI. In such a system there are no etiological factors that are unique to SLI; rather, the same factors that contribute to individual differences in language development among children with normal levels of language development will contribute to SLI. Leonard's (1987) description of SLI conforms rather well to this multifactorial model.

Finally, the third genetic system that can be hypothesized for SLI is the mixed model. As the name states, this mode of transmission involves a mixture of a major genetic locus operating in the context of background multifactorial and/or environmental influence. Mixed models of transmission result in continuous traits that may have a skewed distribution or multimodal distribution.

Analysis of Pedigrees

In order to test for these modes of transmission, it is first necessary for us to obtain data on the phenotype of interest (SLI in this case) from family members, and then test these data against predictions made by models of different mechanisms of transmission. As I mentioned earlier, we are now engaged in a pedigree study of SLI with the objective of using these data to make inferences about the possible mode(s) of inheritance of SLI. The data contained in the pedigrees from these families can be used to test various hypotheses about the transmission of SLI. The preferred method for testing these hypotheses is called complex segregation analysis. Basically, this is a statistical method for obtained phenotypic data from which estimates are made of genotypic parameters such as the frequency of different gene types (alleles), penetrance, etc. Once these parameters can be estimated with confidence, the values can be compared with known modes of genetic transmission. We are currently performing such an analysis, but as yet do not have results to report.

There is a simpler, though less powerful method that we have performed. This is a method proposed by Penrose (1954). With this method, the mode of genetic transmission of diseases can be evaluated by knowing the rate of the disease in the siblings of probands (q) and the rate in the general population (s) and from this computing a relative frequency ($K = s/q$). Penrose has provided expected relative frequency values for two Mendelian autosomal modes – dominant and recessive and a multifactorial mode.

From our family study we were able to compute the rate of SLI in brothers and sisters of SLI probands and found it to be 22%. We are not as sure about the rate of SLI in the general population. If we assume, however, that the prevalence of SLI is 3%, the relative frequency (K) of SLI in the siblings of the SLI probands is 7.33%. The expected relative frequencies for each mode of transmission are contained in Table 2, and we can see that the obtained (K) falls in between the multifactorial mode (5.8) and recessive mode (8.3). A limitation with Penrose's procedure is that it does not provide a means of testing the goodness of fit between the obtained and expected values, and thus we cannot use it to test whether the data fit one of these predictions. It is this type of power that complex segregation analysis provides. These results, however, suggest that SLI is likely to fit some model that will contain a genetic component.

General Population	Obtained Siblings		Dominant	Expected Recessive	Multi-factorial
(q)	(s)	s/q	$(\frac{1}{2}q)$	$(\frac{1}{4}q)$	$(\frac{1}{N}q)$
0.03	0.22	7.33	16.7	8.3	5.8

Table 2: A comparison between observed relative frequency of SLI and relative frequencies expected based upon dominant recessive and multifactorial modes of inheritance. Relative frequency (s/q) is computed by dividing the prevalence of SLI in siblings of SLI probands (s) by the prevalence of SLI in the general population (q). This obtained relative frequency can be compared to the expected values for each mode of genetic transmission. The coefficients for each mode ($1/2$, $1/4$, $1/N$) represent the probablility of a sibling being affected given an affected proband. The expected rate for each mode, then, is the product of the prevalence rate in the general population multiplied by the coefficient for the particular mode.

Conclusions

The epidemiological study of SLI is quite new. However, we can see that two risk factors for SLI have been identified. It is now quite clear that males in some families are much more likely to be SLI than would be expected, based on the prevalence rate in the general population. Each of these factors comes with both a biological and environmental explanation. That is, males could be performing more poorly in terms of language development because of certain gender-based linguistic expectations and interactions of the caregiver that lead to slower rates of language development. Likewise, the familiality of SLI could be explained by invoking the child's linguistic environment. In order for these non-biological explanations to be plausible, it will be necessary for such experiential factors be potent enough to take effect during the first year to 18 months of the child's life, since these language-learning problems begin to surface during that time. Further, these variations in language exposure would need to be greater than those found in different cultures such as those described by Crago in this volume. In other words, there would have to be a rather substantial disruption or variation in the linguistic environment of the child. To date, however, there has been no evidence of a variation in language exposure, and in fact the language experiences of the SLI child seem to be well within the bounds of normal variation as noted earlier.

I suspect that the most prominent aspects of an explanation for SLI will focus on the biological aspects of maleness and some genetic mechanism underlying the familility. Although such a conclusion may narrow the range of possible explanations, there remain numerous ways that genes and other biological factors may interact to influence the neurological substrates of language acquisition. A fundamental question at this time pertains to the manner in which the biology of maleness interacts with the likely genetic basis of SLI. SLI is clearly not a simple X-linked disorder, since there were instances of father-to-son transmission in our families. It is more likely that SLI is sex-influenced such that individuals with a particular genotype will be predisposed to SLI, and this predisposition is increased by biological factors associated with maleness. We are now at the stage where biological and neurodevelopmental theories must be explored to consider ways in which maleness and genotype interact to influence the neural substrates of language. These theories may then provide for a refinement in the epidemiological observations that we should make in the future.

Acknowledgment

This study was supported by a grant from the National Institutes of Health (NIH USPHS R01 DC00612–02).

References

Aram, D.M., M. Hack, S. Hawkins, B.M. Weissman and E. Borawski-Clark (1991). Very-low-birthweight children and speech and language development. *Journal of Speech and Hearing Research* 34: 1169–79

Aram, D.M., and N.E. Hall (1989). Longitudinal follow-up of children with preschool communication disorders: Treatment implications. *School Psychology Review* 18: 487–501

Beitchman, J.H., J. Hood and A. Inglis (April, 1992). Familial transmission of speech and language impairment: A preliminary investigation. *Canadian Journal of Psychiatry – Revue Canadienne de Psychiatrie* 37: 151–56

Benton, A. (1964). Developmental aphasia and brain damage. *Cortex* 1: 40–52

Bishop, D.V., and C. Adams (1990). A prospective study of the relationship between specific language impairment, phonological disorders and reading retardation. *Journal of Child Psychology and Psychiatry and Allied Disciplines* 31: 1027–50

Byrne, J., C. Ellsworth, E. Bowering and M. Vincer (1993). Language development in low birthweight infants: the first two years of life. *Journal of Developmental and Behavioral Pediatrics* 14: 21–27

Clahsen, H. (1989). The grammatical characterization of developmental dysphasia. *Linguistics* 27: 897–920

Creevy, D.C. (1986). The relationship of obstetrical trauma to learning disabilities: An obstetrician's view. In M. Lewis (ed.), *Learning Disabilities and Prenatal Risk*. Chicago: University of Illinois Press

DeFries, J.C. (1989). Gender ratios in children with reading disability and their affected relatives: A commentary. *Journal of Learning Disabilities* 22: 544–45

Drillien, C.M., A.J.M. Thomson and K. Burgoyne (1982). Low birthweight children at early school age: A longitudinal study. *Developmental Medicine and Child Neurology* 22: 26–47

D'Souza, S.W., E. McCartney, M. Nolan and I.G. Taylor (1981). Hearing, speech, and language in survivors of severe perinatal asphyxia. *Archives of Diseases in Childhood* 56: 245–52

Finucci, J.M., and B. Childs (1981). Are there really more dyslexic boys than girls? In A. Ansara, A. Geschwind, A. Galaburda, M. Albert and N. Gartrell (eds.), *Sex Differences in Dyslexia*, 1–9. Towson, MD: Orton Dyslexia Society

Friedman, E.A., and R.K. Neff (1987). *Labor and Delivery: Impact on Offspring.* Littleton, MA: PSG Publishing

Fundudis, T., I. Kolvin and R. Garside (1979). *Speech Retarded and Deaf Children: Their Psychological Development.* New York: Academic Press

Galaburda, A.M., G.F. Sherman, G.D. Rosen, F. Aboitz and N. Geschwind (1985). Developmental dyslexia: Four consecutive patients with cortical anomalies. *Annals of Neurology* 18: 222–33

George, M.S., M.R. Trimble, H.A. Ring, F.R. Sallee and M.M. Robertson (1993). Obsessions in obsessive-compulsive disorder with and without Gilles de la Tourette's syndrome. *American Journal of Psychiatry* 150: 93–97

Geschwind, N., and P. Behan (1982). Left-handedness: Association with immune disease, migraine, and developmental learning disorder. *Proceedings of the National Academy of Sciences of the United States of America* 79: 5097–5100

Gopnik, M. (1990). Feature-blind grammar and dysphagia. *Nature* 344: 715

Gopnik, M., and M.B. Crago (1991). Familial aggregation of a developmental language disorder. *Cognition* 39: 1–50

Hallgren, B. (1950). Specific dyslexia: A clinical and genetic study. *Acta Psychiatrica et Neurologica Scandinavica* 65: 1–287

Johnston, J.R., and T.K. Schery (1976). The use of grammatical morphemes by children with communication disorders. In D.M. Morehead and A.E. Morehead (eds.), *Normal and Deficient Child Language*, 239–58. Baltimore, MD: University Park

Klein, N., M.B. Hack, J. Gallagher and A. Fanaroff (1985). Preschool performance of children with normal intelligence who were very low-birthweight infants. *Pediatrics* 75: 531–37

Leonard, L.B. (1987). Is specific language impairment a useful construct? In S. Rosenberg (ed.), *Advances in Applied Psycholinguistics*, Vol. 1, 1–39. New York: Cambridge University Press

Lewis, B.A., B.L. Ekelman and D.M. Aram (1989). A familial study of severe phonological disorders. *Journal of Speech and Hearing Research* 32: 713–24

Lewis, B.A., and L.A. Thompson (1992). A study of developmental speech and language disorders in twins. *Journal of Speech and Hearing Research* 35: 1086–94

Menyuk, P., J. Liebergott, M. Schultz, M. Chesnick and L. Ferrier (1991). Patterns of early lexical and cognitive development in premature and full-term infants. *Journal of Speech and Hearing Research* 34: 88–94

Morehead, D., and D. Ingram (1973). The development of base syntax in normal and linguistically deviant children. *Journal of Speech and Hearing Research* 16: 330–52

Neils, J., and D.M. Aram (1986, October). Family history of children with developmental language disorders. *Perceptual and Motor Skills* 63: 655–58

Pauls, D.L. (1992). The genetics of obsessive compulsive disorder and Gilles de la Tourette's syndrome. *Psychiatric Clinics of North America* 15: 759–66

Penrose, L.S. (1954). The genetical background of common diseases. *Acta Geneticae Medicae et Gemellologiae. Twin Research* 4: 257–65

Randall, D., J. Reynell and M. Curwen (1974). A study of language development in a sample of three-year-old children. *British Journal of Disorders of Communication* 9: 3–16

Shaywitz, S.E., B.A. Shaywitz, J.M. Fletcher and M.D. Escobar (1990). Prevalence of reading disability in boys and girls. Results of the Connecticut Longitudinal Study. *Jama* 264: 998–1002

Siegel, L. (1982). Reproductive, perinatal, and environmental factors as predictors of the cognitive and language development of preterm and full-term infants. *Child Development* 53: 963–73

Silva, P.A. (1980). The prevalence, stability and significance of developmental language delay in preschool children. *Developmental Medicine and Child Neurology* 22: 768–77

Silva, P.A., S. Williams and R. McGee (1987). A longitudinal study of children with developmental language delay at age three: Later intelligence, reading and behaviour problems. *Developmental Medicine and Child Neurology* 29: 630–40

Stark, R.E., and P. Tallal. (1988). *Language, Speech, and Reading Disorders in Children*. Boston: Little, Brown

Stevenson, J., and N. Richman (1976). The prevalence of language delay in a population of three-year-old children and its association with general retardation. *Developmental Medicine and Child Neurology* 18: 431–41

Tallal, P., R. Ross and S. Curtiss (1989). Unexpected sex-ratios in families of language/learning-impaired children. *Neuropsychologia* 27: 987–98

Tomblin, J.B. (1989). Familial concentration of developmental language impairment. *Journal of Speech and Hearing Disorders* 54: 287–95

—— (1992). Risk factors associated with specific language disorder. In M. Wolraich and D.K. Routh (eds.), *Developmental and Behavioral Pediatrics*, 131–58. Philadelphia, PA: Jessica Kingsley

Tomblin, J.B., P.R. Freese and N.L. Records (1992). Diagnosing specific language impairment in adults for the purpose of pedigree analysis. *Journal of Speech and Hearing Research* 35: 832–43

Tomblin, J.B., J.C. Hardy and H.A. Hein (1991). Predicting poor- communication status in preschool children using risk factors present at birth. *Journal of Speech and Hearing Research* 34: 1096–1105

Vetter, D., W. Fay and H. Winitz (1980). Overview: Perinatal, medical, and growth factors. In F.M. Lassman, P.J. La Benz, and E.S. La Benz (eds.), *Early Correlates of Speech, Language, and Hearing,* 355–78. Littleton, MA: PSG Publishing

Vogler, G.P., J.C. DeFries and S.N. Decker (1985). Family history as an indicator of risk for reading disability. *Journal of Learning Disabilities* 18: 419–21

Wadsworth, S.J., J.C. DeFries, J. Stevenson, J.W. Gilger and B.F. Pennington (1992). Gender ratios among reading-disabled children and their siblings as a function of parental impairment. *Journal of Child Psychology and Psychiatry and Allied Disciplines* 33: 1229–39

Whitehurst, G.J., D.S. Arnold, M. Smith, J.E. Fischel, C.J. Lonigan and M.C. Valdez-Menchaca (1991). Family history in developmental expressive language delay. *Journal of Speech and Hearing Research* 34: 1150–57

6

Familial Language Impairment

Myrna Gopnik, Jenny Dalalakis
Suzy E. Fukuda, Shinji Fukuda

Introduction

In the past 40 years there has been a fundamental change in our understanding of the nature of human language. The view of language as an arbitrary, socially learned animal communication system has been superseded by a view that regards language as a formally constrained, biologically determined, species-specific recursive system. Contemporary linguists, foremost among them Chomsky, hypothesize that all human languages are constructed from a small set of specific principles (the universal grammar) that limit the kinds of grammars that can occur. Evidence for this claim comes from two sources: the linguistic properties of the languages of the world and the way children acquire the language of their environment, whether spoken or signed (see Petitto, this volume). Research into the properties of currently extant languages has appropriately led to some revisions of the particular properties originally proposed for the universal grammar, but the notion that languages do share some fundamental properties has largely been confirmed.

This universal grammar is hypothesized to be innate. In other words, normal children come equipped to acquire languages that manifest the universal grammar; the innate specification of the constraints on grammars allows the child to acquire language so quickly and accurately. If it is true that the universal grammar guides the child in the acquisition of language, then the kinds of errors that a child makes in acquiring language should reflect these innate constraints – and empirical studies of language acquisition have confirmed that they do.

In addition, because no other animal is capable of naturally using a language built on these principles, or even learning such a language under explicit instruction, it has been hypothesized that the innately specified constraints on possible grammars are species-specific and have evolved in the recent past by means of natural selection (Pinker, this volume). Current linguistic theory, therefore, makes very strong and specific claims about the biological foundations of language.

111

The evidence that has been adduced to support these biological hypotheses has consisted largely in patterns of linguistic evidence, but the question of what precisely is inherited or how this heritability is played out has not yet been tested directly. If language is biologically specified by some genetic factor or factors, then a genetic mutation could interfere with the ability to acquire language. Tomblin (this volume) discusses the epidemiological evidence that a developmental disorder of language aggregates in families and that the pattern of aggregation is consistent with the disorder's being inherited. The existence of a population of children whose language does not follow the normal course of development and who appear never to be able to construct a normal grammar constitutes a natural experiment that, for the first time, can directly test the hypothesis that there are innate constraints on the formulation of grammars that guide the normal acquisition of language. This population of developmentally impaired individuals, therefore, allows us to investigate directly the connection between language development and its biological foundations.

This chapter will provide an overview of the research into this disorder in which our team at McGill has been engaged. Some of the alternative explanations which have been proposed to account for the disorder will be discussed critically, and then our own hypothesis and the predictions that follow from it will be presented. The linguistic properties of the disorder in English, Greek and Japanese will then be summarized. It will be shown that the pattern of impairment across these three languages is very similar, and suggests that the disorder affects impaired children's ability to acquire abstract symbolic rules in the grammar (which are implemented unconsciously and automatically) although they are able to learn individual lexical items and explicit rules that can be stored in declarative memory (Paradis and Gopnik 1994).

Definition of Specific Language Impairment

Specific Language Impairment (SLI) is clinically diagnosed in those cases where a child exhibits difficulty in acquiring his or her native language in the absence of any other conditions (such as deafness, gross neurological damage, low intelligence, autism, or motor impairment) that could account for this difficulty. This clinical population is defined in many countries by exclusionary criteria, and does not appear to be characterized by a unitary disorder (Bishop 1992). A wide range of etiologies, levels of severity, stages of resolution and degrees of compensation make the study of this disorder complex and contribute to the range of explanatory theories.

Aram, Ekelman and Nation (1984), for example, have pointed out that longitudinal studies of children diagnosed as SLI have shown that in 20% to 50% of the subjects, the apparent language disorder fully resolves as they get older. In the remainder of the population, language problems persist several years after the original diagnosis and even into adulthood. This means that many preschoolers diagnosed as language impaired will eventually acquire normal grammars. The English-speaking subjects that we will be reporting on here are all adult subjects, ranging in age from 18 to 75, and can therefore be considered members of the population of subjects who do have persistent difficulties with language throughout their lives and who never develop some basic properties of normal grammars.

Specific language impairment presents itself as a symptom, much like fever or fatigue, rather than a well-defined syndrome. Therefore, there is not likely to be a single explanatory theory that can account for all cases in which the development of language appears to be selectively impaired. The data and explanatory hypotheses presented in this paper, therefore, may apply to only a subset of the subjects clinically diagnosed as SLI. The subjects we report on in this paper exhibit a consistent set of linguistic difficulties across languages, which can be accounted for by an impairment in the grammar itself.

The Genetic Hypothesis

Tomblin (this volume) has reviewed the evidence that at least some cases of SLI are inherited. Our own data from the English family that we have been studying and from the Greek and Japanese subjects show similar patterns of familiality. It is nevertheless true that the relationship between the development of language and the genetic substrate is very complex and involves the interaction of multigenetic factors. The pattern of familial aggregation in the English-speaking multigenerational family reported on in this paper is particularly interesting because it is consistent with the hypothesis of genetic etiology by autosomal dominant transmission. However, even if it were unambiguously established that the familial language disorder we are concerned with was linked to an autosomal dominant gene, this would not mean that the single gene was solely responsible for language development in controls. It is clear that in any complex system a malfunction in one part of the system may have extensive consequences for the system as a whole, and yet that single part cannot be said to be responsible for the whole system. Moreover, we have no evidence to demonstrate that this gene (or genes) affects language and only language in every instance. That is, the gene might impair some more general property of neurological development, for example, the pattern of neuronal migration which might, in turn, affect the development of neurological asymmetries (see Plante 1991; Plante et al. 1991). If this were the case, the precise consequences of the genetic disorder might depend on, for example, the precise moment in the development of the brain that it turned on. In some cases, it might spare language but have consequences for some other cognitive system. It is known that other specific cognitive disorders also aggregate in families. We have selected our subjects precisely because they do have a language disorder. Whether this gene is specific to language, and whether it underlies all such cases of language disorders, is still to be determined. Though linkage analysis to find the locus of this gene is underway at several centres, to date it has not been found. Only when this has been accomplished can these more general questions be addressed.

One of the goals of this research is to find out what the contribution of the genetic component is to the biology of language and how it interacts with the linguistic input from the environment. As Kuhl and Meltzoff (this volume) have shown with respect to the development of the phonological system in babies, this interaction is quite complex, and only careful and detailed investigation can distinguish the contribution of each component.

Linguistic Description

In order to study the significance of the linguistic disorder, it is crucial that we provide a detailed and linguistically principled account of the impaired subjects' language, so that any hypothesis about the cause of the disorder can be tested against the empirical evidence of the ways in which their language is affected. In order to do this, some fundamental assumptions about language must guide the characterization of language impairment. These principles are not specific to any particular theory of grammar, but rather are general principles about the nature of language itself.

Underlying Grammar

The first principle is that speakers of a language have an internalized set of abstract rules guiding their utterances. Uttered surface forms provide evidence about the properties of the abstract rules, but do not in themselves constitute language. It is the grammar, the set of abstract rules producing the utterances, that constitutes language, and therefore it is this grammar that must be characterized if we want to understand any language, even impaired language.

Individual surface forms underdetermine the form of the underlying grammar. That is, for any particular surface form, a large number of possible grammars is consistent with it. Only by considering the system as a whole can the abstract representations that underlie the surface forms and the rules that operate to produce them be determined.

It follows that two utterances produced by two different speakers may be identical in their surface form and yet come from two different underlying representations via two different sets of rules. We will argue, for example, that the surface form *walked* can arise from at least two different sources: (1) from a representation containing the stem *walk* and the past morpheme *-ed* and a syntactic rule that obligatorily requires tense to be realized on all main verbs; or (2) an unanalyzed representation *walked* that simply means "to move in the past" and an optional semantic rule that says that a verb with the meaning of past is generally desirable to use when the contextual meaning is in the past.

This paper will present data showing that although the language-impaired subjects sometimes appear to produce the "correct" surface form, further analysis of their performance as a whole shows that these forms are produced not by a hierarchically organized system of abstract rules operating on grammatical categories but rather by very specific compensatory strategies, including memorization of inflected forms as unanalyzed lexical items and the conscious application of learned explicit rules.

Constituents

The second important principle is that the grammar has rules that organize individual items into more complex constituents. It is not the succession of individual items that constitutes language, but rather their organization into larger constituents, themselves organized into more abstract, hierarchically ordered constituents.

For example, subjects are typically reported to have difficulty with *plural* and *past* (see Leonard 1989), but in English, because there is no explicit marker for *singular* or *present*, the unmarked forms that the impaired subjects produce for *singular* and *present* are not reported as errors. While such a description may be accurate in terms of the surface forms, it is clearly not interpretable in terms of an underlying system. The impaireds are also reported to have difficulty with *articles* as well as with *plurals*, but these two facts are reported as if they were independent phenomena – which misses the generalization that they have difficulty with number agreement among constituents in the noun phrase.

Explanatory Models

There have been several different explanations to account for SLI. These fall mainly into three different groups: (1) those that suppose that there is no problem with language itself: the apparent linguistic deficits are believed to be an epiphenomenon of a more basic peripheral problem in perceptual processing or articulatory production; (2) those that suppose that language is not a modular autonomous cognitive system and therefore that this disorder in language is really caused by a deficit in general cognitive processing that also affects other cognitive systems (see Johnston, this volume); (3) those that suppose, as we do, that the impairment is indeed a deficit in the ability to construct a normal grammar. Advocates of this view differ in precisely what aspects of the grammar are affected by this deficit. For example, Clahsen and Hansen (this volume) proposes that the deficit is in the system of agreement, while Wexler and Rice hold that SLI individuals remain in an *optional infinitive stage* that normal children pass through (see Rice and Wexler, 1995)

Peripheral Processing Explanations

Speech Production Hypothesis

One explanation for the apparent problems that these subjects have with grammatical morphemes is that they are really a reflection of problems with "phonological production," a solution specifically proposed by Fletcher (1990) (in a response to Gopnik's 1990 report in *Nature*. Fletcher (1990) proposes that

> the more likely source of the variable performance problems lies in the language-production processing system, rather than in the underlying grammar. Grammatical forms like plural, past tense and third person singular are particularly vulnerable in English, in individuals with phonological problems. Was the phonological ability of the subjects reviewed and eliminated as a factor in the impairment of some or all of them? Until alternative explanations have been explicitly considered, there must be some skepticism about Gopnik's thesis. (Fletcher 1990, 226)

What Fletcher appears to mean by "grammatical forms" is the phonological realization in actual speech of the abstract representation in the grammar. He suggests that what we are interpreting as a deficit in the underlying grammar is more likely an inability to produce the correct surface form. According to this hypothesis, when the impaired members of the family say "Yesterday I walk," instead of "Yesterday I walked," it is not because they have a grammatical problem with tense but only because they have problems producing the final alveolar sound. This hypothesis claims that they understand the underlying grammatical properties of tense, but simply cannot produce the correct surface grammatical form because they have trouble converting their phonological representation of the correctly marked form into the necessary articulatory movements. Because they cannot reliably produce a final alveolar, for instance, we mistakenly believe that they are not producing a past-tense-marked word. This is a perfectly reasonable suggestion, because these subjects do have trouble producing consonant clusters accurately; they often substitute one sound for another and have a great deal of trouble producing polysyllabic words.

However, an investigation of the phonological properties of the spontaneous speech of the impaired subjects (Gopnik 1994b) shows that although they sometimes delete final alveolars in monomorphemic words, they do not do so any more frequently than their unaffected relatives. The deletions that do occur in monomorphemic words therefore appear to be part of their dialect. There is, however, a significant difference between the affected and unaffected members of the family in their errors in producing past-marked verbs in semantically past contexts. As one would expect, though their dialect allows them to delete some final alveolars, the unaffected subjects virtually never delete final alveolars which are serving the morphological function of marking past. The opposite is the case for the affected members. Their rate of omission of final alveolars is much greater in those cases in which these forms would serve to mark the past tense. Moreover, they often produce the stem form instead of the past-tense form for irregular verbs as well as for regular verbs. In order to explain their errors on irregulars in terms of articulatory production, one would need the auxiliary hypothesis that they have difficulties producing the alternations in medial vowels that often signal irregular past. This is clearly unlikely to be the case, but still we examined all of their monomorphemic words that contained the vowels in question. There was not one case in which such a vowel substitution was made.

Therefore, the impaired subjects' production of stems instead of past-marked forms cannot be accounted for in terms of an articulatory deficit for either regular or irregular verbs. The errors that they make in accepting stem forms instead of past-marked forms in temporally past contexts occurs in grammaticality-judgment tasks and in single-word production tasks, in picture-prompted narratives and in on-line lexical judgment tasks. None of these tasks can easily be accounted for by an articulatory deficit. Furthermore, an analysis of evidence from Japanese shows that errors in grammatical marking occur in complex polysyllabic phonological contexts that do not appear to be articulatorily vulnerable in Fletcher's sense and therefore could not possibly be accounted for by any simple articulatory-deficit hypothesis. None of these data are consistent with Fletcher's hypothesis that subjects' apparent problem with tense is caused by their phonological difficulties in language production. All are consistent with the hypothesis of an impairment in the automatic, unconscious rules that guarantee agreement in their grammar.

The Perceptual Processing Hypothesis

Another explanation for SLI is suggested by Leonard and his colleagues (1992):

> Although SLI children might be able to perceive and produce forms such as word final consonants and unstressed syllables in non-morphemic contexts, the already greater perceptual and production demands placed on them by these surface properties limit the resources available to these children for the additional operations of hypothesizing the grammatical function of a form and placing it in a morphological paradigm. (P. 153)

The evidence and arguments presented in that paper were examined in detail (Gopnik, 1994c) and it was shown that (1) the variables needed to express this hypothesis are not well enough defined to be testable; and (2) given any reasonable interpretation of the variables of their theory, the various data from English and other languages are not compatible with an explanation that depends on perceptual processing.

One serious problem with Leonard's hypothesis, as he himself acknowledges, is that it is not well enough defined to be testable. The auditory-processing-deficit hypothesis involves three variables: (1) perceptual deficits in SLI children that make it difficult for them to process certain sounds; (2) a set of sounds in English and in Italian that are difficult to process and (3) the psychological resources needed to construct morphological paradigms. Yet no clear and testable criteria are given to determine any of these three variables independently. If we cannot decide in advance how to determine that the subjects did have a perceptual deficit, then we cannot use "perceptual deficit" as an explanatory principle. Similarly, it is necessary to have clear criteria about which language sounds are likely to be at risk in order to test whether the sounds most at risk perceptually are actually those that are not produced. It is not legitimate to examine which sounds are not produced by SLI children and then, *post hoc*, argue that it is precisely these sounds that are difficult to perceive and process. Finally, to claim that these children cannot build morphological categories because they have insufficient resources to use their impaired perceptual representations to construct morphological paradigms, one must at least outline how the cognitive system uses such information to build paradigms, in what way such a system could be impaired, and how one could determine this.

One way to test this hypothesis is to see if these subjects make errors on structures that involve what would be, within any reasonable definition, a "phonologically salient" segment. We have examined several such forms cross-linguistically. In English we examined the comparative morpheme, because it provides an example of a clear difference between phonologically conditioned variants. If phonological processing difficulties were the determining factor, then one would expect the lexical form *more*, as in "more expensive," to be more likely to be produced than the unstressed ending *-er* that occurs in "bigger." The data on comparatives reported in Dalalakis (1994a) show that this is not the case. The subjects appear to have more difficulty with producing and judging *more*-comparatives than they do with the *-er* comparatives, although in any reasonable theory of perception the unstressed *-er* is less salient than the word *more*. It does not seem likely, therefore, that the difficulty with comparative affixation results from a perceptual-processing deficit. We would hypothesize that the affected subjects' better performance on the *-er* forms results from the greater frequency of these forms. This frequency effect has also been documented in, for example, their production of regular past-tense verbs, and is consistent with the hypothesis that they store marked forms as unanalyzed wholes in declarative memory (Kehayia 1994; Paradis and Gopnik 1994; Ullman and Gopnik 1994).

A similar case can be made for progressive aspect. Aspect in English has two markers, a form of *to be* before the verb and *-ing* added to the verb. Impaired subjects do not, however, consistently produce both forms together as required. The data show three different versions of *progressive*, one with both *to be* and *-ing* , one with just *to be*, and a third with just *-ing*:

(1) Anne is fighting.

(2) Carol is cry in the church.

(3) I walking down the road.

Such data cannot be accounted for in terms of the "low salience" of the forms, but are predictable from the assumption that the subjects lack obligatory agreement rules.

Data from Japanese and from Greek, which are reported in detail in *McGill Working Papers in Linguistics* 10 (S.E. Fukuda and S. Fukuda 1994a; S.E. Fukuda and S. Fukuda 1994b; Fukuda, S. 1994; Dalalakis 1994b) and which will be discussed more briefly in this paper, as well as data from Inuktitut (Crago and Allen 1994), show that language impairment can affect morphological markers that are polysyllabic and that must be characterized as "salient" if this term is to have any constrained and testable interpretation. In sum, the data from Japanese, Inuktitut and English comparative- and aspect-marking suggest that polysyllabic and lexical morphological markers can be impaired, indicating that there is no direct correlation between the perceptual "salience" (which is not clearly defined by Leonard) of a morphological marker and its risk of being impaired. In one sense we agree with Leonard: language-impaired subjects cannot build morphological paradigms. The difference between our theories is that he insists this is because they have an auditory-processing problem, and we believe it is because they have a specific problem in building such paradigms.

The Cognitive Explanation

One interesting question is whether the impairment that is observed in language is a consequence of a language-specific disorder or the result of some more general cognitive problem. One of the clinically defining characteristics of this disorder is that the affected individuals have performance IQs in the normal range. Still, it has been suggested that there may be a more subtle and specific cognitive deficit that causes the observed deficits in language. The problem with establishing such a causal link between a cognitive deficit and the linguistic deficit in this population is that if a gene or genes affects the development of the neural substrate, it might be the case that the same gene could affect neurological development in regions of the brain that were responsible for cognitive abilities other than language. If this were the case, then it should be expected that in some cases this disorder would co-occur with disorders in other cognitive domains. This would not in any way imply that the co-occurring cognitive disorder caused the linguistic disorder. It would only mean that both the cognitive and the linguistic disorder were a consequence of an impaired pattern of neurological development.

To demonstrate that the linguistic disorder was the consequence of some more general cognitive disorder, it would have to be shown that all of the individuals who had this linguistic disorder also had the cognitive disorder and furthermore that there was some principled and predictive relationship between the properties of the cognitive disorder and the specific properties of the disorder in language. In order to do this, it is necessary to have some very clear descriptions of precisely what is wrong with the language of these subjects. That is what we seek to do. We cannot prove the general proposition that in principle there could be no explanation of the data by a more general cognitive deficit, but to date no one has shown that such a cognitive deficit exists.

The Grammatical Hypothesis

Theoretical Model

Over the years, we have been developing a model to account for the range of data that we have analyzed. In the most general terms, the language-impaired subjects appear to be unable to construct automatic implicit rules for morphological and phonological processes within the grammar on the basis of the input that they receive from their native language (Paradis and Gopnik 1994). Non-impaired speakers are able to abstract such implicit rules from the language that they hear (for a very interesting discussion of the construction of implicit rules for phonology in young babies see Kuhl and Meltzoff, this volume). These rules in non-impaired subjects allow them to establish agreement relations among the elements in a sentence and construct productive morphological rules to produce the correctly inflected form for words that they have never before encountered – a task the impaired subjects cannot perform (Goad and Rebellati 1994; Gopnik 1994a; Gillon and Gopnik 1994; Ullman and Gopnik 1994). In the phonology, normal speakers are able to extract from the language that they hear around them the implicit rules that allow them to produce and construct phonological words of any length or complexity that are allowed in their language. A study of the ability of impaired subjects to generate novel polysyllabic words shows that they do not routinely produce polysyllabic words by using the implicit rules that their unimpaired relatives use, although they have developed some compensatory strategies that allow them to produce some forms in which the target polysyllabic word is rendered as a succession of minimal words (Piggott and Kessler Robb 1994). Non-impaired speakers are able to apply these rules at a very young age and without any explicit instruction. They are able to abstract regularities from the language that they hear around them and to formulate the general rules of their language, which they then use in an unconscious, automatic, virtually errorless way. This is what the impaired subjects do not appear to be able to accomplish.

Compensatory Mechanisms

Though the impaired subjects do not have the ability to construct automatic implicit rules, it can be shown that they are able to use compensatory mechanisms to simulate some aspects of normal language function. One of these compensatory mechanisms is memorization. Though they may not be able to produce the regularly inflected form of a word from a rule, there is no reason that they should not be able to learn the word as they learn any other monomorphemic word – as an unanalyzed whole. Though they might not be able to acquire the rule that produces the past tense form of *jump* as *jump+ed*, they can learn the monomorphemic word *jumped* that is not grammatically marked for past, but that carries the meaning of "pastness" in its semantic definition. If this were the case, then one would predict that regularly inflected forms showing no frequency effect in controls would show a frequency effect in the impaired subjects, and that impaireds would have particular difficulty with novel forms. In addition, on-line priming experiments should show that inflected forms appear in impaired subjects' mental lexicon as unanalyzed wholes. For example, it is known that unaffected subjects take longer to decide that *zacked* is not a real word than that *zack* is not a real word, because they are sensitive to the existence of *-ed* as a real inflectional ending. If impaired subjects are not sensitive to the inflectional ending and are processing *-ed* forms as unanalyzed wholes, then there should be no difference in the time that it takes them to decide that they are not real words. Our data from impaireds do show that there is a frequency effect for regular verbs, that producing inflected forms of novel words is very difficult, and that in on-line tasks, there is an insensitivity to inflection.

Another way that impaireds can produce forms with the surface appearance of past tense is by applying pedagogical rules that they are explicitly taught in the special schools they attend and in their speech therapy sessions. An example of such a rule is "you must add *-ed* to the verb to make the past tense" or "you must add *-s* to a noun to make a plural form." These pedagogical rules provide some instruction about what operations must be performed. They unwittingly assume, however, that the speaker has knowledge of other constraints on the morphology that, because they are so basic to the language, are not consciously noticed by unimpaired speakers of the language. For example, all speakers of English realize that "you add an *-ed* to form regular pasts," yet these same speakers are very surprised to learn about the obligatory allophonic variation that requires voicing assimilation between the final consonant of the stem and the *-ed* suffix that marks past: the past tense of "jump" is "jump[t]" with a voiceless alveolar stop, but the past tense of "jog" is "jog[d]," with a voiced alveolar stop. Normal speakers automatically and unconsciously choose the appropriate allophone when they construct regularly inflected forms: in constructing plurals, they say "cat[s]" with a voiceless sibilant, but "dog[z]" with a voiced sibilant, and "glass[əz]" with an epenthetic vowel. Normal speakers also know that the morphological rules in English apply to the bare stem and not to an already inflected form: they do not generally produce forms that are doubly inflected, such as "swam[ed]" or "blows[ed]." The impaired subjects, by contrast, do produce such forms.

Predictions

English

The model given above makes very specific predictions about the kinds of errors that the impaired subjects are likely to make. For one, errors in agreement would be expected. What precisely constitutes agreement in English is the subject of much lively theoretical debate; we will take it here to be any process in which the morphological form of one element is constrained by the form of another element in the relevant domain. This would predict that the impaired subjects should have difficulties with noun-verb agreement, tense, sequence of tenses in texts, anaphor, number, the mass-count distinction and comparatives. In spontaneous speech, they should have difficulty in producing agreement relations among elements within constituents. They should have similar difficulties recognizing that sentences with agreement errors are in fact ungrammatical, and should exhibit these difficulties in both tasks that require them to make explicit grammaticality judgments and tasks in which such judgments play an implicit role.

Because they do not have automatic symbolic rules, the impaired subjects should be impaired in their ability to generate the correct regular, morphologically marked forms for words that they have never before encountered, such as nonsense words. In the phonology, they should have difficulties with language-specific rules that go beyond universal minimal phonological requirements.

As discussed above, the storing of inflected forms as unanalyzed wholes in memory predicts that subjects should perform better on past forms that occur more frequently than their stem forms. This frequency effect should occur for regular verbs as well as for irregulars. The non-impaired controls should exhibit frequency effects only for irregular forms that must be stored in memory, but not for regulars that can be derived productively. Which forms are stored as unanalyzed lexical items should also be detectable by on-line lexical-decision tasks, which can probe the structure of the mental lexicon.

As for the compensatory mechanism of relying on explicitly learned rules, there are several kinds of data that can be used to distinguish between an inflected form that is produced via an explicit rule and one that is produced via an implicit rule. If subjects are consciously applying an explicit rule, then it should take them longer to construct their response than if the response were generated by an automatic, unconscious process. This predicts that the impaired subjects should take much longer to construct their responses than do their unimpaired relatives. In addition, the pattern of errors made in producing inflected forms should reflect the constraints on the rule (as possessed by controls) that are absent from the formulation of the explicit pedagogical rule. Therefore, if the impaired subjects are not constructing the rule by abstracting it from the pattern in which it actually occurs in English, but rather are learning it as an explicit rule, such as "to change a singular noun to a plural noun add an -s," then there should be errors in the allomorphs that they produce.

Japanese

We will assume that the behaviour of the Japanese developmentally language-impaired will resemble that of the English developmentally language-impaired. Since the impairment in the above hypotheses is assumed to be in the underlying grammar, the linguistic manifestations of the disorder should be of virtually the same type across diverse languages; the assumption that the behaviour of these two populations should be similar follows as a logical consequence.

Like the English impaired subjects, the Japanese subjects should be unable to construct abstract implicit rules for morphological and phonological processes within the grammar. This would predict that the Japanese impaireds should have difficulties with the marking of tense, sequence of tenses in texts and anaphora. Japanese, unlike English, is primarily a language without obligatory concordance; thus, the issue of noun-verb agreement is not relevant. A phonological process that should be problematic for the Japanese impaireds is *rendaku* (sequential voicing in compounds), because it is governed by a set of implicit obligatory rules. The impaired subjects should be able to recognize and produce compounds that occur frequently in the language that exemplify this pattern of sequential voicing, but be unable to extract the implicit obligatory rule of voicing from the existing forms and apply it when forming new compounds (S.E. Fukuda and S. Fukuda 1994).

Greek

Greek is a language rich in morphological affixation that requires the use of obligatory concordance rules every time a noun, adjective, pronoun or verb is used; bare stems of verbs, nominals and adverbs cannot surface as real words. As a result, the impaired subjects, who are assumed to be using lexically learned unanalyzed items (rather than stems and affixes) should have difficulty co-ordinating words for rule-dependent grammatical features such as case, gender, number, tense, person and so on. This in turn, predicts that the Greek impaired subjects will consistently produce ungrammatical utterances where items seem to be mismarked, but never produce totally unmarked stems as we see in English since that would result in nonexistent forms.

Linguistic Evidence

The data that we will be discussing in this chapter come from the analysis of spontaneous speech as well as from a wide range of tests of comprehension, production and grammaticality judgments in writing, listening and speaking. The results of any single test might be accounted for by some property of the test itself. For example, it might be the case that these subjects have some undetected difficulties with reading, and therefore the results of tests that required them to read might be compromised. But by looking at converging data from tests of very different designs which call upon very different competencies, we can eliminate these test-dependent variables. If the same linguistic deficit is evident in comprehension, production and grammaticality judgments during listening, writing and speaking, then it seems reasonable to suppose that the deficit is in the grammar itself. In addition to these tests, we have begun to investigate the subjects' language processing through reaction-time experiments (Kehayia 1994). The results of these studies are consistent with the results of our other tests.

Our research team investigated the impaired subjects' abilities on a wide range of linguistic variables in English, including tense, noun-verb agreement, determiner-noun agreement, number, comparatives, morphophonological variation, phonological word formation, perception of consonants in monomorphemic words and categorical perception. We have also conducted tests of similar linguistic variables in Greek and in Japanese. These data are reported in detail in a special issue of *McGill Working Papers in Linguistics* (Volume 10). Only a brief summary of those data can be presented here.

The question that will be addressed in this section is what processes the language-impaired subjects use in order to produce surface morphological forms such as *children, boys, talked, took, bigger* or *more expensive.* One current language-acquisition model (Pinker 1991) posits that normal speakers use two very different processes to produce the morphologically marked surface form: a general symbolic rule that produces regular forms and a memory-based association network that produces irregular forms. The symbolic rule is implicit, automatic and unconscious; it can take any sequence, even nonsense words, as input and produce an appropriately marked form. Such rules are learned by quite young normal children without any explicit instruction, and once children learn an implicit linguistic rule, they can automatically produce all regular forms, independently of their frequency. The data given below support the argument that language-impaired subjects do not use implicit symbolic rules in any context, but that their behaviour is precisely that which would be predicted if they were using a memorized association network.

Subjects in This Study

English

This chapter reports on data from three different languages: English, Japanese and Greek. The English-speaking subjects in our research are all members of a single multigenerational family whose pedigree is reproduced in Figure 1. There are 36 members in the family that was studied, extending over three generations. Of these, 16 members have been diagnosed as language impaired.

The language disorder in this family is very apparent and is almost equally distributed among males and females. All of the subjects that we are considering to be language impaired, except for the grandmother, were diagnosed as such by the school system (Hurst et al. 1990; Pembrey 1992). The members of the middle generation were treated for their language disorder within the normal school system, and report that they received language therapy from a special teacher about once a week. The 11 grandchildren who were diagnosed as language impaired attend a special school for language-impaired children and have received language therapy since they were four years old.

The language-impaired members of this family appear to have no hearing loss; some of them do have articulatory problems. As discussed above, however, a careful analysis of their language performance over a wide range of tests shows that these articulatory problems cannot account for their language problems. The mean performance IQ of the impaired members of the family was first reported to be 95 (80-112) as determined by the WAIS-R/WISC-R scales (Pembry 1992). Another report suggests that their mean performance IQ is somewhat lower, 86 (range 71-111) (Vargha-Khadem et al. 1995). In either case it is clear that most of the language impaired subjects have performance IQs within the normal range. The real question is whether the lower IQs of some of the language impaired members of the family are the cause of their problems with language. Bishop has studied twins with language impairment and has concluded that "there is no fundamental difference between children who have a large discrepancy between IQ and verbal functioning and those who do not." (1994, p. 6) These data are consistent with our hypothesis that in addition to affecting language, this disorder can affect areas of the developing brain that are responsible for other cognitive functions.

The normal controls are the unimpaired members of the same family. In this way we can ensure that the controls have the same dialect and sociolinguistic background as the impaired subjects and that the ob-

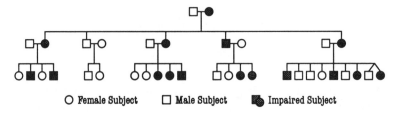

Figure 1: Family tree of English-speaking subjects extending over three generations.

served differences in their language are solely the result of the disorder. Some of the tests were administered to unaffected subjects who were not members of the family, and the performance of these extra-family controls was just the same as that of the controls within the family. Therefore, we have confidence that the unimpaired members of the family do have normal language skills.

Cross-linguistic Subjects

There are 10 Japanese-speaking subjects reported on in this study, ranging in age from 8;9 to 12;1. They were selected from various speech-language laboratories of elementary schools throughout Japan according to the same criteria for developmental language impairment used to identify the English subjects. Three of these subjects have a known family history of language impairment; the other seven family pedigrees are still under investigation. Similarly to the English subjects mentioned above, the Japanese subjects have received language therapy since diagnosis, have no hearing loss and have a performance IQ above 80 as determined by the WISC-R scale and above 90 as determined by the Tanaka-Binet scale.

There are 13 Greek subjects ranging in age from 5;2 to 17;0. They were also selected from a language-impaired population with no known hearing impairment, and within a normal range performance IQ on the Greek versions of WISC-R/Griffiths tests. All subjects were referred to us by their language therapists. Of the 13 subjects, 7 subjects are known to have a positive family history of language impairment, 1 is known not to have any affected relations, and the family histories of the rest are still under investigation.

Data

In order to provide a principled description of the language deficits in this population, we will distinguish three different levels at which errors occur.

1. Obligatory Feature-marking

Speakers of a language must learn which abstract elements in the representation of a sentence are marked for specific properties. For example, in English, all count nouns must be marked for number as either [+singular] or [+plural] and all main verbs must be marked for tense as either [+present] or [+past]. In Japanese, verbs must be marked for tense, aspect and voice, and nouns for case (nominative, accusative, genitive or dative). In Greek, nominals (nouns, adjectives, pronouns) must be marked for number, gender, person (for pronouns) and case, and verbs for tense, person, number, aspect and voice. These abstract grammatical markers are necessary for rules of agreement in the syntax to operate.

2. Morphology

The second level of analysis concerns the morphological processes that produce the correct surface form from the marked syntactic category. Pinker (1991) has argued that two different processes are used by normal speakers of English to produce morphological forms: for example, in English pluralization, regular forms are derived from symbolic rules that take any stem as input and add -s for those entries that are marked [+plural]; in English tense marking, -ed marks [+past]; irregulars, on the other hand, are memorized as entries in an association network. We are assuming that normal speakers of Japanese, Greek or any other language rely on the same morphological processes.

3. Agreement

In addition, speakers of English must learn agreement rules that guarantee concordant marking among various elements of the sentence – for example, determiners with nouns, and sequence of tenses in sentences. Speakers of Japanese need not learn rules of agreement, but they must learn to control sequence of tense within as well as across sentences. Greek speakers must learn that all constituents of a phrase must be in concordance for the features marked.

Our data show that English, Japanese and Greek developmentally language-impaired subjects are impaired at all three levels. They do not recognize that the grammatical markers, such as tense in English, are obligatory; they do not construct productive morphological rules; and they do not have the necessary agreement among elements in a sentence.

Obligatory Marking

If the language-impaired subjects do not know that specification of the feature tense is obligatory, they should then make errors of the following kind in their spontaneous speech: they should demonstrate uncertainty with respect to tense-marking; they should be insensitive to the ungrammaticality of sentences that are missing the obligatory marking; and they should be unable to produce the correct tense marking on demand. The data presented below show that the language-impaired subjects manifest all of these difficulties in all three languages.

At the outset, a distinction must be made between syntactic processes for [+past] tense marking and the semantic concept of "pastness." A wide range of data from spoken and written comprehension and production tasks, rating tasks and spontaneous speech all reveal that the impaired subjects do not lack the semantic concept of pastness. They can and do use several different means to indicate that an event took place in the past: (1) verb forms such as *went* and *talked*; (2) temporal adverbs such as *last week* or *the other day*; (3) the form *used to* to refer to past habitual action. It is clear that they have developed a grammar in which the semantic idea of pastness can be encoded.

Though they have developed the capacity to use some devices of language to indicate pastness, the data from spontaneous speech, grammaticality-rating tasks and tense-changing tests in all three languages are consistent in giving no evidence that the impaired subjects have the syntactic knowledge that there is an abstract *obligatory* category tense that *must* occur on all verbs that are in semantically past contexts.

In English, normal children acquire the knowledge about obligatory tense-marking at a very young age. It has been shown that normal English-speaking children know that tense is obligatory by 3;6 years (Marcus et al. 1992). The morphological processes that produce the correct surface form appear to be acquired at more or less the same time. They have also suggested that these two processes may be connected and that as children acquire the knowledge that there is an obligatory rule that requires that tense always be marked, they also develop a productive rule that allows them to produce a past-tense form for any new verb they may encounter.

Spontaneous Speech

If the language-impaired subjects have an impaired underlying grammar, then one would expect to see some reflections of the problem in their spontaneous speech as well as in testing situations. However, the evidence of their underlying problem may be mitigated by compensating strategies that they have adopted over their lifetimes. If this is the case, then one should expect to see an improvement of apparent tense-marking with age without full competency ever being achieved. This is precisely what the data show. In clearly past contexts in spontaneous speech, English and Japanese language-impaired subjects all produce some temporally past sentences in which the stem form of the verb is used, instead of the correct past form.[1] The normal controls virtually always mark tense correctly. In the large English family, in which we have a wide spectrum of ages represented, the older subjects are generally better at producing the correct past form in temporally past contexts than their younger relatives.

One explanation that might be offered is that these subjects actually do know that there is a category, "tense," and that it is obligatory, but that they simply made an error in marking the verb [+present] instead of [+past]. In English, the unmarked stem form and the present-tense form are identical in all but one case: third-person singular, which requires a final -s (*The boy jumps.*) If the English language-impaired subjects are using verbs marked [+present] instead of [+past] in past contexts, then they should be using -s-marked forms for third-person singular subjects. If, on the other hand, they are producing verbs that are unmarked for tense, then they should produce the stem form in all cases. The data from spontaneous speech show that the English language-impaired subjects produced 75 forms with no overt past-tense marking in semantically past contexts. Thirty-one of these verbs had third-person singular subjects. In only 3 cases was the verb marked with the third-person singular -s. Therefore the forms with no overt marking are not [+present] forms mistakenly used in past contexts, but rather stem forms with no overt tense marking.

Elicited Data

Grammaticality Ratings

Several tests were given that required the subjects to rate the grammaticality of sentences that had errors of various kinds. For some tasks there was no significant difference between the impaired and unimpaired subjects, while for other tasks there was a significant difference. The fact that the impaired subjects were just like their unimpaired relatives on some tasks means that they understood the nature of the task and were able to perform it. In general they were very good at judging that a sentence contained a non-word, and they were also very good at judging that grammatical sentences were indeed grammatical. Their greatest problem, as one would predict, was in judging sentences that contained unmarked forms and were in fact not acceptable. Unmarked stems in contexts of obligatory marking were consistently not recognized as wrong and so were not corrected, similar to undetected production errors seen in spontaneous speech where stems surfaced unmarked.

One rating task required the subjects to rate the acceptability of written sentences in explicitly past contexts from 1 (unacceptable) to 7 (perfectly acceptable). The sentences were arranged in sets of three that varied only in the form of the verb: one sentence occurred with the stem form of the verb (e.g., *wipe, take*); one with the regular past *-ed* ending (*wiped; taked*); and the third with the stem with an internal vowel change (*wope, took*). The forms were presented in writing and all three variants of the same verb were in front of the subject at once so that their performance on this task could not be attributed to auditory processing or to short-term memory difficulties.

The subjects were not significantly different in judging that sentences with past-tense marking were very acceptable or that sentences with nonexistent forms like *wope* were unacceptable. They differed significantly, however, in their rating of the unmarked stem form for both regular and irregular verbs. Normal speakers judge the unmarked stem form of the verb in temporally past contexts to be unacceptable, and rate it near the bottom of the scale; impaired speakers judge the stem form of the verb in temporally past contexts to be acceptable, and rate it above the middle of the rating scale (control mean = 1.28; language-impaired mean = 4.28; $p < .001$).

An analogous rating task was administered to the Japanese impaired subjects. Subjects were again required to judge a series of sentences for grammaticality. The stimulus sentences were either correctly or incorrectly marked for tense. Performance was similar to that of English subjects; for example, incorrect sentences in past-tense context with present-tense verbs were judged to be acceptable (control mean: 93% correct vs. impaired mean: 46% correct; $p < .001$).

Greek impaired subjects also performed poorly on identifying incorrect sentences on a grammaticality rating task standardized across the three languages. Their performance was better on correct stimuli (77% correct acceptance) compared to the incorrect stimuli (only 26.1% correct identification as incorrect).

Although we have concentrated on verbs here, similar rating-task results have been observed in judgments of comparatives (Dalalakis 1994a) and in the judgment of sentences with incorrect noun phrases (Gillon and Gopnik 1994)

Tense-changing Test

The English impaired subjects could not change from one tense to another in a tense-changing task that required them to complete a sentence of the form:

(4)   Everyday he walks eight miles. Yesterday he ____.

They often produced sentences that were ungrammatical with respect to tense. The controls had no difficulty with this task and did not produce sentences that were ungrammatical with respect to tense (control mean = 91.7%; impaired mean = 38.3%; $p < .001$).

The behaviour of the Japanese and Greek impaired subjects closely resembled that of the English subjects on the same task. They too produced sentences that were incorrectly marked for tense (control mean = 98%; Japanese impaired mean = 48% and Greek impaired mean = 40%).

The data from spontaneous speech and elicited production data in the form of self-correction, verb-form ratings and tense-changing are all consistent with the hypothesis that the language-impaired subjects do not have an internalized grammar that requires that all verbs in English must *obligatorily* be marked for tense. According to this hypothesis they may have the abstract syntactic category tense in their underlying grammar, but they do not always mark it on the verb.

These data are also consistent with the more radical hypothesis that these subjects do not construct the syntactic category tense at all but have adopted lexical strategies for producing the surface forms that appear to be the result of a verb that is marked [+past]. One empirical consequence of the subjects' not having tense at all is that the agreement rules and the symbolic morphological rules that operate on this category would necessarily also be impaired.

The English subjects were given lexical decision-reaction time tests to see if they were sensitive to tense marking in processing, even though they clearly were insensitive to them in spontaneous speech and grammaticality ratings. These tests indicate that the impaired subjects do not have an internal representation for tense (Kehayia 1994).

Morphology

The question to be considered in this section is whether the impaired subjects use morphological rules to productively form new polymorphemic words from stem forms. A subsidiary question is whether the polymorphemic words in their vocabulary are in fact represented in their mental lexicon as complex forms or whether they are merely listed as morphologically unanalyzed lexical items.

Nonsense Words

In order to show that the impaired subjects are truly unable to construct symbolic rules and apply them implicitly, we designed a series of tests using novel (nonsense) words which we presented to the subjects as nouns, verbs, compounds or adjectives in such a context that they had to mark them for features such as number, tense or comparison. Overall, impaired subjects across the three languages failed to correctly apply the appropriate grammatical rules to the novel words. Non-impaired controls, on the other hand, implicitly applied such rules to these words without hesitation or delay.

In one test subjects were presented with an illustration of a nonsense figure and told: "This is a *wug*. These are ____?" The non-impaired subjects were able to do this task, but the impaired subjects were not. In those cases where the impaired subjects did produce some phonological ending on the novel word, a careful phonological analysis demonstrates that they do not have control of the morphophonological rules that should guide such productions. For example, they sometimes produced forms without the universally obligatory voicing assimilation and in other cases they produced geminated sibilants. The overall pattern of phonological errors that they make demonstrates that even when they do produce a final sibilant it is not incorporated into the word as an inflectional ending, but rather is conjoined with the stem as a compound (Goad and Rebellati 1994). Similarly, they fail when the nonsense word is presented as a verb in a present-tense context and they are required to produce the verb in a past context: "Every day I *prame* quite well. Yesterday, I ____ quite well" (Ullman and Gopnik 1994), or when presented as an adjective in a comparative construction: "This bag is *bimmy*. This one here is even ____?" (Dalalakis 1994a). Non-impaired speakers as young as 4 years of age can perform such tasks without hesitation, thus showing an implicit ability to manipulate grammatical rules across word categories.

Japanese subjects similarly fail to apply implicit phonological rules as evidenced in the operation of compounding. For example, in the process of *Rendaku*, which requires voicing of the word-initial obstruent of the second member of a compound (except under certain conditions) as in: *ori + kami = origami,* impaired subjects consistently produce compound forms analogous to *orikami*. When presented with novel compounds, the impaired subjects, unlike the non-impaired controls, exhibit the same behaviour: they do not voice the appropriate word-initial obstruent (S.E. Fukuda and S. Fukuda 1994).

In the Greek equivalent to the "Wug" test (Dalalakis 1994b), when Greek impaired subjects are cued to produce plural forms of novel nouns, they respond by repeating the singular form, just as the English subjects do, or by inappropriately marking the stimulus for plural. For example, to the stimulus

(5)   Aftos   ine   enas   *vitoras.   Afti   ine dhio ____?
       This-masc. is one-masc. novel noun. These-masc. are two ____?

the response may be *dhio *vitoras* (two novel noun-sing.) or *dhio *vitoria* (two novel noun-pl. but wrong gender).

In sum, we see the impaired subjects failing to apply grammatical rules to words that could not have been learned lexically, regardless of the category to which they belong (verb, noun, adjective, compound), which implies that the impairment affects their ability to construct morphological rules.

The question then is whether they are using a rule to produce existing regularly inflected forms or whether they are learning these forms as unanalyzed lexical items. As mentioned above, in a timed lexical-decision task the impaired subjects, in contrast with the controls, took no longer to decide that *zack* was not a word than to decide that *zacked* was not a word. In a priming task that was designed to investigate the structure of the mental lexicon, it has been shown that normal controls, in several different languages, show a greater priming effect when the stem form is used to prime the inflected form than when the inflected form is used to prime the stem form. This difference was not present in the language-impaired subjects: the stem displayed no priming advantage over the inflected form. These results are consistent with the hypothesis that the impaired subjects do indeed store regular past-tense verbs as lexical items with no internal structure (Kehayia 1994).

Agreement

Intuitively, the concept of agreement can be simply stated: an agreement relation holds between elements if a property of one element of a sequence constrains properties of the other element of the sequence. There are many examples of this kind of relationship: a verb must agree with its subject in number and person; a determiner must agree with its noun with respect to number and mass; a pronoun must agree with its antecedent in number, person and gender; under stipulated conditions verbs must agree with respect to tense. Some of these relationships hold within sentence boundaries and others hold across sentence boundaries. The problem is that in current linguistic theory the concept of agreement is much more constrained and there is no variable that governs all of these relationships in a similar way. Clahsen and Hansen (this volume) hypothesize that the linguistic deficit affects agreement relationships in the narrower sense, but that it does not affect morphological productivity. In the previous section we have shown that our impaired subjects, cross-linguistically, do have problems productively using morphological rules. The data in this section will show that our subjects have difficulties with a wide range of agreement relationships: agreement between nouns and verbs, agreement between anaphors and their antecedents, and sequence of tenses are also impaired in these subjects.

General Agreement Errors

In a general test that included several kinds of agreement, there was a significant difference between the controls' and the impaireds' ability to judge whether sentences were grammatical with respect to agreement and to correct sentences that they judged as incorrect (grammatical judgment of 29 sentences: control mean = 95%; impaired mean = 59%; $p < .00001$). The impaired subjects were at the level of chance in deciding whether the stimulus sentences were grammatical. Scoring the corrections was much more difficult because, while the normal subjects appear to recognize the nature of the error and correct just that error, the impaired subjects often changed properties of sentences that were already correct or irrelevant with respect to the agreement error:

(6) Roses grow in the garden.

is judged ungrammatical and changed to:

The roses grow in the garden.

(7) A pretty girl smile at me.

is judged ungrammatical and changed to:

> The pretty girl smiled at me.

(8) The boy eats three cookie.

is judged ungrammatical and changed to:

> The boys eat *four* cookie.

We adopted a generous scoring procedure: the subject was credited for a correction that resulted in a grammatical sentence whether or not that correction demonstrated that the subject understood the feature error. Even with this generous scoring procedure the impaired subjects performed significantly worse than the controls (corrections of the 21 ungrammatical sentences: control mean = 18.33; impaired mean = 7.83; $p < .00001$). These data show that the language impaired subjects did not recognize and could not correct errors in agreement.

The same task was given to the Japanese impaired subjects (S. Fukuda and S.E. Fukuda 1994). Their performance was very similar to that of the English impaired subjects in that they too were at the level of chance in judging whether or not the stimuli were grammatical. They also often focused on elements of the sentence that were grammatical and changed them, which resulted in new ungrammatical sentences. For example,

(9) Otousan-*wa kaettara,   minna-de   o-matsuri-ni ikimashou.
     Father-Topic   returns everyone-with festival-to   go-let's
     When father returns, let's all go to the festival.

which should be:

> Otousan-*ga* kaettara, minna-de o-matsuri-ni ikimashou.

is judged as ungrammatical and is changed to another ungrammatical sentence:

(10) Otousan-*wa kaettara,   issho-ni   o-matsuri-ni ikimashou.
                        together-with

Out of a total of 60 sentences, the control mean was 92% compared to the impaired mean which was 43.3% correct ($p < .0002$).

We observed the same behaviour in Greek. Again, impaired subjects failed to notice ungrammaticalities, and incorrectly modified phrases that were correct to begin with. In the following example, the noun phrase is incorrect for gender agreement:

(11) Adhiasa   *to *meghalo kanata stin   avli.
     Emptied-I the   large   pitcher in-the courtyard.
              *neutr. *neutr. fem.
     I emptied the large pitcher in the courtyard.

was corrected as:

(12)   Adhiaza   *to *meghalo kanata stin   avli.
        Was emptying-I the   large   pitcher in-the courtyard.
        I was emptying the large pitcher in the courtyard.

The impaired subject's attempted correction failed to target the error in gender agreement, focusing rather on the correct verb.

In sum, corrections of ungrammatical sentences in the grammaticality-judgment tasks reported above were poor. The English subjects achieved a mean of 33.3% correct, Japanese subjects 17.8% and Greek subjects 26.1%.

Sequence of Tenses

The subjects told a narrative in response to a series of six pictures. The impaired adults produced the correct morphological form of both regular and irregular past-tense verbs in their narratives. Although there is no problem with the surface forms that are used, there is a crucial difference between the normal and impaired speakers in the pattern of occurrence of these forms. All of the impaired speakers use both past- and present-tense verbs in the same narrative while the normal speakers always use only one tense consistently throughout the narrative. The impaired subjects do not change tenses for semantic purposes to indicate a change in story "time" but rather just seem to lack the notion that there is a rule that requires that tenses agree. Consider the following utterances by impaired subjects.

(13) They call the ambulance and the ambulance came.

(14) He *did* it then he *fall.*

(15) The neighbors *phoned* an ambulance because the man *fall* off the tree.

Errors in tense agreement occur in narratives in spontaneous speech as well as in the picture-prompted narratives. This difficulty is also observed in Japanese and Greek.

Anaphora

Another aspect of the construction of narratives that provides insights into the use of agreement rules is pronominal anaphora. In order to determine the pattern of anaphora in the picture-prompted narratives described above, the number of full noun phrases (as in *the boy*) and the number of pronominal noun phrases (as in *he*) was determined. In order to control for the differences in the length of the stories, the percentage of noun phrases in the story that were full noun phrases was calculated. The impaired subjects used significantly fewer anaphors than did the controls (control mean = 55.17%; impaired mean = 91.2%; $p < .00001$). It appears that the impaired subjects avoid using pronominal anaphor and prefer instead to use the full noun phrase.

Their difficulty in handling pronominal anaphora was confirmed in a test that compared their ability to answer questions about a narrative with full noun phrases as compared to an identical story with pronominal anaphor. The subjects had no trouble answering questions about the full-noun-phrase versions of the stories. They were able to understand and remember the relationships and events in the stories. If the pronominal version of the story was given to the subject before the full-noun-phrase version of that story, then the subjects had a great deal of trouble answering the questions. However, if the-full-noun phrase version was given before its pronominal version then the subjects did not have trouble answering the questions even though the two versions were separated by other stories. They were able to remember and use the information established in the full-noun-phrase version to figure out the relationships in the pronominal version. This difficulty with pronominal agreement also occurs in spontaneous speech:

(16) It's a flying finches they are.

(17) so I help // it help me.

The data clearly show that a broad range of agreement relations present particular difficulty for these subjects. Similar difficulties with agreement have been reported in German-speaking language-impaired children (Clahsen 1991). Our Japanese and Greek subjects also have problems with agreement, so this phenomenon is not a result of any language-specific particularities.

Subject-Verb Agreement

In the discussion in the previous section about obligatory tense marking in past-tense contexts it was shown that in spontaneous speech the subjects often produce sentences in which the verb does not agree with its subject. This pattern of lack of subject-verb agreement occurs in spontaneous-speech sentences in present contexts as well as past contexts:

(18) My eyes goes really funny.

Talking about her visit to the doctor the previous week, one impaired subject produced:

(19) He say, "Oh, it's your age."

(20) Tricky questions isn't it?

Japanese, unlike English, is primarily a language without obligatory concordance, so we do not see instances of subject-verb agreement. Greek, on the other hand, always has obligatory, overt subject-verb agreement. Impaired subjects produce utterances within which the subject and verb do not correctly agree for number and person. For example, in the sentence:

(21) Dhen prepi na ghinonde polemi yati   khanonde *ikoyenia.
     Neg. must part. take-place   wars because get lost-they family
     Wars should not take place because family get killed.

the final verb requires a subject that is in the plural ("families"), but it actually occurs in the singular.

Conclusion

The fact that there is a disorder of language that is associated with a genetic factor or factors provides us with a natural experiment that allows us to obtain direct evidence about the properties of the innate abilities that are necessary for the acquisition of language. The cross-linguistic data that we have briefly discussed here provide clear evidence that this familial disorder can affect a wide variety of processes in language. The subjects appear unable to learn the automatic unconscious rules that govern these aspects of language, but the pattern of compensatory mechanisms that they use suggests that these subjects are able to use their other cognitive skills to simulate some aspects of language.

The crucial questions to be dealt with now are identifying the extent of the linguistic deficit, the genetic factor or factors and the consequences for the development of the neurological substrate. We are now involved in a research project that is investigating the linguistic, genetic and neurological aspects of this disorder and we trust that this research will begin to provide insights into these very fundamental questions in the near future.

Acknowledgments

We would like to thank all of our colleagues who have been so helpful in the development of the linguistic aspects of this project: Heather Goad, Brendan Gillon, Eva Kehayia, Glyne Piggott and Michel Paradis. We would also like to thank Martine Kessler Robb, Kie Ross, Jacob Brostoff and Catherine Rebellati for all of their assistance. This work was supported by grants from the Social Sciences and Humanities Research Council of Canada, 410–90–1744 and 410–93–0252.

Note

1 In Greek and Japanese, where bare verbal stems are not acceptable, subjects produced forms with inflectional marking that was inappropriate for the context.

References

Aram, D.M., B.L. Ekelman and J.E. Nation (1984). Preschoolers with language disorders: Ten years later. *Journal of Speech and Hearing Research* 27: 232–44

Bishop, D.V.M. (1992). The underlying nature of specific language impairment. *Journal of Child Psychology and Psychiatry* 33 (1): 3–66

Clahsen, H. (1991). German plurals in adult second language development: Evidence for a dual mechanism model of inflection. Paper presented at the Twelfth Second Language Research Forum, Los Angeles, CA

Crago, M., and S. Allen (1994). Morphemes gone askew: Linguistic impairment in Inuktitut. *McGill Working Papers in Linguistics* 10: 206–15

Dalalakis, J. (1994a). English adjectival comparatives and Familial Language Impairment. *McGill Working Papers in Linguistics* 10: 50–66

——— (1994b). Developmental language impairment in Greek. *McGill Working Papers in Linguistics* 10: 216–27

Fletcher (1990). Speech and language defects. *Nature* 346: 226

Fukuda, S. (1994). Lexical representation of Japanese complex verbs: A theoretical model and implications from dysphasic children. *McGill Working Papers in Linguistics* 10: 194–205

Fukuda, S..E., and S. Fukuda (1994a) Developmental language impairment in Japanese: A linguistic investigation. *McGill Working Papers in Linguistics* 10: 150–77

——— (1994b). To voice or not to voice: The operation of *Rendaku* in the Japanese developmentally language-impaired. *McGill Working Papers in Linguistics* 10: 178–93

Gillon, B.S., and M. Gopnik (1994). Grammatical number in subjects with Specific Language Impairment. *McGill Working Papers in Linguistics* 10: 41–49

Goad, H. and C. Rebellati (1994). Pluralization in Familial Language Impairment. *McGill Working Papers in Linguistics* 10: 24–40

Gopnik, M. (1990). Feature-blind grammar and dysphasia. *Nature* 344: 715

Gopnik, M. (1994a). Impairments of syntactic tense in a familial language disorder. *McGill Working Papers in Linguistics* 10: 67–80

—— (1994b). The articulatory hypothesis: Production of final alveolars in monomorphemic words. *McGill Working Papers in Linguistics* 10: 129–34

—— (1994c). The auditory perception/processing hypothesis revisited. *McGill Working Papers in Linguistics* 10: 135–41

Hurst, J.A., M. Baraitser, E. Auger, F. Graham and S. Norell (1990). An extended family with an inherited speech disorder. *Developmental Medicine and Child Neurology* 32: 347–55.

Kehayia, E. (1994). Whole-word access or decomposition in word recognition in Familial Language Impairment: A psycholinguistic study. *McGill Working Papers in Linguistics* 10: 123–28

Leonard, L.B. (1989). Language learnability and specific language impairment in children. *Applied Psycholinguistics* 10: 179–202

Leonard, L.B., U. Bortolini, M.C. Caselli, K.K. McGregor and L. Sabbadini (1992). Morphological deficits in children with specific language impairment: The status of features in the underlying grammar. *Language Acquisition* 2: 151–79

Marcus, G.F., S. Pinker, M. Ullman, M. Hollander, T.J. Rosen and F. Xu (1992). Overregularization in language acquisition. *Monographs of the Society for Research in Child Development* 57, 4, serial no. 228

Paradis, M., and M. Gopnik (1994). Compensatory strategies in Familial Language Impairment. *McGill Working Papers in Linguistics* 10: 142–49

Pembrey, M. (1992). Genetics and language disorders. In P. Fletcher and D. Hall (eds.), *Specific Speech and Language Disorders in Children*. San Diego, CA: Singular Publishing Group

Piggott, G., and M. Kessler Robb (1994). Prosodic organization in Familial Language Impairment: Evidence from stress. *McGill Working Papers in Linguistics* 10: 16–23

Pinker, S. (1991). Rules of language. *Science* 253: 530–35

Plante, E. (1991). MRI findings in the parents and siblings of Specifically Language-Impaired boys. *Brain and Language* 41: 67–80

Plante, E., L. Swisher, R. Vance and S. Rapcsak (1991). MRI findings in boys with Specific Language Impairment. *Brain and Language* 41: 52–66

Rice, M., and K. Wexler (1995). Tense over time: The persistence of optional infinitives in English in children with SLI. Paper presented at the Twentieth Annual Boston University Conference on Language Development, Boston, MA

Ullman, M., and M. Gopnik (1994). Past tense production: Regular, irregular, and nonsense verbs. *McGill Working Papers in Linguistics* 10: 81–88

7

The Grammatical Agreement Deficit in Specific Language Impairment: Evidence from Therapy Experiments

Harald Clahsen and Detlef Hansen

1. Introduction

Some children demonstrate great difficulty in the acquisition of grammar. These children are labelled "specifically-language impaired" (SLI) if they show delays and/or disorders in the normal acquisition of grammar despite any clear non-linguistic deficit – that is, these children have normal non-verbal IQs, no hearing deficits and no obvious emotional or behavioural disturbances. SLI children cannot be considered to be "mentally retarded," since SLI children do not show a discrepancy between chronological age and mental age on non-verbal intelligence. SLI children can also be distinguished from autistic children, because the SLIs do not show a lack of responsiveness to humans and other characteristics of autistic children. Thus, there seems to exist a group of children who demonstrate difficulty acquiring grammar but for whom no clear non-linguistic cause can be found.

A focus of recent SLI research has been to characterize the grammatical deficits of these children in linguistic terms, by adopting different notions from linguistic theory and from theories of the normal acquisition of grammar. The general working hypothesis that is shared among linguistic investigations of SLI is that the observed grammatical impairments can be explained by assuming selective disruptions of the normal development of central grammatical modules, (e.g. problems with syntactic features). Furthermore, there seems to be a consensus that SLI children have problems with grammatical function words and bound morphemes encoding case, gender, number, person and so forth. SLI children often omit these elements or use them incorrectly. It also seems to be the case that in SLI children, the development of inflectional morphology comes to standstill at an early stage, and that beyond that point the acquisition process cannot advance without difficulties. By contrast, it is controversial whether SLI also involves deficits in phrase structure and word order (Grimm and Weinert 1990).

In current SLI research, three different linguistic approaches are discussed most extensively: (i) the surface deficit (Leonard et al. 1992), according to which SLI children are said to have difficulties acquiring grammatical morphemes with low phonetic substance; (ii) the rule-deficit model (Gopnik and Crago 1991), according to which SLI subjects do not have access to regular rules of inflection; (iii) the grammatical agreement deficit (Clahsen 1989, 1991), according to which SLI children have problems establishing agreement relations between two elements in phrase structure. An overview and discussion of these approaches can be found in Bishop (1992) and Clahsen (1993).

In the present paper we will report on recent research testing the grammatical agreement deficit in SLI children. The first part of the paper presents a summary of the grammatical agreement account and of the main empirical findings on which it is based. The second part will report on a set of experiments that were designed to explore predictions derived from the grammatical agreement deficit in SLI therapy (Hansen 1993). The linguistic phenomenon to be investigated is the relationship between word order and agreement morphology. Previous findings from our project indicate that although word order in general is correct, German-speaking SLI children typically produce root-clause infinitives, that is, verb-final patterns instead of the verb-second (V2) patterns required by adult German. We will argue that the frequent root-clause infinitives and the lack of generalized V2 are indirect effects of the children's problems with agreement, rather than an indication of a linguistic disorder in word order or head movement. Based on that, we can make an interesting prediction for our therapy experiments: if the agreement system is systematically taught in therapy, then those SLI children who acquire agreement as a result of the therapy should also have the adult-like distribution of verb-placement patterns without any additional effort. This prediction is easy to falsify, namely, by children who acquired agreement during therapy, but who still use many root-clause infinitives. In Hansen's longitudinal therapy experiments such cases were not found (Hansen 1993). Rather, all the children who developed into subject-verb agreement system dominantly produced V2 patterns after therapy. This finding will be interpreted as supporting the grammatical agreement deficit.

2. The Grammatical Agreement Deficit in SLI

2.1. Basic Assumptions and Predictions

The agreement account emerged from our project on German-speaking children and has not yet been systematically tested from a cross-linguistic perspective. In Clahsen (1993), however, several results from recent SLI studies on languages other than German were shown to be derivable from the agreement hypothesis.

The major claim of the agreement hypothesis is that SLI can be characterized in terms of a selective impairment of an otherwise intact grammatical system. It is assumed that SLI children have problems establishing the structural relationship of agreement between two phrase-structure categories. There are of course different ways of theoretically defining the notion of grammatical agreement. Somewhat tentatively, we have adopted the notion of agreement from Generalized Phrase Structure Grammar (GPSG) (Gazdar et al. 1985). In GPSG, a distinction is made between the level of phrase-structure configuration and the level of control and percolation of grammatical features. Phrase-structure geometry is determined by principles of X-bar syntax, that is, by configurational rules of immediate dominance and linear precedence. The most important principle in GPSG determining the choice of grammatical features is the Control-Agreement Principle (or CAP) (Gazdar et al. 1985, 89). In this view, agreement is an asymmetrical relation between two categories, where one is a functor and the other is an argument controlling the functor.

Given the grammatical agreement deficit, the following linguistic phenomena should cause problems for SLI children:

(1) Subject-verb agreement, for example, the third person singular -s in English or the person and number suffixes that appear on finite verbs in Italian and German;

(2) Auxiliaries, that is, the finite forms of "to be" and "to have" that co-occur with participles, gerunds and so forth;

(3) Overt structural case markers, for example, accusative case-marking of the direct object in German;

(4) Gender marking on determiners and adjectives as, for example, in German.

Consider subject-verb agreement. In terms of the Control-Agreement Principle, person and number are not primary features of finite verbs. They are only realized on finite verbs (= the functor), but provide information about the subject and, in this way, can be said to be controlled by the subject (= the argument). Therefore, given that the CAP is not accessible to SLI children, subject-verb agreement should be impaired in SLI. Similarly, auxiliaries in English and German are lexical fillers of subject-verb agreement features, and, if the agreement account of SLI is correct, these children should have problems with auxiliaries.

Structural case marking also falls under the CAP. In a language with morphological case marking, such as in German, structural case is realized on NPs, but it is a syntactic feature of lexical and or functional categories (V, Infl, Det). Therefore, German-speaking SLI children should have problems acquiring the overt structural case markers of adult German.

Gender is a lexical feature of nouns, but in German it is morphologically realized on determiners and adjectives, and not on nouns. Thus, gender marking can be subsumed under the general notion of control-agreement. By contrast, notions such as definiteness are inherent features of determiners and can be acquired even without the CAP, for example, through semantic bootstrapping. Therefore, we would expect that SLI children have definite and indefinite articles and other determiners, but that they have problems with the use of correct gender markings on determiners.

In contrast to the subsystems of inflection mentioned above, noun plurals in English and German, past tense marking in English and participle inflection in German do not fall under the CAP, since, rather than being controlled by an argument category, these are marked directly on the noun or verb and contribute to its meaning (along with other features). Therefore, we expect that these phenomena should be unimpaired in SLI children. In addition, we expect SLI children not to have any genuine word-order difficulties. They should not have any problems acquiring the correct placement of, for example, articles in relation to NPs, prepositions in relation to their complements and other kinds of constituent-internal word order.

2.2. Results

In this section we will summarize empirical findings from various SLI studies focusing on subject-verb agreement and word order.

Subject-Verb Agreement and Participle Inflection. Studies from English, German and Italian show that person and number agreement is impaired in SLI. A summary of these studies can be found in Clahsen (1993). Here our focus is on subject-verb agreement in German-speaking SLI children.

Based on cross-sectional and longitudinal data, Clahsen (1991, 165ff.) found that only one child out of 10 SLI children examined (mean age: 5;6; range: 3;2 to 9;6) acquired the correct paradigm for person and number inflection on the finite verb; in this child (Petra), subject-verb agreement emerged at the age of about 4 years – that is, considerably later than in normal children (Clahsen and Penke 1992). None of the other nine children acquired the system of subject-verb agreement

during the period of observation. Typically, these children used zero affixation or -*n* forms (= infinitives) irrespective of the person and number of the subject. Consequently, the rates of correct overt marking of
these forms are rather low. Moreover, only a limited set of affixes occurs
in the children's utterances; in particular, the second person singular
suffix -*st* is not acquired, although this affix is the only unique form in
the German agreement paradigm.

Similar results were obtained in a longitudinal study with 19 SLI
children (mean age: 5;4; range: 3;11 to 6;11) studied over a period of one
year (Rothweiler and Clahsen 1993). It was found that 11 out of these
19 children had problems acquiring the subject-verb agreement paradigm. In this regard, they differed considerably from language-unimpaired controls matched to them on the basis of Mean Length of Utterance (MLU). Rothweiler and Clahsen found, for example, that the
percentage of correct use of the second-person singular suffix -*st* in
obligatory contexts was 55%, weighing each child equally. Moreover, it
was found that the infinitive form -*n* was often used as a default affix
to replace finite verb forms (mean rate of incorrect -*n* = 49%).

In order to determine whether the grammatical impairment of SLI
children affects other areas of inflectional morphology, Rothweiler and
Clahsen (1993) compared the rates of correct agreement markings in
obligatory contexts with those of the regular and the irregular participle suffixes -*t* (= regular) and -*n* (= irregular) in these 11 children. High
rates of correct participle suffixation were found in the SLI children: irregular participles with marked stems (which require the participle
suffix -*n* in German) were correctly marked in most cases (83%), and
regular participles were correctly marked with the participle suffix -*t*
in 86%. Moreover, Rothweiler and Clahsen (1993) found the same kinds
of errors for both SLI children and normal controls. Apart from occasional cases of zero suffixation (below 10%), the only source of error
was that strong verbs in German were categorized by the children as
regular verbs, and were suffixed with the default affix -*t* instead of the
irregular affix -*n*, for example **gegeht* ("**goed*") instead of *gegangen*
("gone") or **gebratet* ("**frie-n*") instead of *gebraten* ("fried"). There were
no errors in the stems of irregular participles; examples such as **ge-
fanden* ("**fand*") instead of *gefunden* ("found") did not occur. Moreover,
all irregular participles, that is, those with ablaut stems were suffixed
with -*n* as required in German; there were no errors such as **gefundet*
("**founded*") or the like. Finally, regular participles were correctly suffixed with -*t*, and not with the irregular affix -*n*.

In general, these findings show that in inflecting participles, SLI children are similar to normal MLU controls, both quantitatively (in terms
of error frequencies) and qualitatively (in terms of types of errors).

These results contrast with problems the same SLI children have with subject-verb agreement. Taken together, these observations suggest that SLI children do not have a general deficit with inflectional morphology, but that the impairment is restricted to agreement.

Word Order. The acquisition of word order, specifically of verb placement, has been an important focus of research in studies on German-speaking SLI subjects.

On the basis of data from 10 SLI children, Clahsen (1991) found no constituent-internal word order errors in NPs, PPs and APs. By contrast, none of the 10 children had the adult-like distribution of verb-placement patterns;[1] rather, the children dominantly produced root-clause infinitives with non-finite verbs in clause-final position. Quantitative analyses revealed that the proportions of verb-second and verb-final patterns varied, but that verb-final patterns were dominant for most of the children (mean = 64%; range: 36% to 84% counting each child equally). More importantly, qualitative differences were found between verb-final patterns on the one hand and verb-initial and verb-second patterns on the other hand: verb-final patterns are typically used with uninflected verbal elements (stems), infinitives and participles, whereas the first or second verb position is dominantly covered by a restricted class of finite verbal elements, that is, modals and auxiliaries as well as some verbs inflected with the suffix -*t*, plus some imperatives. These asymmetries between verb-final and verb-second patterns were found in 9 out of 10 children. One child, Petra, diverged from this distribution in that she produced verb-final patterns for both non-finite and finite verbs in root clauses. Recall that Petra was the only child studied in Clahsen (1991) who acquired subject-verb agreement during the period of observation. However, in contrast to normal children, she did not raise finite verbs to the V2 position. Rather, the V2 position is filled with a restricted set of (finite) verbs only, particularly with modals, while other kinds of finite verbs remain in clause-final position. A case similar to Petra has been reported in Kaltenbacher and Lindner (1990, 7). Clahsen (1991) discusses different accounts for the specific pattern found in Petra.

Grimm (1987) and Grimm and Weinert (1990), based on longitudinal data from 8 German-speaking SLI children (age 3;9 to 4;8), found that in 69% of the sentences produced by the SLI children, either the verb or the subject was in clause-final position, resulting in incorrect word-order patterns in 53% of the cases (Grimm 1987). Similar results were obtained in a sentence-imitation task that was carried out with the same set of 8 SLI children. Grimm and Weinert (1990) found that in 61% of the presented stimuli, the SLI children changed the given word orders to incorrect patterns, typically to SOV. These figures for verb-final patterns are within the same distribution as those found in Clahsen (1991), suggesting that the children studied by Grimm and Weinert do not have the adult-like distribution of verb-placement patterns either.

Collings et al. (1989) studied one SLI child (Dieter) longitudinally from age 6;1 to 6;11. They showed that Dieter dominantly used V2 patterns in the final recording, at age 6;11, that is, about 4 years later than language-unimpaired children (cf. Clahsen and Penke 1992). Before that point, verb-final patterns were clearly dominant (cf. Table 8 in Collings et al., 139). Interestingly, Dieter did not acquire subject-verb agreement throughout the whole period of observation. Even at age 6;11, when he produced V2 at a rate of more than 90%, Dieter still did not use the second-person singular suffix -st, and produced many sentences with the infinitive ending -n replacing a finite verb form. In contrast to what is known from language-impaired children, these verb forms, which are non-finite in terms of their morphological shape, appeared in the V2 position. Collings et al. argued that this child must have acquired the V2 rule without having access to the finite/non-finite distinction.

Overall, these results indicate that V2, as in adult German, is hard to acquire for SLI children. Most SLI children lack regular subject-verb agreement and, consequently, produce many root-clause infinitives instead of V2-patterns. Some SLI children (Petra, Dieter) seem to acquire a version of V2 that diverges from the one in adult German.

The observation that German-speaking SLI children frequently use verb-final patterns in main clauses has been made in several studies. The interpretation of these "errors," however, is controversial. According to Grimm and Weinert (1990, 224) the verb-final patterns indicate that SLI children have problems of dealing with word order per se. In addition to the observations mentioned above, they quote some sample utterances from different children with auxiliaries or modals in clause-final position and separable prefix verbs in second position which, they claim, never occur in normal development (ibid., 221), and argue that these "deviant syntactic structures are the result of insufficient language processing" (ibid., 225).

We think that this conclusion is premature and that the claims on which it is based are incorrect. First, verb-final patterns are not deviant in German. Rather, verb-final is the normal position of non-finite verbs in German. Thus, the general figures presented in Grimm and Weinert indicating that SLI children prefer the verb-final pattern do not mean that word order per se is impaired. Second, with respect to their claim that SLI children produce deviant sentences with finite verbs appearing in clause-final positions and non-finite verbs in second position, neither Grimm and Weinert (1990) nor Grimm (1987) present any quantitative figures indicating how many such cases occurred in the data. It is true that SLI children sometimes produce such "deviant" word orders, but (i) such cases have also been reported for normal children (Fritzenschaft et al. 1990), and (ii) the figures presented in Clahsen (1991) and Clahsen and Penke (1992) indicate that such word-order patterns are extremely rare in both SLI children and normal controls – that is, they occur in less than 10%. Third, the idea that word-order "errors" result from deficits of language processing, specifically from the SLI children's "difficulties in separating units that are semantically linked and in placing separated parts in different positions" (Grimm and Weinert 1990, 225) does not explain their preference for the verb-final pattern. If Grimm and Weinert were right, we would expect verb placement to be random.

Alternatively, we suggest that the apparent word-order errors result from the children's problems with subject-verb agreement: SLI children do not have a general paradigm of person and number inflection. Thus, their grammars do not allow them to generate a corresponding finite form for any given verb. Instead, these children only have a small set of (stored) finite verb forms (e.g., modals, a restricted class of verbs appearing with the suffix -t and a few auxiliaries). The grammatical agreement deficit correctly predicts that for this restricted class of verbal elements, V2 is possible, but that generalized V2 as in adult German, with all main clauses having a finite verb form in the second structural position, is not possible for SLI children.

2.3. *Preliminary Summary*

The empirical results summarized in this section demonstrate that SLI cannot be characterized in terms of global disturbances of inflectional morphology. We found that participle inflection is unimpaired (Rothweiler and Clahsen 1993). The same holds for other areas of inflection that do not fall under agreement, such as noun plurals in English- and German-speaking SLI children (Ötting 1992, Clahsen et al. 1992). In contrast to that, it was found in several studies that subject-verb agreement is typically impaired in SLI children (Clahsen 1991; Rothweiler and Clahsen 1993). Similarly, other areas of inflection, such as structural case marking and gender inflection which involve agreement relationships have also been shown to cause major difficulties for SLI children (cf. Clahsen 1993). Finally, it has been reported that word order is in general correct, but that word-order phenomena such as German Verb-Second are hard to acquire for SLI children. These findings support the view that SLI may be characterized in terms of a selective deficit of an otherwise normal grammatical system, and that the deficit crucially affects the area of grammatical agreement relationships.

3. Therapy Experiments with SLI Children

The results summarized in the previous section suggest that German-speaking SLI children typically do not have the subject-verb agreement paradigm and generalized V2. It was proposed that both phenomena are connected and can be derived from assuming a grammatical agreement deficit in SLI. There is, however, a certain weakness in this conclusion, since it has not yet been shown that the two phenomena developmentally co-vary in SLI children. Suppose, for example, that at some point in language development an SLI child acquires the subject-verb agreement paradigm but does not have generalized V2. Then, one might argue that the two phenomena are in fact based on independent impairments rather than deriving from a joint source.

Therapy experiments with SLI children provide one possibility of testing the developmental relationship between subject-verb agreement and generalized V2. Hansen (1993) carried out such therapy experiments in connection with our project. The SLI children involved in Hansen's experiments did not have subject-verb agreement at the beginning of the therapy. He designed and administered therapy sessions with the children, one goal of which was to teach them the regular subject-verb agreement paradigm. Under the grammatical agreement hypothesis we would expect that those children who were successful in acquiring agreement would also have generalized V2. If the two phenomena were developmentally independent, however, some children should acquire agreement but not V2. In this way, Hansen's therapy experiments provide for a crucial test case of the grammatical agreement deficit.

3.1. Subjects

Four German-speaking SLI children (Dennis, Max, Sebastian and Sonja) with ages ranging from 6;1 to 6;11 (mean age: 6;5) were involved in the therapy study. About 90 therapy sessions per child were held over a period of 14 months. In addition to their grammatical impairments, three children are reported to having had articulatory problems (Denis, Max and Sebastian). These children received therapy on articulation and did not have any articulatory deficits at the beginning of the therapy experiments. Independently from Hansen's studies, speech therapists diagnosed the four children as SLI. Their linguistic diagnosis was based on the results of standardized language assessments tests (Landauer Sprachentwicklungstest für Vorschulkinder [LSV], cf. Götte 1976; Heidelberger Sprachentwicklungstest [HSET], cf. Grimm and Schöler 1978). According to the clinical documents, none of the children was mentally retarded or had hearing deficits, nor did any of them have behavioural and/or communicational disorders. Finally, the clinical assessment revealed no obvious signs of neurological dysfunctions.

The four children have received individual therapy on their grammatical problems from the age of approximately 4;5 up to the beginning of the therapy experiments. During that period, speech therapists made use of several different remedial methods ranging from pattern drills to highly unspecified exercises of general communication abilities, perceptual training and so forth. It is reported in the clinical documents of the four children (Hansen 1993) that the various therapy efforts did not improve the children's grammatical competence, and the speech therapists made it clear that no further progress in the area of grammatical development was to be expected from these children.

3.2. Method

Before the therapy experiments were started, Hansen assessed the four children's level of grammatical development using a computerized version of the profile analysis (COPROF, described in Clahsen and Hansen 1991) as a descriptive tool. The assessment was based on a spontaneous speech sample of approximately 100 grammatically analyzable utterances per child.[2]

The goal of the therapy experiments was to help the children acquiring the agreement system, but they should not provide the children with any direct evidence for V2. Therapy sessions were designed which created felicitous situational conditions for the use of different verbal inflections of the same lexical verb. The therapy sessions were administered by the speech therapist with whom the particular child was familiar.

3.3. Materials

The linguistic materials used in the therapy experiments were designed to provide the children with selected input focusing on subject-verb agreement forms; the items involved isolated verbs, verbal paradigms and simple Subject + Verb sentences. Hansen (1993) designed games in which the speaker role and/or discourse perspective switched from one turn to the next, but the lexical verbs used in the input sentences remained constant throughout. In one of these situations, the therapist and the child had several puppets (father, mother, a boy and a girl) and played the game "Getting Up in the Morning":

Therapist: Der Wecker klingelt. Ich stehe auf. Die Mutter steht auf.
(The alarm-clock is ringing. I get up. Mother gets up.)

Child: Vater auch.   (Daddy too.)

Therapist: Der Vater steht auf, die Mutter steht auf und ich stehe auf.
(Daddy gets up, mother gets up and I get up.)

Child: Raus.   (Out.)

We advised the therapist (i) to use the same lexical verb throughout the games, (ii) to change the sentential subjects and (iii) not to add material other than subjects and verbs to the input sentences.

In another situation, two children plus the therapist were involved. One of the children was encouraged to produce non-verbal actions, sounds or events which the therapist and the second child should describe. In order to avoid elliptical answers, the therapist introduced her utterance by the sentence "I guess he drives/walks/coughs ..." After the child had correctly described the action, the therapist used the same lexical verb with a different subject. (Child A, Peter, is performing an action.)

Child B:	Peter lauft.	(Peter runs)
Therapist:	Peter läuft?	(Peter runs?)
Child B:	Du laufen?	(You run?)
Peter:	Nein. Nicht ganz.	(No. Not quite)
Therapist:	Oder er tanzt.	(Or he dances)
Child B:	Peter tanzt.	(Peter dances)
Therapist:	Peter tanzt?	(Peter dances?)
Child B:	Peter tanz?	(Peter dance?)
Peter:	Ja. Ich tanze.	(Yes. I dance)
Therapist:	Ja. Peter tanzt.	(Yes. Peter dances)

In these games, the SLI children were confronted with many different finite verb forms of the same lexical verb. In addition, the therapists were instructed to apply modelling techniques, for example, stressing agreement endings in their input utterances, extending children's non-finite verbs into simple Subject + Verb sentences or forced alternative questions. In this way the therapists provided the children with highly transparent input on the subject-verb agreement paradigm of adult German.

3.4. Results

In the following, we will briefly describe the children's grammatical system and level of grammatical development before we began with the therapy experiments. Then we will describe the development of subject-verb agreement and V2 that occurred during the therapy experiments.

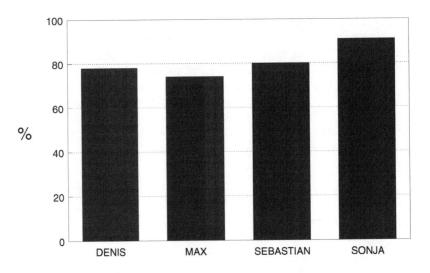

Figure 1: Aux and Cop Omissions before Therapy Experiments

The Children's Grammatical System before the Therapy Experiments. We analyzed the first recording for each child using COPROF profiles. The profiles demonstrate that the children have problems with the linguistic structures of the later phases IV and V (which are acquired by linguistically normal children at about 3 years of age), whereas the patterns of the early phases I and II do not cause any specific difficulties; see Clahsen (1991, 118ff.) for a detailed description of the abbreviations used in the profile charts. Interestingly, however, not all the structures of the later phases are inaccessible to the SLI children. Rather, we find that some structures, even of the latest phase V, are used by the children, and that others (belonging to earlier phases in linguistically normal children) have not been acquired. This holds particularly for certain inflectional affixes and grammatical function words, such as case markings, person and number affixes, gender markings, articles and auxiliaries. Consider, for example, the proportions of auxiliary and copula omissions in the children's corpora at the beginning of the study; the percentages in Figure 1 are calculated based on the profile charts as follows:

$$\frac{\text{number of overtly realized auxiliaries and copulas}}{\text{obligatory contexts for aux. and cop.}}$$

Figure 1 shows that the children had considerable difficulties with auxiliaries and copulas before the therapy experiments: auxiliaries and

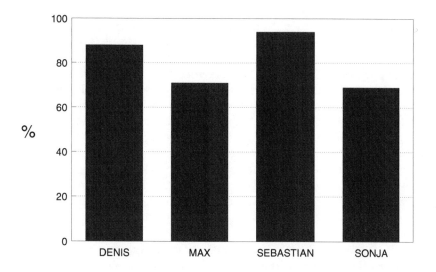

Figure 2: Verb Placement before Therapy Experiment: Proportion of Verb-final Patterns.

copulas were very rare in general and were omitted in most of the obligatory contexts (mean rate: 81%). By contrast, the proportions of omissions of lexical verbs were significantly less frequent, with a mean rate of 15%. Auxiliaries and copulas are lexical instantiations of person and number features in German. Thus, the relatively high rates of aux. and cop. omissions reflect the children's problems with subject-verb agreement at the beginning of Hansen's study. Furthermore, the children did not have the paradigm of regular verb inflection forms encoding subject-verb agreement at the beginning of the study: in 76% of the sentences with verbs, verbs appeared in the stem or infinitive form. Most importantly, the second-person singular suffix -*st* did not occur at all in the SLI children's data.

In contrast to the children's problems with subject-verb agreement, constituent-internal word order was generally correct: prepositions and articles are placed before their complements, attributive adjectives are always in the correct prenominal position and so forth. V2 patterns (which are obligatory in German main clauses) are, however, used extremely rarely as can be seen from Figure 2. In this figure, we calculated the proportion of verb-placement patterns in main clause that deviated from the V2 property of adult German; note that (S)XV patterns are incorrect with respect toV2, whereas V2 and V1 patterns are correct.

$$\frac{\text{frequency of (S)XV}}{\text{frequencies of (S)XV plus V2 plus V1}}$$

Figure 2 shows that most of the children's sentential utterances with verbs fall into the (S)XV pattern, with percentages ranging from 69% to 94%. (S)XV patterns, which are sometimes called "root clause infinitives" (Wexler 1994), typically occur in language-unimpaired German-speaking children before the subject-verb agreement paradigm has been acquired – that is, before the age of approximately 2;5. It has been argued that root clause infinitives in normal children result from the fact that the children do not yet have a productive paradigm for generating finite verb forms. Therefore in cases in which children do not retrieve a finite verb form from the lexicon, they produce a non-finite verb form in clause-final position and leave the V2 position empty. The same reasoning seems to hold for the SLI data: the occurrence of root clause infinitives is taken to indirectly result from the children's not yet having acquired the subject-verb agreement paradigm.

The Development of Subject-Verb Agreement and V2 during Therapy. The data from the first recording of each child indicates that the children had not acquired the paradigm of subject-verb agreement and generalized V2. The major goal of the therapy experiments was to provide the children with systematic input designed to help them in acquiring subject-verb agreement. Hansen did not explicitly teach generalized V2; our expectation, however, was that once the agreement paradigm had been acquired, V2 should have been the dominant word-order pattern, and this should have been possible without any additional learning.

Table 1 presents frequencies of occurrence of regular verb inflection forms in corpora I to IV for each child. Recall that the therapy experiments started after corp. I and that the time intervals between corp. II, III and IV were approximately four months each. The figures in Table 1 show frequencies of occurrence of the German person and number suffixes. Table 1 demonstrates that the children extended their initially

	Denis					Max					Sebastian					Sonja				
	0	n	t	e	st	0	n	t	e	st	0	n	t	e	st	0	n	t	3	st
Corp. I	6	33	3	–	–	25	11	12	2	–	6	21	7	3	–	17	11	9	5	–
Corp. II	21	24	2	1	–	22	18	7	1	–	17	19	2	2	–	20	18	7	6	–
Corp. III	22	13	12	10	–	26	10	10	3	–	18	12	9	6	–	16	20	8	10	1
Corp. IV	17	7	11	12	11	18	9	6	3	5	12	15	18	6	8	16	19	10	13	12

Table 1: Regular Verb Inflection Endings

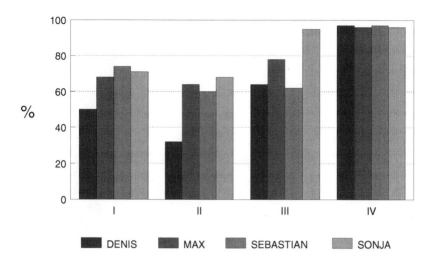

Figure 3: Development of Subject-Verb Agreement during Our Therapy Study

reduced system of verbal suffixes throughout the therapy experiments, and that they acquired the complete inventory of regular agreement suffixes at the end of the study. As can be seen, the second-person singular suffix -*st* is acquired after all other affixes. This developmental sequence is identical to that of language-unimpaired children (Clahsen 1986).

Figure 3 contains percentages of correct usage of the person and number affixes in obligatory contexts; the figures were calculated as follows:

$$\frac{\text{total number of correct agreement affixes}}{\text{total number of clauses requiring agreement affixes}}$$

Figure 3 shows relatively low rates of correct subject-verb agreement in corp. I and II, ranging from 26% to 68%. In corp. IV, however, the use of agreement suffixes is adult-like in the four children (mean: 97%). Notice that the data on which these graphs are based come from spontaneous speech samples that were taken outside of the actual therapy sessions.

This development coincides with the children's discovery of -*st* as an agreement marker. These results demonstrate that the children acquired the subject-verb agreement paradigm during Hansen's therapy experiments, and that this takes place when -*st* is acquired, similarly to what has been found for language-unimpaired children.

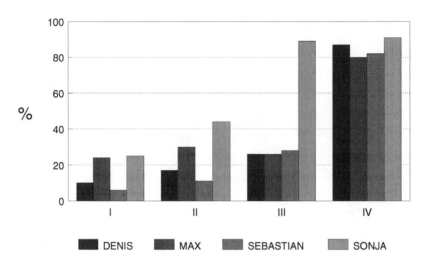

Figure 4: Development of Verb-Second during Our Therapy Experiments

With respect to the development of generalized V2, Figure 4 presents the proportions of sentences containing finite verbs in the V2-position; the figures are calculated as follows:

$$\frac{\text{total number of V2 patterns}}{\text{total number of verb-final, V2 and V1 patterns}}$$

Figure 4 shows a close developmental relationship between subject-verb agreement and V2: as long as the regular agreement paradigm has not been acquired (i.e., before corp. IV for Denis, Max and Sebastian and before corp. III for Sonja), the proportions of V2 patterns are low, ranging from 6% to 44%. During this period, the preferred word order is the verb-final pattern. However, once subject-verb agreement has been acquired (i.e., between corp. III and IV), the figures for V2 drastically increase to more than 80% for all the children. This development is parallel to the connection between the acquisition of agreement and that of V2 in language-unimpaired children (Clahsen and Penke 1992).

Summarizing the results of the therapy experiments, we found that the children acquired both the subject-verb agreement paradigm and generalized V2 during the period of investigation. We suggest that the acquisition of agreement directly results from Hansen's therapy experiments, whereas the development of generalized V2 is a secondary effect of the children's acquisition of the agreement paradigm. Recall that in Hansen's therapy experiments we did not provide the children with direct evidence for V2; the agreement suffixes were rather presented in simple Subject + Verb sentences or even in isolated finite verb forms. This rules out the possibility that the observed development of V2 is a direct therapy effect. We conclude that the linguistic impairment of the four children is restricted to processes of grammatical agreement and does not affect word order per se.

4. Discussion

Recent SLI research has focused on characterizing the grammatical deficits of SLI children in linguistic terms, by adopting different notions from linguistic theory and from theories of the normal acquisition of grammar. According to the approach developed in our project, many of the grammatical problems of SLI children involve an impairment of grammatical agreement (i.e., the process by which two phrase-structure elements are coindexed with respect to some grammatical feature such as person or number). In the present paper we reported on recent results of tests of the grammatical agreement deficit.

The hypothesis developed in our project predicts that SLI children have a selective deficit that affects grammatical agreement, whereas grammatical processes which do not fall under agreement should be unimpaired. This prediction is supported by the observed dissociation between participle inflection and subject-verb agreement in German-speaking SLI children (cf. Rothweiler and Clahsen 1993 and section 2.2 above). The grammatical agreement deficit also predicts that syntactic effects of agreement such as generalized V2 in adult German should be available to SLI children once subject-verb agreement has been acquired. This prediction is supported by the results of Hansen's therapy experiments: those SLI children who acquired agreement as a result of the therapy also had correct V2 without any additional effort. This (together with the fact that there were no constituent-internal word-order errors) demonstrates that the acquisition of word-order regularities, even of V2, is unimpaired in SLI children, but that the adult-like distribution of V2 patterns has to await the children's acquisition of the regular subject-verb agreement paradigm.

Let us finally consider our results in the light of other linguistically oriented approaches to SLI. Leonard et al. (1992) proposed that SLI children have problems with perceptually non-salient morphemes, such as non-syllabic consonantal segments. Our results are not compatible with this approach. If SLI children had general problems with such morphemes, the observed dissociation between subject-verb agreement and participle suffixation should not occur, because the same phonetic form (e.g., the -n affix) is correctly used on participles but incorrectly with respect to agreement. Moreover, the surface hypothesis does not explain the children's low performance of V2 patterns in the early recordings and the observed (indirect) therapy effects.

Gopnik (1992) and Gopnik and Crago (1991) proposed that SLI subjects memorize and store inflected word forms rather than constructing and applying inflectional rules. Thus, SLI subjects are said to treat regular and irregular forms in the same way – that is, both are stored in memory. Our results on correct -t participle suffixation and overregularization go against this approach, because they clearly demonstrate that SLI children develop regular rules of inflection, just like normal children do. Moreover, Gopnik's hypothesis is purely morphological and does not provide an account of the observed problems with V2.

In conclusion, we found support for the hypothesis that SLI children have a very specific grammatical problem with agreement. The deficit affects the acquisition of subject-verb agreement and leaves other areas of inflectional morphology, such as noun plurals and participle inflection, unimpaired. Moreover, we found that a specific therapy helps the children to acquire subject-verb agreement, and that this triggers development in other areas of the children's grammars which were not subject to the therapy.

Acknowledgments

The research in this paper is supported by German Science Foundation grants Cl 97/5–1 and Cl 97/1.1–1.2 to Harald Clahsen, and grant Wu 86/9.1–9.4 to Dieter Wunderlich and Harald Clahsen. We thank the members of our research group, in particular Monika Rothweiler, Andreas Woest and Jutta Pollmann for their contributions.

Notes

1 In German main clauses, all finite verbs appear in the second structural position, whereas in embedded clauses, they are in final position. Non-finite verbs always appear in clause-final position. In syntactic analyses of adult German, the clause-final position is normally taken to be the basic pattern, while the main clause word order is said to be a derived pattern, resulting from a rule that moves all finite verbs to the second structural position. This rule is called generalized verb-second (V2).

2 Linguistic profiles have been developed for use in the assessment of language disorders, particularly with regard to grammatical disabilities in children (Crystal 1982). The best-known profile currently available came to be known as LARSP, the Language Assessment Remediation and Screening Procedure (Crystal et al. 1976). Based on a descriptive synthesis of the L1/English-acquisition literature, a set of seven developmental stages is suggested. At each stage, LARSP provides those grammatical structures which are commonly used by normal children. The profile chart for German child

language which has been developed in our research group (Clahsen 1986) consists of five developmental phases, ranging from the period when children predominantly use one-word utterances up to the time when embedded clauses occur. For each phase, the profile provides the most typical grammatical structures which have been documented in empirical studies on normal German child language.

References

Bishop, D. (1992). The underlying nature of specific language impairment. *Journal of Child Psychology and Psychiatry* 33 (1): 3–66

Clahsen, H. (1982). *Spracherwerb in der Kindheit.* Narr: Tübingen

—— (1986). *Die Profilanalyse.* Marhold: Berlin

—— (1989). The grammatical characterization of developmental dysphasia. *Linguistics* 27: 897–920

—— (1991). *Child Language and Developmental Dysphasia. Linguistic Studies of the Acquisition of German.* Amsterdam: Benjamins

—— (1993). Linguistic perspectives on specific language impairment. *Working Papers Series "Theorie des Lexikons"* 37. Düsseldorf: University of Düsseldorf

Clahsen, H., and D. Hansen (1991). *COPROF [Computerunterstützte Profilanalyse].* Cologne: Focus

Clahsen, H., and M. Penke (1992). The acquisition of agreement morphology and its syntactic consequences. In J. Meisel (ed.), *The Acquisition of Verb Placement,* 181–224. Dordrecht: Kluwer

Clahsen, H., and M. Rothweiler (1993). Inflectional rules in children's grammars: evidence from German participles. *Yearbook of Morphology* 1992: 255–88

Clahsen H., M. Rothweiler, A. Woest and G.F. Marcus (1992). Regular and irregular inflection in the acquisition of German noun plurals. *Cognition* 45: 225–55

Collings, A. (1989). Zum Kasuserwerb beim Dysgrammatismus. Unpublished paper. Department of Linguistics, University of Düsseldorf

Collings, A., B. Puschmann and M. Rothweiler (1989). Dysgrammatismus: Ein Defizit der grammatischen Kongruenz. *Neurolinguistik* 2: 127–43

Crystal, D. (1982). *Profiling Linguistic Disability.* London: Arnold

Crystal, D., Fletcher, P. and M. Garman (1976). *The Grammatical Analysis of Language Disability.* London: Arnold

Fritzenschaft, A., I. Gawlitzek-Maiwald, R. Tracy and S. Winkler (1990). Wege zur komplexen Syntax. *Zeitschrift für Sprachwissenschaft* 9: 52–134

Gazdar, G., E. Klein, G. Pullum and I. Sag. (1985). *Generalized Phrase Structure Grammar.* Cambridge, MA: Harvard University Press

Götte, R. (1976). *Landauer Sprachentwicklungstest für Vorschulkinder (LSV).* Weinheim: Beltz

Gopnik, M. (1990). Feature-blind grammar and dysphasia. *Nature* 344: 715

────── (1992). Linguistic properties of genetic language impairment. Unpublished paper. Montréal: McGill University

Gopnik, M., and M. Crago (1991). Familial aggregation of a developmental language disorder. *Cognition* 39: 1–50

Grimm, H. (1987). Developmental dysphasia: New theoretical perspectives and empirical results. *The German Journal of Psychology* 11: 8–22

Grimm, H., and H. Schöler (1978). *Heidelberger Sprachentwicklungstest (HSET)*. Braunschweig: Thieme

Grimm, H., and S. Weinert (1990). Is the syntax development of dysphasic children deviant and why? New findings to an old question. *Journal of Speech and Hearing Research* 33: 220–28

Hansen, D. (1993). Sprachtherapie bei Dysgrammatismus. Empirische Studien zur Therapieforschung. Doctoral dissertation, Dortmund: University of Dortmund

Kaltenbacher, E., and K. Lindner (1990). Some aspects of delayed and deviant development in German children with specific language impairment. Paper presented at the Second Conference of the European Group for Child Language Disorders, Röros, Norway

Leonard, L., L. Sabbadini, J. Leonard and V. Volterra (1987). Specific language impairment in children: a cross-linguistic study. *Brain and Language* 32: 233–52

Leonard, L., L. Sabbadini, V. Volterra and J. Leonard (1987). Some influences on the grammar of English- and Italian-speaking children with specific language impairment. *Applied Psycholinguistics* 9: 39–57

Leonard, L., U. Bertolini, M. Caselli, K. McGregor and L. Sabbadini (1992). Morphological deficits in children with specific language impairment. The status of features in the underlying grammar. *Language Acquisition* 2: 151–79

Ötting, J. (1992). Language-Impaired and Normally Developing Children's Acquisition of English Plural. Unpublished Ph.D. dissertation, University of Kansas

Ouhalla, J. (1991, March). Functional categories and the head parameter. Glow Colloquium, Leiden

Rothweiler, M. (1988). Ein Fall von Dygrammatismus: Eine linguistische Analyse. *Frühförderung Interdisziplinär* 3: 114–24

Rothweiler, M., and H. Clahsen (1993). Dissociations in SLI children's inflectional systems: A study of participle inflection and subject-verb-agreement. *Journal of Logopedics and Phoniatrics* 18: 169–79

Wexler, K. (1994). Optional infinitives, head movement and economy of derivation. In N. Hornstein and D. Lightfoot (eds.), *Verb Movement*. Cambridge: Cambridge University Press, pp. 305–350.

8

Specific Language Impairment, Cognition and the Biological Basis of Language

Judith R. Johnston

The title of this chapter reminds me of the "great Question of Life, the Universe, and Everything" in *The Hitch Hiker's Guide to the Galaxy* (Adams 1979). Like Adams, I intend to talk about particular events, big questions and other matters pulled along in the course of argument. The purpose of this symposium is to sample diverse bodies of research that have bearing on our understanding of the biological bases for human language. For some years, I have been studying children who have difficulty learning their first language, in spite of apparently normal sensory and motor mechanisms, normal social relationships and normal non-verbal intelligence. These children are often described as having a *specific language impairment* (SLI), and they provide researchers with a unique opportunity to observe the developmental dissociation of language and other aspects of knowledge and behaviour. Such dissociations are never easy to interpret (Shallice 1991), but in conjunction with other data, they can contribute to our models of the mind.

For the last decade, my experimental work has focused on non-verbal cognition in SLI children. In the pages to follow, I will share with you what we have found, and then I will use these findings to argue for a particular view of our biological preparation for language. The paper is divided into three major sections. In the first, I review findings from various studies of non-verbal cognition, distinguishing between two sorts of tasks, those that entail language competence and those that do not. In the second section, I relate findings from studies of non-verbal cognition in SLI children to what we know of their language learning patterns. In the third section, I will draw out the larger theoretical implications of this research for our understanding of the biological basis of language.

Non-Verbal Performance in SLI Children

Higher-Level Problem Solving: The Role of Language Deficits

I begin with a brief comment on complex conceptual thought. Some eighteen studies have looked at the ability of SLI children to solve

161

higher-level cognitive problems, and most of them have reported poor performance relative to age-matched controls (see Johnston 1992 and Ellis Weismer 1993 for reviews). SLI children have shown difficulty in drawing inferences from pictured texts, formulating and testing hypotheses about class membership and solving Piagetian problems in the domains of class, number and space. A recent study by Ellis Weismer (1991) conveys the flavour of this research. Sixteen SLI children, aged 7;1, were matched by mental age to children with normally developing language. Each child was presented with a series of reasoning problems in which they needed to determine which of two geometric forms was the "correct" one. Forms varied in two dimensions such as size and colour, and the correct answer was always a single value on one dimension, for example, the red one. Across trials the child was expected to infer the selection rule from observing the examiner's choices, and from explicit feedback on the correctness of his answers. The SLI children were able to solve only 23% of the problems, while the control children solved 65%. After analyzing response patterns, Ellis Weismer concludes that "language impaired children display inefficient use of problem solving skills ... in that they are less likely to spontaneously and reliably apply available strategies for processing information" (Ellis Weismur 1991, 1335).

The studies on higher-level cognition are interesting in their own right, but they may not tell us much about the biological bases of language. Despite the effort of experimenters to minimize verbal demands, *language* disabilities most probably contributed to the findings – not so much in the instruction given or the response required as in the cognitive strategies that were employed. This point must remain speculative, since the data concern only final products, not the processes used to create them. It is easy to imagine, however, that the solution of many of these problems would be facilitated by the "inner" use of language codes. The problems require complex mental calculations in the absence of manipulable objects or material feedback. They force children to consider possible states and relations, linked by various logical and physical operations. Language can assist in such tasks by representing interpretations of the physical world, by summarizing thought over time and by supporting the application of pre-compiled mental routines. The results of such facilitation would be increased focus and economy of thought. Poor facility with language may or may not limit cognitive development in any ultimate sense, but it undoubtedly impedes learning and slows cognitive growth. From this perspective, the higher-level cognitive delays seen in SLI children must reflect to some degree their difficulty using language as an intellectual tool (see Siegel et al. 1981 for related arguments).

Thinking Out Loud. To my knowledge there have been no studies that look directly at the way SLI children use language for thought. One of my students, Arlene Sturn, recently completed an initial exploration of this topic (Sturn 1993). In her study, 3- and 4-year-olds were given various construction materials and told to build a bridge over a painted "river." One third of the children were language impaired; the others were matched to the SLI group by either age or language level. Children played in pairs, each pair composed of children who knew each other, with at least one member having normal language development (NL). Two sets of building supplies were piled on the floor on opposite sides of the "river," and each child was seated by a pile. Sessions were audio- and video-taped, but Sturn otherwise avoided any substantive interaction with the builders.

Not surprisingly, the preschoolers in this study frequently talked as they worked, sometimes to themselves and sometimes to their playmate. A portion of this talk was about events that had nothing to do with the building task, but much of it directly concerned the plans, activities and worries of the children as they constructed their bridges. The following excerpts illustrate these data:

M (SLI, 4;8, talking to self):
Oh Oh.
Well, put these down for –
Put these down first, and and then, and, okay and –
Put these down first, and –
First.

C (NL, 4;9, collaborating with playmate):
Make a, may, maybe I can, maybe I can, s, some, maybe I can –
I know, but, I, maybe we can, I got a good idea we can do.
We can *straw it* like that so that thing doesn't, um come off the string.

Notice how M uses language to hold on to his plan as he works, and C lexicalizes his good idea. Language of this sort appears to have just the simplifying and focusing effects that should facilitate problem solving.

One of our interests in this study was to see whether the SLI children made use of language for problem solving to the same extent as children with normally developing language. Perhaps one of the reasons SLI children show cognitive delays is that they fail to apply their verbal resources to intellectual tasks. At the initial level of analysis, the answer is clearly No. Figured either absolutely or proportionally, the language impaired preschoolers used as many task-related utterances as their age peers with normal language. Despite the late onset and slow development of their speech, they were employing verbal tools to help them solve intellectual problems. Whatever cognitive difficulties may result from their language deficits must stem from inefficiency or limitations in repertoire, not from functional propensity.

In summary, experimenters have frequently found children with SLI to be less adept than their age mates in tasks that require higher-level conceptual problem solving. Task analysis suggests that much of this delay can be attributed to the covert role of language in thought, although the mechanisms for this influence require further study. Those of us with theoretical interests in the developmental relationships between language and thought, or clinical interests in the consequences of language disability, will want to pursue this topic. For now, however, this line of research provides little insight into the biological bases of language. I turn now to consider aspects of cognition which have a less verbal character.

Cognitive Processing: Limitations Not Attributable to Language

The importance of language as a tool for thought is virtually unarguable. The importance of cognition for language learning is, on the other hand, a matter for vigorous argument. As scholars have tried to explain children's remarkable success with language learning, they have considered the mental functions and capabilities that exist, or develop, prior to speech. Could general cognitive processes, or at least nonverbal cognitive processes, in concert with the child's language experience, account for the Child Language facts? After 30 years, the literature on language acquisition contains every possible answer to this question. It may be that children with SLI can contribute to this debate by drawing our attention to cognitive dysfunctions or limitations which are associated with their language delays. These affected areas of cognition can then serve as candidate determinants in models of language learning. Recent studies of SLI provide us with four likely candidates.[1]

Early Symbolic Play. Research with normally developing children indicates that words and gesture symbols emerge during the same period of development – but also that the order of onset for the two systems is variable, and that they initially express different sets of meanings (Shore et al. 1990). Although further observations are needed, a similar picture seems likely for deaf infants despite the fact that they are developing signs and gestures in the same, manual, mode (Petitto, this volume). The importance of the data on early language and gesture symbols is that they imply independent domains of development as well as some common origin. At least 10 studies to date have reported that children with specific language impairment engage in less, or less sophisticated, symbolic play than their age peers. (Rescorla and Goossens 1992; others reviewed in Johnston 1992). Researchers have generally concluded that the co-occurrence of language deficits and pretend-play deficits reflects the common symbolic nature of these activities. However, a closer look at the literature raises a question about this conclusion. Most of the studies have measured only language and play in any depth; other cognitive functions have been presumed normal on the basis of performance IQ. Since we now know that IQ scores are often misleading as indices of intellectual function, it remains possible that the deficits in symbolic play are part of a broader picture of cognitive impairment rather than a symptom of some special symbol deficiency.

A recent study by one of my students at the Univeristy of British Columbia begins to answer this question. Capreol (1994) designed her study with two goals in mind. First, she wanted to see whether the same association between delays in language learning and delays in non-verbal symbolic behaviour would be true for language-disordered children at different stages of language learning. Second, she wanted to investigate the relations between symbolic play and non-symbolic problem solving. Although she ruled out children with profound developmental delays, Capreol did not limit her study to children with SLI. Six of her 2- and 3-year-olds, however, fell into this category, and the data from these subjects present an intriguing picture. Each of the children completed standardized language tests and the Symbolic Play Test (Lowe and Costello 1976), did a series of block construction problems (developed by Joan Stiles, University of California at SanDiego, personal communication 1991), and contributed samples of spontaneous symbolic play and spontaneous language. From these observations, Capreol developed a 3-point profile: expressive language level, symbolic play level and manipulative problem-solving level. For the SLI children, all of the profiles show age-appropriate performance in block constructions, as well as the expected developmental gap between block building and language skills. The key finding concerns the level of symbolic play. For three of the children, symbolic play levels are similar to language levels; for the other three, symbolic play scores are at the level of block building. Neither age nor language comprehension distinguishes the two groups, but the children with stronger play skills have larger vocabularies and more word combinations. This finding is corroborated in a recent longitudinal study of four late talkers whose play scores likewise lagged until vocabulary reached 50 words (Ellis Weismer, Murray-Branch and Miller 1991).

Given small sample size and the vagaries of identifying SLI children in the presyntactic period (e.g., Thal and Tobias 1992), Capreol's results cannot be taken as conclusive. They suggest, however, that some children with SLI do manifest *early* symbolic play deficits despite age level performance on other tasks requiring constructive intelligence. Although later stages of symbolic play seem likely to require language skill, in earlier stages the two systems seem to develop quite independently. This being so, early play deficits can be construed as non-verbal in character, perhaps as symptoms of some special problem with symbolic functions.

Perception of Brief Events. The second set of observations concerns the perception of brief events. The earliest findings in this line of investigation come from a 1965 study reported by Lowe and Campbell. These researchers presented school-age SLI children with two brief auditory stimuli at varying interstimulus intervals (ISI). The ISI values at which the language impaired children could decide whether one or two events *had occurred* did not differ from normal, but the ISI necessary for accurate *judgments of order* was 10 times longer than normal. There is now a considerable literature on the perception of brief events by SLI children, due in large part to the work of Tallal and her colleagues (e.g., Tallal and Piercy 1974; Tallal, Stark, Kallman and Mellits 1981; Tallal 1990). This literature has been reviewed extensively and I will not do so again here (see Leonard 1987; Johnston 1988 for reviews). Certain features of the data, however, are important for the present discussion. Note first, that while the early projects indicated a modality-specific, auditory deficit, later studies of somewhat younger children revealed analogous difficulties with visual stimuli such as lights and nonsense figures. Such data make it clear that the perceptual deficits of SLI children are not uniquely auditory, and are not limited to linguistic material nor to any perceptual systems genetically designed for speech signals.

Tallal and other researchers often speak of deficits in "temporal processing," but the nature of these perceptual problems is actually not well understood. Among other issues, the phenomena may or may not involve short-term memory function. In Tallal and Stark (1981), for example, SLI children succeeded in recognizing brief vowel segments, when they were not immediately followed by other stimuli. From this we might conclude that stimuli must be both brief and rapidly sequenced to cause perceptual difficulty, or alternatively, that brief, rapidly sequenced stimuli cause problems only when subjects need to note and remember their sequence. On the other hand, Elliot, Hammer and Scholl (1989) have recently reported findings with a Just-Noticeable-Difference paradigm that indicate perceptual deficits even when memory demands are virtually nonexistent. Resolution of this and related matters will require further study. There is now little doubt, however, that SLI children perceive brief sequential events less well than their age peers.

Visual Imagery. The third set of observations comes from a study of visual imagery that Susan Ellis Weismer and I reported in 1983 (Johnston and Ellis Weismer 1983). In this experiment, 6- and 9-year-old children, with and without specific language impairment, were asked to make similarity judgments about arrays of geometric forms. In each trial, the child would simultaneously view two arrays. During training, both of the arrays were presented in vertical orientation. During the experiment proper, one remained vertical, but the other array was oriented at a 0, 45, 90 or 135 degree angle to the first. On half of the trials, the two arrays contained the same shapes in the same order; on the other half, the order of the shapes differed. The children's task was to decide whether the arrays were identical or not, and to press a button indicating their decision. Reaction times were taken as an index of proficiency.

All of the children demonstrated a good understanding of order concepts, and there were no group differences in speed or accuracy during the training trials. Results from the experiment proper, however, indicated that the SLI children at both ages responded more slowly than their normal peers. This remained true when we took the added precaution of using reaction times from the training trials as a covariate (see also Savich 1984).

One fact about the mental rotation paradigm makes this study particularly interesting for the present discussion. Although it is usually impossible to determine the nature of the cognitive strategy that a child uses to solve a given problem, mental rotation data allow us to do so (Kosslyn 1980). If the viewer solves the problem by creating and manipulating mental images, response times are a direct function of the degree of rotation (i.e., extended rotations require more time). If on the other hand the viewer solves the problem by using verbal symbols, the relationship between response time and degree of rotation does not hold. Our findings were unambiguous on this point. For all four groups of children, reaction times increased as the rotation distance increased, providing strong evidence that all of the children were using imagistic strategies. Whatever difficulties led the SLI children to perform more slowly on this task appear to have been non-verbal in character. Our original report of this study took the findings as indicative of symbolic deficit, but I am now inclined to interpret them as evidence of processing limitations.

Attentional Capacity. The clinical literature on specific language impairment has frequently linked this condition to deficits in attention (*Proceedings* 1960, 43). However, only a handful of studies have investigated attentional processes in this population, and with mixed findings, due in part to a failure to consider task difficulty (Apel and Kamhi 1988). Two themes are nevertheless emerging from this work.

SLI children seem to show difficulties: (1) orienting to environmental change and (2) encoding perceived stimuli. Both of these problems have obvious implications for attentional capacity. In a limited capacity (Bower and Clapper 1989) cognitive system, inefficiency or ineffectiveness with any component of a calculation reduces the resources available for some other component and thereby places limits on the amount or nature of the mental work that can be done.

My colleague Laura Riddle wrote a dissertation study of attention that illustrates these themes and connections. Riddle (1992) asked 4- and 5-year-olds to complete a visual classification task and a concurrent auditory detection task. All of the children had earned normal range performance IQs; half of them evidenced serious delays in language development, the other half did not. On each trial of the experiment, the children received a visual alerting signal. They then viewed a slide depicting an object from one of 16 basic-level categories (e.g., a cat). After a brief interval, this was replaced by a second slide depicting two objects: another object from the same basic category and an object from an entirely different superordinate family (e.g., a cat and a shoe). The child was to choose the object which matched the original target by pressing a button at the corresponding side of the screen. On a random half of the trials, a buzzer sounded during one of three phases of the visual task: the *alerting* period, the viewing of the target (*encoding*) or the viewing of the response choices (*responding*). The child was to press a button and stop the buzzer as quickly as possible while remembering to "play the picture game." Auditory reaction times in the dual task presentation were compared with baseline times to determine any "concurrence costs."

According to the logic of the dual-task paradigm, a child's reaction time in the secondary task (i.e., buzzer detection) reveals the proportion of attentional capacity needed to complete the primary task (i.e., picture classification). In our case, if the demands of the classification task were high, "spare" capacity should decrease, resulting in slower auditory reaction times. Riddle's major findings concerned the younger children, ranging in age from 3;10 to 4;9. When the buzzer occurred during either the alerting or the encoding phase, the younger SLI children responded more slowly than the children with normally developing language.

These findings cannot be explained by any simple appeal to differences in the ability level of the children or in their understanding of the tasks. The language-impaired and normally developing children had similar baseline reaction times on both tasks, and maintained high levels of accuracy throughout the experiment. Instead, the findings point to differences in attentional capacity. The SLI children could do the classification task, but it apparently consumed a high proportion of their cognitive resources, leaving them less free to respond to the auditory probe.

Slow responses during the alerting phase seem to indicate some difficulty with rapid orientation to environmental change. The visual signal for readiness, a red plus sign, was still consuming resources for the SLI children at a point when the children witi normal language had completed their orientation and achieved a fully alert state. Macworth et al. (1973) reported similar findings in a study of eye-gaze patterns. Children in that study watched a matrix of blinking geometric forms, one of which turned red after a period of viewing. Seven of the 10 SLI children were slow to orient to the visual novelty; the other 3 children oriented quickly but stared at the red form for an unusually long time.

Slow responses during the encoding phase seem to indicate a second sort of attentional problem. Riddle's young SLI subjects, like Macworth's three, seemed fully consumed by the need to interpret and code the target picture. Could this reflect their inept use of verbal symbols? Additional data suggest a more interesting story. In half of the trials, the target picture and the correct response picture were identical (e.g., a cat, the same cat); in the other half of the trials, the two pictures showed physically different members of the same basic category (e.g., a cat, a different cat). The SLI children were more accurate when the pictures were identical, but the normally developing children showed no such difference. This data pattern is what would be expected if the SLI children, at least some of the time, encoded the target visually rather than verbally. Use of verbal codes would negate the distinction between an identical cat and a merely similar cat; both would be true instances of the verbal category "cat." Only use of visual memory codes would maintain the distinction between the identical and the similar.

If the younger SLI children relied on non-verbal coding strategies, their slow responses in the encoding phase indicate either that they were poor non-verbal coders, or that non-verbal strategies are inherently more costly. A recent study by Townsend and Tallal (1989) may help us choose between these alternatives. Seven-year-olds were asked to listen to an auditory signal (a high- or low-frequency moving tone), and then to detect all instances of that target in a five minute series of single tones. This task was repeated with visual squiggles and with short auditory or visual sequences of the same stimuli (J. Townsend, personal communication, 1993). All of the stimuli were designed to minimize the utility of verbal codes. Although the SLI children did less well than the normally developing children with the auditory items, a finding reminiscent of the auditory perception research cited earlier, their performance on the visual items was age appropriate. This suggests that the encoding problems seen in the Riddle study were inherent in their non-verbal coding strategy and not due to limits in competence. Further research using the selective attention task with younger children will be needed to confirm this conclusion (cf. Tallal and Stark 1981).

In summary, data from studies of symbolic play, visual imagery, perception and attention strongly suggest that the cognitive dysfunctions and/or limitations of SLI children do extend to non-verbal areas. All but the play studies clearly implicate basic information-processing mechanisms, and point to abnormalities in the rate and/or efficiency with which information is handled. The SLI children in these studies could make the similarity decisions, the order judgments or the classifications that the experimenters required, but they needed more time to orient, more time between stimuli, or more time to respond. It is worth noting that such differences in processing rate and efficiency could easily, in other contexts, translate into limitations on the nature and complexity of the problems that could be solved at all

Information Processing Deficits and the Developmental Profiles of Children with Specific Language Disorder

Our task at this symposium is to consider the nature of the biological basis of human language. Like many of the participants here, I believe that we can use the language patterns of children with SLI to inform our general theories of language. If we choose this strategy, however, good science requires us to pay attention to the non-verbal deficits as well as the verbal ones. Here we have two options. We can argue that the non-verbal and verbal deficits are brought about by a common developmental misfortune but are otherwise independent. Or, we can look for connections between the two areas of dysfunction. Since the latter option strikes me as more interesting, I turn now to consider the possible consequences of a slow and/or inefficient processing mechanism for language acquisition. This discussion is in no way meant to be a sufficient account of language development. I certainly recognize the importance and plausibility of domain-specific competencies, and further, I believe that any satisfying account of language learning will need to consider "top-down" processes as well as data-driven cognition. We do, however, need a starting place, and the available studies invite us to begin by considering the possible significance of deficiencies in basic information-processing mechanisms.

When we look at the language profiles of children with specific language disorders, we find two main phenomena that invite explanation: (1) a general pattern of late onset and slow development and (2) specific patterns of strength and weakness in various linguistic domains. How could cognitive processing deficiencies be related to these facts?

Late and Slow Language Development. Consider first the general pattern of late and slow language development. Although acquisition theories differ in the emphasis placed on cognitive processing mechanisms, virtually all of them do invoke notions of attention, perception and input analysis at some point in the model. Pinker (1989) for example, posits one early learning process in which "verb meanings correspond to concepts given by the child's perceptual and cognitive mechanisms ... [and] to acquire them, the child ... map[s] a sound uttered in the presence of an exemplar of a concept onto the mental representation of that concept" (Pinker 1989, 253–54). The initial semantic structure that results from that mapping is refined, as needed, by hypothesis-testing activities in which the child eliminates "any incorrect hypotheses as a result of observing how the verb is used across situations" (ibid., 255). The implicit cognitive demands of such learning would be considerable, including at one point the simultaneous activation and co-ordination of a lexical representation, a pool of candidate semantic features, and an specific event interpretation. If we assume (Schacter 1989) that mental resources are needed to access stored information and maintain it for comparative analyses, then slow or inefficient processing could increase the resource demands of the verb-learning task. This would leave the child vulnerable to error or incomplete analysis. Some such scenario might explain Kelly's (1992) recent finding that SLI preschoolers make more semantic verb errors than either age-matched or language-matched peers, both within and across major categories of meaning.

As a second example, consider the findings from a miniature language system experiment that I and my colleagues conducted (Johnston et al. 1990). In this study we asked school-age children with varying language proficiency to learn two different artificial languages. Both languages had phonetically balanced vocabularies of seven words, expressed the same sort of relational meaning (Action: Agent, Patient/Theme),[2] and had grammars consisting of a word-order rule and a suffix marking the Patient/Theme. The word-order rules differed such that the inflectional morpheme was either utterance final or utterance medial: Action + Ag + P/T + suffix (Language 1); Ag + P/T + suffix + Action (Language 2). Illustrative sentences in the two languages are as follows:

Language 1 (VSO)	Hev	zune	fak	oo
	Act	Ag	P/T	Sx
Language #2 (SOV)	Kaze	shup	o	waf
	Ag	P/T	Sx	Act

Children learned the languages incidently, from fluent speakers, while playing an interactive communication game. Both production and comprehension data were collected across the course of learning.

Five of the children proved to be poor language learners. (Three of these five had been previously identified as having a specific language impairment.) In contrast to the other children, these poor learners were successful with only one of the languages, and took more than twice as many trials to learn even that one. Their error patterns were particularly interesting for the present discussion: on Language 1, they tended to include the suffix in its sentence-final position, but made many errors on word order; for Language 2, they generally omitted the suffix and made few word-order errors. Presumably, the different positions of the Patient/Theme made the suffix more and less perceptually salient, accounting for the fact that suffix errors were associated with Language 2. The very existence of these strongly differentiated error patterns is, however, the real finding of interest. Why did the low-proficiency learners focus on one aspect of the grammar and ignore the other, both within and across trials? Limitation in attentional resources again seems like a useful explanation. Whatever aspect of the grammar captured their attention first continued to drive the learning process. Other features of the grammar were ignored, preventing the child from arriving at broader conclusions about the language *system*. In the case of Language 1, this selectivity was particularly damaging: children learned to place the "oo" syllable in the sentence final position, but since they did so without regard for word order, they were unlikely to note the association between the particle and the Patient/Theme. This meant that the "oo" syllable was not analyzed as a suffix. In a more complex language, failures of this sort would certainly impede the course of acquisition.

In short, when we look at the fine detail of language learning – either by careful modelling or by microdevelopmental data – we discover a process that makes heavy demands on attentional resources. It is not surprising that children with processing deficiencies would acquire language late and slowly.

Strengths and Weaknesses in Specific Linguistic Domains. Children with SLI not only learn to speak at a late age and make slow progress, they also seem to have special difficulty with specific sorts of linguistic forms. The best documented instances come from studies of grammatical morphology. Since our own work in the 1970s (Johnston and Schery 1976), a number of investigators have confirmed that SLI children learning English do not use inflectional morphemes, auxiliaries, articles and other functors as well as would be expected from MLU

(Leonard et al., in press; others reviewed in Johnston 1988) or lexical knowledge (Moore and Johnston 1993). One explanation for this fact arises from the observation that "English grammatical morphemes are difficult perceptually because, as nonsyllabic consonant segments and unstressed syllables, they are shorter in duration than adjacent morphemes" (Leonard 1992, 188). Children who have difficulty perceiving brief acoustic events should find these forms especially challenging. Not only will the primary data be noisy, but the "extra" resources required for perceptual processing will reduce the mental energy available for building morphological paradigms.

If this line of argument is valid, grammatical morphemes with more salient acoustic properties should be easier to learn. Recent cross-linguistic studies of SLI children largely confirm this prediction (Leonard 1992; Leonard et al. 1992; Dromi, Leonard and Shteiman 1993). Grammatical morphemes in Italian tend to be word-final vowels, or word final multisyllabic forms ending in vowels, that are longer than the English consonantal forms, and further, can benefit from clause-final vowel lengthening. Grammatical inflections in Hebrew tend to occur in stressed syllables and also to benefit from lengthening. SLI children who are learning these two languages show little difficulty with the grammatical morphemes that conform to these acoustic profiles. They do have difficulty learning morphemes that, like the English set, are unstressed.

The role of perceptual dysfunction in our accounts of morphological deficits is a matter of considerable current debate. The papers by Gopnik and Clahsen in this volume capture the spirit of this discourse. I fear, however, that two misunderstandings threaten to disrupt the productivity of our collective efforts. The first concerns the important distinction between *acquisition* and *use*. The explanatory argument I have presented above applies to the *acquisition* of language patterns by SLI children, not to the *use* of these patterns once they are learned. Perceptual dysfunction could strongly influence a child's analysis of the primary linguistic data and hence her rate of learning, but have little effect once the morphological paradigms have been built. Production errors at that point would reflect other performance factors such as attentional capacity, memory recall or the co-ordination of various utterance formulation processes. The possibility that morphological errors could arise from two different sources has not received adequate attention in attempts to confirm or disconfirm the "perceptual" account. From a dual factor perspective, for example, there is no reason to be surprised when the morphological error patterns of older SLI speakers fail to reflect the acoustic characteristics of the morphemes (see Gopnik, this volume, for a differing view).

This raises a second and more general topic of concern. It seems to me that, as researchers and theoreticians, we have much to learn about argumentation in multi-factor causal models. The debates over SLI morphology are illustrative. The full range of data strongly suggest that perceptual deficits alone cannot explain the learning of grammatical morphemes. Note, for example, that while German and English inflections are quite similar in their acoustic properties, German SLI children seem to have less difficulty with them. We have argued elsewhere that the functional importance of inflections in German may draw children's attention to these forms and compensate for their perceptual difficulty (Lindner and Johnston 1992). Similar arguments are made by Dromi et al. (1993) to explain unexpected successes with the Hebrew definite prefix. Rice and Oetting (1993), in a separate line of argument, invoke differences in the scope and nature of syntactic agreement rules to explain why English-speaking SLI children have more difficulty with the third person singular verb inflection -s than with the plural -s (see Clahsen, this volume, for further discussion of scope of agreement). Rather than argue as if these various explanations were in competition, I suggest that it would make more sense to find ways of integrating them into a broader acquisition model. For me, the data on SLI grammatical morphology, taken as a whole, point to exactly that interplay of perceptual, cognitive, semantic and syntactic factors that is posited by most theories of child language. It is more difficult to confirm that there is or is not an effect of a factor that, at best, could account for only a portion of the variance, but that is the real nature of our task. If we assume such a multi-factor perspective, the association between acoustic facts, perceptual deficits and morphological learning patterns that can be seen in studies of SLI children actually seems remarkably strong.

To summarize, studies of non-verbal cognition in children with SLI point to the existence of information-processing deficits, particularly in the areas of perception, processing rate and attentional capacity. In the preceding sections, I have tried to show how deficits of this sort could account for the characteristic language patterns of SLI children, namely the late and laboured course of acquisition and the relative difficulty of English grammatical morphemes.

Specific Language Disorder, Cognition and the Biological Basis of Language

I return now to the Great Question of Life, the Universe and Everything. What do children with specific language impairment tell us about the biological basis of language? The easy answer was, of course, provided many years ago by thoughtful clinicians (McCready 1926;

Ingram 1959) who collected family histories and concluded that specific language disorder, and hence language, has a biological basis. Our
task now, as Pennington and Smith describe it, is to "identify pure subtypes of disorder and relate each disorder to dysfunction in a particular
component or components of the complex neuropsychological system
subserving language development" (Pennington and Smith 1983, 383).
This task will be difficult given the many possible paths between genetic endowment, or other causal agents, and behaviour – especially in
a developing organism (Sejnowski and Churchland 1989). Some
progress is being made. Tallal, Townsend, Curtiss and Wulfeck (1991),
for example, have recently reported a correlation between family history of SLI, attentional deficit and severe morphosyntactic delays.
Tomblin's current investigation of family pedigrees is likely to illumi-
nate the nature of the genetic mechanisms involved (Tomblin 1989 and
this volume). And, a possible physical basis for this linkage is suggested by new MRI data showing atypical perisylvian asymmetries associated with morphosyntactic delays (Plante and Swisher 1991). Relationships between this cluster of findings and the larger literature on
SLI have yet to be determined. It may be, for example, that attentional
systems can be compromised by genetic *or* environmental agents, but
that this distinction has no bearing on language outcomes since the important learning constraints arise out of the attentional dysfunction,
whatever its cause.

Faced with this complexity, researchers cannot afford to aim their
lines of investigation and argument in the wrong direction. Here is
where the research on non-verbal cognition in SLI children becomes
important. However we may interpret particular findings, we are
forced to the general conclusion that Specific Language Impairment is
not very specific. There is evidence of developmental dissociation, but
little evidence of "sparing" – at least not as we have traditionally defined it. SLI children perform better on some learning tasks than on others, but this does not, in fact, translate neatly into "verbal" deficits and
"non-verbal" strengths. Instead, it seems that young SLI children do
relatively well when tasks are biased toward visual perceptual analysis
and static stimuli, when they allow for trial and error manipulation,
and/or when chains of reasoning are short. They do less well when
problems reward linguistic coding, stimuli are brief and sequenced,
perceptual analyses must occur over time, mental calculations are complex and/or the problem space is symbolic.

I am convinced that an important key to understanding the developmental profiles of SLI children lies in the study of their cognitive
processing limitations. In this chapter I have provided evidence of
these limitations and have tried to illustrate how they could affect

language learning. Analogous arguments could be made to explain poor performance in symbolic play, imagery and other non-verbal domains. Eventually, with correct descriptions of the compromised mechanisms and the problem spaces, we should be able to predict the entire array of learning outcomes. I readily admit that we are nowhere near reaching this goal.

What we do know is this: any attempt to observe SLI children and infer some general truth about human language must contend with the *non-specificity* of their impairment. SLI children do show significant delays in language acquisition, but they also show difficulties with many aspects of cognitive function that cannot easily be explained by the language facts. My general truth of the moment is that the same set of neuropsychological systems can account for delays – and learning – in both the language and the non-language domains. To readers who find this conclusion unsatisfying, I offer the following from *The Hitch Hiker's Guide*:

> "Alright," said Deep Thought. "The Answer to the Great Question of Life, the Universe and Everything ... is ... Forty-two." "Forty-two!" yelled Loonquawl. "Is that all you've got to show for seven and a half million years' work?" "I checked it very thoroughly," said the computer, "and that quite definitely is the answer. I think the problem, to be quite honest with you, is that you've never actually known what the question is." (Adams 1979, 135–136)

Notes

1 Findings in regard to perception of simultaneous tactile stimuli (Tallal, Stark and Mellits 1985), spatial memory (Wyke and Asso 1979; Doehring 1960), analysis of rhythm (Kracke 1975), and hierarchical construction (Cromer 1983) are undoubtedly of equal importance, but have not attracted as much research attention and will not be considered here. Petitto's focus (this volume) on the role of temporal patterning – and Morgan and Meier's (1987) recent arguments on prosodic bootstrapping – suggest that further attention to rhythmic perception would be particularly valuable.
2 This notation is meant to indicate that one of the arguments of the verb was both directly involved in the action of the Agent and underwent a change of state or location (Pinker 1989).

References

Adams, D. (1979). *The Hitch Hiker's Guide to the Galaxy.* London: Pan Books
Apel, K., and A. Kamhi (1988, November). Selective attention skills of normal and language-impaired children. Paper presented to the American Speech-Language-Hearing Association, Boston, Massachusetts

Bower, G. and J. Clapper (1989). Experimental methods in cognitive science. In M. Posner (Ed.) *Foundations of Cognitive Science*, 245–300. Cambridge, MA: MIT

Capreol, C. (1994). The Relationship between Symbolic Play and Constructive Problem Solving in Young Children with Significant Language Delay. Unpublished M.Sc. thesis, University of British Columbia

Clahsen, H. (1989) The grammatical characterization of developmental dysphasia. *Linguistics* 27: 897–920

—— (this volume)

Cromer, R. (1983). Hierarchical planning disability in the drawings and constructions of a special group of severely aphasic children. *Brain and Cognition* 2: 144–64

Doehring, D. (1960). Visual spatial memory in aphasic children. *Journal of Speech and Hearing Research* 3: 138–49

Dromi, E., L. Leonard and M. Shteiman (1993). The grammatical morphology of Hebrew-speaking children with specific language impairment: Some competing hypotheses. *Journal of Speech and Hearing Research* 36: 760–71

Elliott, L., M. Hammer and M. Scholl (1989) Fine-grained auditory discrimination in normal children and children with language-learning problems. *Journal of Speech and Hearing Research* 32: 112–19

Ellis Weismer, S. (1991). Hypothesis testing abilities of language impaired children. *Journal of Speech and Hearing Research* 34: 1329–38

—— (1993). Perceptual and cognitive deficits in children with specific language impairment (developmental dysphasia): Implications for diagnosis and intervention. In H. Grimm and H. Skowronek (eds.), *Language Acquisition Problems and Reading Disorders: Aspects of Diagnosis and Intervention*. New York: De Gruyter

Ellis Weismer, S., J. Murray-Branch and J. Miller (1991, November). Language development patterns in late talkers and typically developing children. Paper presented to the American Speech-Language-Hearing Association, Atlanta, Georgia

Gopnik, M. (this volume)

Ingram, T. (1959). Specific developmental disorders of speech in childhood. *Brain* 82: 450–67

Johnston, J. (1988). Specific language disorders in the child. In N. Lass, L. McReynolds, J. Northern, and D. Yoder (eds.), *Handbook of Speech-Language Pathology and Audiology*, 685–715. Toronto: B.C. Decker

—— (1991) Questions about cognition in children with specific language impairment. In J. Miller (ed.), *Research on Child Language Disorders*, 299–308. Austin, TX: Pro-Ed

—— (1992) Cognitive abilities of language impaired children. In P. Fletcher and D. Hall (eds.), *Specific Speech and Language Disorders in Children*, 105–17. London: Whurr

Johnston, J., M. Blatchley and G. Streit Olness (1990). Miniature language system acquisition by children with different learning proficiencies. *Journal of Speech and Hearing Research* 33: 335–42

Johnston, J., and S. Ellis Weismer (1983). Mental rotation abilities in language disordered children. *Journal of Speech and Hearing Research* 26: 397–403

Johnston, J., and T. Schery. (1976). The use of grammatical morphemes by children with communication disorders. In D. Morehead and A. Morehead (eds.), *Normal and Deficient Child Language*, 239–58. Baltimore, MD: University Park

Kelly, D. (1992, November). Semantic verb errors in SLI and normally developing preschoolers. Poster presentation, American Speech-Language-Hearing Association, San Antonio, Texas

Kosslyn, S. (1980). *Image and Mind*. Cambridge, MA: Harvard University Press

Kracke, I. (1975). Perception of rhythmic sequences by receptive aphasic and deaf children. *British Journal of Disorders of Communication* 10: 43–51

Leonard, L. (1987). Is specific language impairment a useful construct? In S. Rosenberg (ed.), *Advances in Applied Psycholinguistics*, Vol. 1, *Disorders of First-Language Development*, 1–39. Cambridge: Cambridge University Press.

———— (1992). The use of morphology by children with specific language impairment: Evidence from three languages. In R. Chapman (ed.,) *Processes in Language Acquisition and Disorders*, 186–201. St. Louis: Mosby Year Book

Leonard, L., U. Bortolini, M.C. Caselli, K. McGregor and L. Sabbadini (1992). Morphological deficits in children with specific language impairment: The status of features in the underlying grammar. *Language Acquisition* 2: 151–79

Lindner, K., and J. Johnston (1992). Grammatical morphology in language-impaired children acquiring English or German as their first language: A functional perspective. *Applied Psycholinguistics* 13: 115–30

Lowe, A., R. and Campbell (1965). Temporal discrimination in aphasoid and normal children. *Journal of Speech and Hearing Rese arch* 8: 313–14

Lowe, M., and A. Costello (1976). *The Symbolic Play Test*. Windsor:NFER

MacWorth, N., N. Grandstaff and K. Pribam (1973). Orientation to pictorial novelty by speech-disordered children. *Neuropsychologia* 2: 443–50

McCready, E. (1926). Defects in zone of language and their influence in education and behaviour. *American Journal of Psychiatry* 6: 267–77

Moore, M.E., and J. Johnston (1993). Expressions of past time by normal and language disordered children. *Applied Psycholinguistics* 14: 515–34

Morgan, J., and R. Meier (1987). Structural packaging in the input to language learning: Contributions of prosodic and morphological marking of phrases to the acquisition of language. *Cognitive Psychology* 19: 498–550

Pennington, B., and S. Smith (1983). Genetic influences on learning disabilities and speech and language disorders. *Child Development* 54: 369–87

Petitto (this volume)

Pinker, S. (1989). *Learnability and cognition*. Cambridge, MA: MIT Press

Plante, E., and L. Swisher (1991). MRI findings in boys with specific language impairment. *Brain and Language* 41: 52–66

Proceedings of the Institute on Childhood Aphasia (1960, September). Stanford University School of Medicine. San Francisco: California Society for Crippled Children and Adults

Rescorla, L., and L. Goossens (1992). Symbolic play development in toddlers with expressive specific language impairment. *Journal of Speech and Hearing Research* 35: 1281–89

Rice, M., and J. Oetting (1993) Morphological deficits of SLI children: Evaluation of number marking and agreement. *Journal of Speech and Hearing Research* 36: 1249–57

Riddle, L. (1992). The attentional capacity of children with specific language impairment. Unpublished doctoral dissertation, Bloomington, IN: Indiana University

Savich, P. (1984). Anticipatory imagery in normal and language disabled children. *Journal of Speech and Hearing Research* 27: 494–501

Sejnowski, T., and P. Churchland (1989). Brain and cognition. In M. Posner (ed.), *Foundations of Cognitive Science*, 301–56. Cambridge, MA: MIT

Schacter, D. (1989). Memory. In M. Posner (ed.), *Foundations of Cognitive Science*, 683–725. Cambridge, MA: MIT

Shallice, T. (1991). Precis from T. Shallice, *From Neuropsychology to Mental Structures*. *Behavioral and Brain Sciences* 14: 429–69

Shore, C., E. Bates, I. Bretherton, M. Beeghly and B. O'Connell (1990) Vocal and gestural symbols: Similarities and differences from 13 to 28 months. In V. Volterra and C. Erting (eds.), *From Gesture to Language in Hearing and Deaf Children*. New York: Springer-Verlag

Siegel, L., A. Lees, L. Allan and B. Bolton (1981). Non-verbal assessment of Piagetian concepts in preschool children with impaired language development. *Educational Psychology* 1: 153–58

Sturn, A. (1993). Thinking outloud: The problem solving language of preschoolers with and without language impairment. Unpublished M.Sc. thesis. Vancouver, BC: University of British Columbia

Tallal, P. (1990). Fine-grained discrimination deficits in language learning impaired children are specific neither to the auditory modality nor to speech perception. *Journal of Speech and Hearing Research* 33: 616–21

Tallal, P., and M. Piercy (1974). Developmental aphasia: rate of auditory processing and selective impairment of consonant perception. *Neuropsychologia* 12: 83–93

Tallal, P., and R. Stark (1981). Speech acoustic cue discrimination abilities of normally developing and language impaired children. *Journal of the Acoustical Society of America* 69: 569–74

Tallal, P., R. Stark, C. Kallman and D. Mellits (1981). A reexamination of some non-verbal perceptual abilities of language-impaired and normal children as a function of age and sensory modality. *Journal of Speech and Hearing Research* 24: 351–57

Tallal, P., R. Stark and D. Mellits (1985). Identification of language impaired children on the basis of rapid perception and production skills. *Brain and Language* 25: 314–22

Tallal, P., J. Townsend, S. Curtiss and B. Wulfeck (1991). Phenotypic profiles of language impaired children based on genetic/family history. *Brain and Language* 41: 81–95

Thal, D., and S. Tobias (1992). Communicative gestures in children with delayed onset of oral expressive vocabulary. *Journal of Speech and Hearing Research* 35: 1281–89

Tomblin, B. (1989). Familial concentration of developmental language impairment. *Journal of Speech and Hearing Disorders* 54: 287–95

——— (this volume)

Townsend, J., and P. Tallal (1989, June). Auditory attentional capacity deficits in disorders of language acquisition. Paper presented to the American Psychological Society, Alexandria, Virginia

Wyke, M., and D. Asso (1979). Perception and memory for spatial relations in children with developmental dysphasia. *Neuropsychologia* 17: 231–39

9
Evolutionary Biology and the Evolution of Language

Steven Pinker

The elephant's trunk is six feet long and one foot thick and contains 60,000 muscles. Elephants can use their trunks to uproot trees, stack timber or carefully place huge logs into position when recruited to build bridges. They can curl their trunk around a pencil and draw characters on letter-size paper. With the two muscular extensions at the tip, they can remove a thorn, pick up a pin or a dime, uncork a bottle, slide the bolt off a cage door and hide it on a ledge, or grip a cup, without breaking it, so firmly that only another elephant can pull it away. The tip is sensitive enough for a blindfolded elephant to ascertain the shape and texture of objects. In the wild, elephants use their trunks to pull up clumps of grass and tap them against their knees to knock off the dirt, to shake coconuts out of palm trees and to powder their bodies with dust. They use their trunks to probe the ground as they walk, avoiding pit-traps, and to dig wells and siphon water from them. Elephants can walk underwater on the beds of deep rivers, or swim like submarines for miles, using their trunks as snorkels. They communicate through their trunks by trumpeting, humming, roaring, piping, purring, rumbling and making a crumpling-metal sound by rapping the trunk against the ground. The trunk is lined with chemoreceptors that allow the elephant to smell a python hidden in the grass or food a mile away (Williams 1989; Carrington 1958).

Elephants are the only living animals that possess this extraordinary organ. Their closest living terrestrial relative is the hyrax, a mammal that you would probably not be able to tell from a large guinea pig. Until now you have probably not given the uniqueness of the elephant's trunk a moment's thought. Certainly no biologist has made a fuss about it. But now imagine what might happen if some biologists were elephants. Obsessed with the unique place of the trunk in nature, they might ask how it could have evolved, given that no other organism has a trunk or anything like it. One school might try to think up ways to narrow the gap. They would first point out that the elephant and hyrax share at least 90% of their DNA, so they could not be all that different. They might say that the trunk must not be as complex as everyone thought; perhaps the number of muscles had been miscounted. They might further note that the hyrax really does have a trunk, but it has somehow been overlooked; after all, it does have nostrils. Though their attempts to train hyraxes to pick up objects with their nostrils have failed, some might trumpet their success at training the hyraxes to push toothpicks around with their tongues, noting that stacking tree trunks or drawing on blackboards differ from it only in degree. The opposite school, maintaining the uniqueness of the trunk, might insist that it appeared all at once in the offspring of a particular trunkless elephant ancestor, the product of a single dramatic mutation. Or they might say that the trunk somehow arose as an automatic by-product of the elephant's having evolved a large head. They might add another paradox for trunk evolution: the trunk is absurdly more intricate and better coordinated than any ancestral elephant would have needed.

These arguments might strike us as peculiar, but every one of them has been made by scientists of a different species about a complex organ that that species alone possesses, language. Noam Chomsky and some of his fiercest opponents agree on one thing: that a uniquely human language instinct seems to be incompatible with the modern Darwinian theory of evolution, in which complex biological systems arise by the gradual accumulation over generations of random genetic mutations that enhance reproductive success. Either there is no specific human language instinct or it must have evolved by other means. Since I have argued extensively that there is one (Pinker 1994), but would certainly forgive anyone who would rather believe Darwin than believe me, I would like to show that one does not have to make such a choice. Though we know few details about how language evolved, there is no reason to doubt that the principal explanation is the same as for any other complex instinct or organ: Darwinian natural selection. (For related arguments, see Pinker and Bloom, 1989; Pinker, 1995; Hurford, 1989, 1991; Newmeyer, 1991; Brandon and Hornstein, 1986; Corballis, 1991.)

Could Language Be Unique to Humans?

Language is obviously as different from other animals' communication systems as the elephant's trunk is different from other animals' nostrils. Non-human communication systems are based on one of three designs: a finite repertory of calls (one for warnings of predators, one for claims to territory, and so on), a continuous analog signal that registers the magnitude of some state (e.g., the livelier the dance of the bee, the richer the food source that it is telling its hivemates about) or a series of random variations on a theme (like a birdsong repeated with a new twist each time – Charlie Parker with feathers; see Wilson 1972; Gould and Marler 1987). Human language, of course, has a very different design. The discrete combinatorial system called "grammar" makes human language infinite (there is no limit to the number of complex words or sentences in a language), digital (this infinity is achieved by rearranging discrete elements in particular orders and combinations, not by varying some signal along a continuum like the mercury in a thermometer) and compositional (each of the infinite combinations has a different meaning that is predictable from the meanings of its parts and the rules and principles arranging them).

Even the seat of human language in the brain is special. The vocal calls of primates are controlled not by their cerebral cortex but by the phylogenetically older neural systems in the brainstem and limbic system that are heavily involved in emotion. Human vocalizations other than language, like sobbing, laughing, moaning and shouting in pain are also controlled subcortically. Language itself, of course, is seated in the cerebral cortex, primarily the left perisylvian regions (Deacon, 1988, 1989; Caplan 1987; Myers 1976; Robinson 1976).

Some psychologists believe that changes in the vocal organs and in the neural circuitry that produces and perceives speech sounds are the *only* aspects of language that evolved in our species. On this view, there are a few general learning abilities found throughout the animal kingdom, and they work most efficiently in humans. At some point in history, language was invented and refined, and we have been learning it ever since. According to this view, chimpanzees are the second-best learners in the animal kingdom, so they should be able to acquire a language, too, albeit a simpler one. All it takes is a teacher, and a sensorimotor channel that chimpanzees can control. Indeed, beginning in the late 1960s, several famous projects claimed to have taught language to chimpanzees (e.g., Sarah: Premack and Premack 1972; Premack 1985; Kanzi: Savage-Rumbaugh 1991; Greenfield and Savage-Rumbaugh 1991; Washoe: Gardner and Gardner 1969, 1974; see Wallman 1992 for a review).

These claims have not only captured the public's imagination (they have been played up in many popular science books, magazines and television programs) but have captivated many scientists, who see the projects as a healthy deflation of our species' arrogant chauvinism (Sagan and Druyan 1992). Some psycholinguists, recalling Darwin's insistence on the gradualness of evolutionary change, seem to believe, moreover, that a detailed examination of chimps' behaviour is unnecessary: they must have language, as a matter of principle. For example, Elizabeth Bates, Donna Thal and Virginia Marchman have written:

> If the basic structural principles of language cannot be learned (bottom up) or derived (top down), there are only two possible explanations for their existence: either Universal Grammar was endowed to us directly by the Creator, or else our species has undergone a mutation of unprecedented magnitude, a cognitive equivalent of the Big Bang...
>
> We have to abandon any strong version of the discontinuity claim that has characterized generative grammar for thirty years. We have to find some way to ground symbols and syntax in the mental material that we share with other species. (Bates et al. 1991, 30, 35)

When chimps' abilities are looked at on their own, though, free from theoretical and ethical preconceptions, different conclusions emerge (Terrace et al. 1979; Seidenberg and Petitto 1979, 1987; Petitto and Seidenberg 1979; Wallman 1992). For one thing, the apes most definitely have not "learned American Sign Language," as has been frequently announced; this preposterous claim is based on the myth that ASL is a crude system of pantomimes and gestures, rather than a full language with complex phonology, morphology and syntax. Furthermore, the chimps' grammatical abilities are close to nil. Whereas typical sentences from a two-year-old child are *"Look at that train Ursula brought"* and *"We going turn light on so you can't see,"* typical sentences from a language-trained chimp are *"Me banana you banana me you give"* and *"Give orange me give eat orange me eat orange give me eat orange give me you."*

Recently, Sue Savage Rumbaugh and her collaborators have claimed that even though common chimps cannot be taught sign language, pygmy chimps (bonobos) can be taught a language that uses visual lexigrams. (Why they should be expected to do so much better than members of their sibling species is not clear; contrary to frequent suggestions, pygmy chimps are no more closely related to humans than common chimps are). Kanzi's crowning linguistic achievement was said to be a kind of three-symbol "sentence" – but the so-called sentences are all chains like the symbol for chase, followed by the symbol for hide, followed by a point to the person Kanzi wants to do the chasing and hiding. That is, they are fixed formulas with no internal structure and are not even three symbols long.

But let us put aside the empirical question of what chimpanzees in fact have accomplished, and return to the theoretical question of whether evolutionary theory requires that they must have acquired some version of language. I will show that if human language is unique in the modern animal kingdom, as it appears to be, the implications for a Darwinian account of its evolution would be as follows: none. A language instinct unique to modern humans poses no more of a paradox than a trunk unique to modern elephants. No contradiction, no Creator, no big bang.

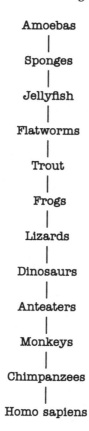

Figure 1: The Wrong Theory

Modern evolutionary theorists are alternately amused and annoyed by a curious fact. Though most educated people profess to believe in Darwin's theory, what they really believe is a slightly modified version of the ancient theological notion of the Great Chain of Being: that all species are arrayed in a linear hierarchy with humans at the top. Darwin's contribution, according to this belief, was showing that each species on the ladder evolved from the species one rung down, instead of being allotted its rung by God. Dimly remembering their high-school biology classes that took them on a tour of the phyla from "primitive" to "modern," people think roughly as follows: amoebas begat sponges which begat jellyfish which begat flatworms which begat trout which begat frogs which begat lizards which begat dinosaurs which begat anteaters which begat monkeys which begat chimpanzees which begat us (Figure 1). (I have skipped a few steps for the sake of brevity.) Hence the paradox: humans enjoy language while their neighbours on the immediately adjacent rungs have nothing of the kind. We expect a fade-in, but we see a big bang.

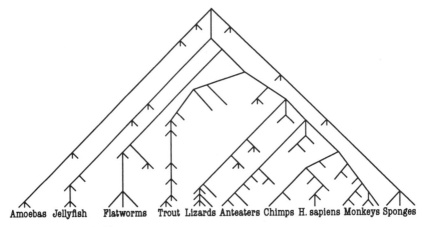

Amoebas Jellyfish   Flatworms   Trout Lizards Anteaters Chimps H. sapiens Monkeys Sponges

Figure 2: The Right Theory

But evolution did not make a ladder; it made a bush (Mayr 1982; Dawkins 1986; Gould 1985). We did not evolve from chimpanzees. We and chimpanzees evolved from a common ancestor, now extinct. The human-chimp ancestor did not evolve from monkeys but from an even older ancestor of the two, also extinct. And so on, back to our single-celled forebears. Paleontologists like to say that to a first approximation, all species are extinct (99% is the usual estimate). The organisms we see around us are distant cousins, not great-grandparents; they are a few scattered twig-tips of an enormous tree whose branches and trunk are no longer with us. Simplifying a lot, I outline the right theory of phylogeny in Figure 2.

Zooming in on our branch, we see chimpanzees not sitting on top of us (A: *Wrong Theory*, Figure 3), but off on a separate sub-branch (B: *Right Theory*, Figure 3).

We also see that a form of language could first have emerged at the position of the arrow, after the branch leading to humans split off from the one leading to chimpanzees. The result would be languageless chimps and approximately 5 to 7 million years in which language could have gradually evolved. Indeed we should zoom in even closer (Figure 4), because species do not mate and produce baby species; organisms mate and produce baby organisms. Species are abbreviations for chunks of a vast family tree composed of individuals, such as the *particular* gorilla, chimp, australopithecine, *erectus*, archaic *sapiens*, Neanderthal and modern *sapiens* I have named in the family tree in Figure 4.

So if the first trace of a proto-language-ability appeared in the ancestor at the arrow, there could have been on the order of 350,000 generations between then and now for the ability to have been elaborated and fine-tuned to the Universal Grammar we see today. For all we

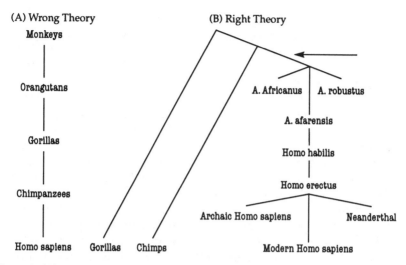

Figure 3: (A) The Wrong Theory and (B) the Right Theory

know, language could have had a gradual fade-in, even if no extant species, not even our closest living relatives, the chimpanzees, have it. There were plenty of organisms with intermediate language abilities, but they are all dead.

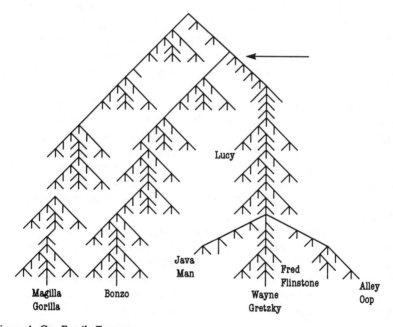

Figure 4: Our Family Tree

Here is another way to think about it. People see chimpanzees, the living species closest to us, and are tempted to conclude that they, at the very least, must have some ability that is ancestral to language. But because the evolutionary tree is a tree of individuals, not species, "the living species closest to us" has no special status; what that species is depends on the accidents of extinction. Try the following thought experiment. Imagine that anthropologists discover a relict population of *Homo habilis* in some remote highland. *Habilis* would now be our closest living relatives. Would that take the pressure off chimps, so it is not so important that they have something like language after all? Or, do it the other way around. Imagine that some epidemic wiped out all the apes several thousand years ago. Would Darwin be in danger unless we showed that monkeys had language? If you are inclined to answer "yes," just push the thought experiment one branch up: imagine that in the past some extraterrestrials developed a craze for primate fur coats, and hunted and trapped all the primates to extinction except hairless us. Would insectivores like anteaters have to shoulder the proto-language burden? What if they went for mammals in general? Or developed a taste for vertebrate flesh, sparing us because they like the sitcom reruns that we inadvertently broadcast into space? Would we then have to look for talking starfish? Or ground syntax in the mental material we share with starfish?

Obviously not. Our brains – and chimpanzee brains and anteater brains – have whatever wiring they have; the wiring cannot change depending on which other species a continent away happen to survive or go extinct. The point of these thought experiments is that the gradualness that Darwin made so much about applies to lineages of individual organisms in a bushy family tree, not entire living species in a great chain. For reasons that we will cover soon, an ancestral ape with nothing but hoots and grunts is unlikely to have given birth to a baby who could learn English or Kivunjo. But it did not have to; there was a chain of several hundred thousand generations of grandchildren in which such abilities could gradually blossom. To determine when in fact language began, we have to look at people, and look at animals, and note what we see; we cannot use the idea of phyletic continuity to legislate the answer from the armchair.

The difference between bush and ladder also allows us to put a lid on a fruitless and boring debate. That debate is over what qualifies as True Language. One side lists some qualities that human language has but that no animal has yet demonstrated: reference, use of symbols displaced of in time and space from their referents, creativity, categorical speech perception, consistent ordering, hierarchical structure, infinity, recursion and so on. The other side finds some counter-example in the animal kingdom (perhaps budgies can discriminate speech sounds, or dolphins or parrots can attend to word order when carrying out commands, or some songbird can improvise indefinitely without repeating itself), and gloats that the citadel of human uniqueness has been breached. The Human Uniqueness team relinquishes that criterion but emphasizes others or adds new ones to the list, provoking angry objections that they are moving the goalposts. To see how silly this all is, imagine a debate over whether flatworms have True Vision or houseflies have True Hands. Is an iris critical? Eyelashes? Fingernails? Who cares? This is a debate for dictionary-writers, not scientists. Plato and Diogenes were not doing biology when Plato defined man as a "featherless biped" and Diogenes refuted him with a plucked chicken.

The fallacy in all this is that there is some line to be drawn across the ladder, the species on the rungs above it being credited with some glorious trait of ours or its precursor, those below lacking it. In the tree of life, traits like eyes or hands or infinite vocalizations can arise on any branch, or several times on different branches, some leading to humans, some not. There is an important scientific issue at stake, but it is not whether some species possesses the true version of a trait as opposed to some pale imitation or vile impostor. The issue is which traits are *homologous* to which other ones.

Biologists distinguish two kinds of similarity. "Analogous" traits are ones that have a common function but arose on different branches of the evolutionary tree and are in an important sense not "the same" organ. The wings of birds and the wings of bees are a textbook example; they are both used for flight, and are similar in some ways because anything used for flight has to be built in those ways, but they arose independently in evolution and have nothing in common beyond their use in flight. "Homologous" traits, in contrast, may or may not have a common function, but they descended from a common ancestor, and hence have some common structure that bespeaks their being "the same" organ. The wing of a bat, the front leg of a horse, the flipper of a seal, the claw of a mole and the hand of a human have completely different functions, but they are all modifications of the forelimb of the ancestor of all mammals, and as a result share non-functional traits like the number of bones and the ways they are connected. To distinguish analogy from homology, biologists usually look at the overall architecture or plan of the organs, and focus on their most useless properties, because the useful ones could have arisen independently in two lineages *because* they are useful, a nuisance to taxonomists called convergent evolution. We deduce that bat wings are really hands because we can see the wrist and count the fingers, and because that is not the only way that nature could have built a wing.

The interesting question is whether human language is homologous to – biologically "the same thing as" – anything in the modern animal kingdom. Discovering some similarity like sequential ordering is pointless, especially when it is found on a remote branch like some bird species that is surely not ancestral to humans. Here primates are relevant, but the ape-trainers and their fans are playing by the wrong rules. Imagine that their wildest dreams are realized and some chimpanzee can be taught to produce real signs, to group and order them consistently to convey meaning, to use them spontaneously to describe events and so on. Does that show that the human ability to learn language evolved from the chimp ability to learn the artificial sign system? Of course not, not any more than seagulls evolved from mosquitos. The symbol system that the chimp learned would have been useful to him, and indeed, the structure was provided by the human inventors. To check for homology with human language, one must find some inherent property (not just taught by the experimenters) that reliably emerges in ape sign systems and in human language, but that could just as easily have been otherwise. One could look at development, checking for some echo of the standard sequence from syllable babbling to jargon babbling to first words to two-word sequences to a grammar explosion. One could look at the developed grammar, seeing if apes develop or favour some version of nouns and verbs, inflections, X-bar syntax, roots and stems, or auxiliaries in second position inverting to form questions. (These structures are not so abstract as to be undetectable; they leapt out of the data when linguists first looked at American Sign Language and creoles, for example.) And, one could look at neuroanatomy, checking for control by the left perisylvian regions of the cortex, with grammar more anterior, dictionary more posterior. This line of questioning, routine in biology since the nineteenth century, has never been applied to chimp signing, though one can make a good prediction of what the answers would be.

Can New Modules Evolve?

How plausible is it that the ancestor to language first appeared after the branch leading to humans split off from that leading to chimps? Not very, says Philip Lieberman, who believes that vocal tract anatomy and speech control are the only things that were modified in evolution, not a grammar module: "Since Darwinian natural selection involves small incremental steps that enhance the present function of the specialized module, the evolution of a 'new' module is logically impossible" (Lieberman 1990, 741–42). Now, something has gone seriously awry in this logic. Humans evolved from single-celled ancestors. Single-celled ancestors had no arms, legs, heart, eyes, liver and so on. Therefore eyes and livers are logically impossible.

The fallacy is that although natural selection involves incremental steps that enhance functioning, the enhancements do not have to be to an existing module. They can slowly build a module out of some previously nondescript stretch of anatomy, or out of the nooks and crannies between existing modules, which the biologists Stephen Jay Gould and Richard Lewontin call "spandrels," from the architectural term. An example of a brand-new module is the eye, which has arisen *de novo* some 40 separate times in animal evolution. It can begin in an eyeless organism with a patch of skin whose cells are sensitive to light. The patch can deepen into a pit, cinch up into a sphere with a hole in front, grow a translucent cover over the hole, and so on, each step allowing the owner to detect events a bit better. An example of a module growing out of bits that were not originally a module is the elephant's trunk. It is a brand new organ, but homologies suggest that it evolved from a fusion of the nostrils and some of the upper lip muscles of the extinct elephant-hyrax common ancestor, followed by radical complications and refinements (see Mayr 1982).

Language could have arisen, and probably did arise, in a similar way: by a revamping of primate brain circuits that originally had no role in vocal communication, and by the addition of some brand new ones. Al Galaburda (Galaburda and Panya 1982) and Terrence Deacon (1988, 1989) have discovered areas in monkey brains that correspond in location, input-output cabling and cellular composition to the human language areas. For example, there are homologues to Wernicke's and Broca's areas of the brain, and an arcuate fasciculus connecting the two, just as in humans. The regions are not involved in producing the monkeys' calls, nor are they involved in producing their gestures. The monkey seems to use the regions corresponding to Wernicke's area and its neighbour in order to recognize sound sequences and to discriminate the calls of other monkeys from its own calls. The Broca's homologues are involved in control of the muscles of the face, mouth, tongue and larynx, and various subregions of these homologues receive inputs from the parts of the brain dedicated to hearing, the sense of touch in the mouth, tongue and larynx, and areas in which information from all the senses converge. No one knows exactly why this arrangement is found in monkeys and, presumably, in their common ancestor with humans, but it gave evolution some parts it could tinker with to produce the human language circuitry, perhaps exploiting the confluence of vocal, auditory and other signals there.

Brand-new circuits in this general territory could have arisen, too. Neuroscientists charting the cortex with electrodes have occasionally found mutant monkeys who have one extra visual map in their brains compared to standard monkeys. A sequence of genetic changes that duplicate a brain map or circuit, reroute its inputs and outputs, and twiddle and tweak its internal connections could manufacture a genuinely new brain module.

Brains can only be rewired if the genes that control their wiring have changed. This brings up another bad argument about why chimp signing must be like human language. The argument is based on the finding that chimpanzees and humans share 98% to 99% of their DNA. The implication is that we must be 99% similar to chimpanzees.

But geneticists are appalled at such reasoning and take pains to stifle it in the same breath that they report their results. The recipe for the embryological soufflé is so baroque that small genetic changes can have enormous effects on the final product. And a 1% difference is not even so small. In terms of the information content in the DNA it is 10 megabytes, big enough for Universal Grammar with lots of room left over for the rest of the instructions on how to turn a chimp into a human. Indeed, a 1% difference in total DNA does not even mean that only 1% of human and chimpanzee genes are different. It could, in theory, mean that 100% of human and chimpanzee genes are different, each by 1%. DNA is a discrete combinatorial code, so a 1% difference in the DNA for a gene can be as significant as a 100% difference, just as changing one bit in every byte, or one letter in every word, can result in a new text that is 100% different, not 10% or 20% different. The reason, for DNA, is that even a single amino-acid substitution can change the shape of a protein enough to alter its function completely; this is what happens in many fatal genetic diseases. Data on genetic similarity are useful in figuring out how to connect up a family tree (for example, did gorillas branch off from a common ancestor of humans and chimps, or did humans branch off from a common ancestor of chimps and gorillas?), and perhaps even to date the divergences using a "molecular clock." But they say nothing about how similar the organisms' brains and bodies are.

Did Language Evolve by Natural Selection?

In a chapter of *On the Origin of Species*, Darwin painstakingly argued that his theory of natural selection could account for the evolution of instincts as well as bodies. If language is like other instincts, presumably it evolved by natural selection, the only successful scientific explanation of complex biological structure.

Chomsky, one might think, would have everything to gain by grounding his controversial theory about a language organ in the firm foundation of evolutionary theory, and in some of his writings he has hinted at a connection. But more often, he is sceptical:

It is perfectly safe to attribute this development [of innate mental structure] to "natural selection," so long as we realize that there is no substance to this assertion, that it amounts to nothing more than a belief that there is some naturalistic explanation for these phenomena ... In studying the evolution of mind, we cannot guess to what extent there are physically possible alternatives to, say, transformational generative grammar, for an organism meeting certain other physical conditions characteristic of humans. Conceivably, there are none – or very few – in which case talk about evolution of the language capacity is besides the point. (Chomsky 1972, 97–98)

Can the problem [the evolution of language] be addressed today? In fact, little is known about these matters. Evolutionary theory is informative about many things, but it has little to say, as of now, of questions of this nature. The answers may well lie not so much in the theory of natural selection as in molecular biology, in the study of what kinds of physical systems can develop under the conditions of life on earth and why, ultimately because of physical principles. It surely cannot be assumed that every trait is specifically selected. In the case of such systems as language ... it is not easy even to imagine a course of selection that might have given rise to them. (Chomsky 1988, 167)

What could he possibly mean? Could there be a language organ that evolved by a process different from the one we have always been told is responsible for the other organs? Many psychologists, impatient with arguments that cannot be fit into a slogan, pounce on such statements and ridicule Chomsky as a crypto-creationist. They are wrong, though I think Chomsky is wrong too.

To understand the issues, we first must understand the logic of Darwin's theory of natural selection. Evolution and natural selection are not the same thing. Evolution, the fact that species change over time because of what Darwin called "descent with modification," was already widely accepted in Darwin's time, but was attributed to now-discredited processes like Lamarck's inheritance of acquired characteristics and an internal urge or striving to evolve in a direction of increasing complexity, culminating in humans. What Darwin and Alfred Wallace discovered and emphasized was a particular cause of evolution, natural selection. Natural selection applies to any set of entities with the properties of *multiplication*, *variation* and *heredity*. Multiplication means that the entities copy themselves, that the copies are also capable of copying themselves, and so on. Variation means that the copying is not perfect; errors crop up from time to time, and these errors may give an entity traits that enable it to copy itself at higher or lower rates relative to other entities. Heredity means that a variant trait produced by a copying error reappears in subsequent copies, so the trait is perpetuated in the lineage. Natural selection is the mathematically necessary outcome that any traits that foster superior replication will tend to spread through the population over many generations. As a result the entities will come to have traits that appear to have been designed for effective replication, including means to this end like gathering energy and materials from the environment and safeguarding them from competitors. These replicating entities are what we recognize as "organisms," and the replication-enhancing traits they accumulated by this process are called "adaptations" (for discussion of the logic of natural selection, see Darwin 1859/1964; Williams 1966; Mayr 1983; Dawkins 1986; Tooby and Cosmides 1990; Maynard Smith 1984, 1986; Dennett 1983).

At this point many people feel proud of themselves for spotting what they think is a fatal flaw. "Aha! The theory is circular! All it says is that traits that lead to effective replication lead to effective replication. Natural selection is 'the survival of the fittest' and the definition of 'the fittest' is 'those who survive'." No! The power of the theory of natural selection is that it connects two very different ideas. The first idea is the appearance of design. By "appearance of design" I mean something that an engineer could look at and surmise that its parts are shaped and arranged so as to carry out some function. Give an optical engineer an eyeball from an unknown species, and the engineer could immediately tell that it is designed for forming an image of the surroundings: it is built like a camera, with a transparent lens, contractible diaphragm, and so on. Moreover, an image-forming device is not just any old piece of bric-à-brac, but a tool that is useful for finding food and mates, escaping from enemies, and so on. Natural selection explains how this design came to be, using a *second* idea: the actuarial statistics of reproduction in the organism's ancestors. Take a good look at the two ideas:

(1) A part of an organism appears to have been engineered to enhance its reproduction.
(2) That organism's ancestors reproduced more effectively than their competitors.

Note that (1) and (2) are logically independent. They are about different things: engineering design, and birth and death rates. They are about different organisms: the one that interests you and its ancestors. You can say that an organism has good vision and that good vision should help it reproduce (1) without knowing how well that organism, or any organism, in fact, reproduces (2). Since "design" merely implies an enhanced *probability* of reproduction, all things being equal, a particular organism with well designed vision may, in fact, not reproduce at all. Maybe it will be struck by lightning. Conversely, it may have a myopic sibling that in fact reproduces better, if, for instance, the same lightning bolt killed a predator who had the sibling in its sights. The theory of natural selection says that (2) (ancestor's birth and death rates) is the explanation for (1) (organism's engineering design) – so it is not circular in the least.

This means that Chomsky was too flip when he dismissed natural selection as having no substance, as nothing more than a belief that there is some naturalistic explanation for a trait. In fact, it is not so easy to show that a trait is a product of selection. The trait has to be hereditary. It has to enhance the probability of reproduction of the organism, relative to organisms without the trait, in an environment like the one its ancestors lived in. There has to have been a sufficiently long lineage of similar organisms in the past. And because natural selection has no foresight, each intermediate stage in the evolution of an organ must have conferred some reproductive advantage on its possessor. Darwin noted that his theory made strong predictions and could be easily be falsified. All it would take is the discovery of a trait that showed signs of design but that appeared somewhere other than at the end of a lineage of replicators that could have used it to help in their replication. One example would be a trait designed only for the beauty of nature, such as a peacock's beautiful but cumbersome tail evolving in moles, whose potential mates are too blind to be attracted to it. Another would be a complex organ that can exist in no useful intermediate form, such as a part-wing that could not have been useful for anything until it was 100% of its current size and shape. A third would be an organism that was not produced by an entity that can replicate, such as some insect that spontaneously grew out of rocks, like a crystal. A fourth would be a trait designed to benefit an organism other than the one that created the trait, such as horses evolving saddles. In the comic strip *Li'l Abner*, the cartoonist Al Capp featured selfless organisms called shmoos that laid chocolate cakes instead of eggs and that cheerfully barbecued themselves so that people could enjoy their delicious boneless meat. The discovery of a real-life shmoo would instantly refute Darwin.

Hasty dismissals aside, Chomsky raises a real issue when he brings up alternatives to natural selection. Thoughtful evolutionary theorists since Darwin have been adamant that not every beneficial trait is an adaptation to be explained by natural selection. When a flying fish leaves the water, it is extremely adaptive for it to re-enter the water. But we do not need natural selection to explain this happy event; gravity will do just fine. Other traits, too, need an explanation different from selection. Sometimes a trait is not an adaptation in itself, but a consequence of something else that is an adaptation. There is no advantage to our bones being white instead of green, but there is an advantage to our bones being rigid; building them out of calcium is one way to make them rigid, and calcium happens to be white. Sometimes a trait is constrained by its history, like the S-bend in our spine that we inherited when four legs became bad and two legs good. Many traits may just be impossible to grow within the constraints of a body plan and the way the genes build the body. The biologist J.B.S. Haldane once said that there are two reasons why humans do not turn into angels: moral imperfection and a body plan that cannot accommodate both arms and wings. And sometimes a trait comes about by dumb luck. If enough time passes in a small population of organisms, all kinds of coincidences will be preserved in it, a process called genetic drift. For example, in a particular generation all the stripeless organisms might be hit by lightning, or die without issue; stripedness will reign thereafter, whatever its advantages or disadvantages.

Stephen Jay Gould and Richard Lewontin (1979) have accused biologists (unfairly, most believe) of ignoring these alternative forces and putting too much stock in natural selection. They ridicule such explanations as "just-so stories," an allusion to Kipling's whimsical tales of how various animals got their parts. Gould and Lewontin's essays have been influential in the cognitive sciences, and Chomsky's scepticism that natural selection can explain human language is in the spirit of their critiques.

But Gould and Lewontin's pot shots do not provide a useful model of how to reason about the evolution of a complex trait. One of their goals was to undermine theories of human behaviour whose political implications they disagreed with. The critiques also reflect their day-to-day professional concerns. Gould is a paleontologist, and paleontologists study organisms after they have turned into rocks. They look more at grand patterns in the history of life than the workings of an individual's long-defunct organs. When they discover, for example, that the dinosaurs were extinguished by an asteroid slamming into the earth and blacking out the sun, small differences in reproductive advantages understandably seem beside the point. Lewontin is a geneticist, and geneticists tend to look at the raw code of the genes and their statistical variation in a population, rather than the complex organs they build. Adaptation can seem like a minor force to them, just as someone examining the 1's and 0's of a computer program in machine language without knowing what the program does might conclude that the patterns are without design. The mainstream in modern evolutionary biology is better represented by biologists like George Williams, John Maynard Smith and Ernst Mayr, who are concerned with the design of whole living organisms. Their consensus is that natural selection has a very special place in evolution, and that the existence of alternatives does *not* mean that the explanation of a biological trait is up for grabs, depending only on the taste of the explainer (Dawkins 1986; Mayr 1983; Maynard Smith 1988; Tooby and Cosmides 1990; Pinker and Bloom 1990; Dennett 1983).

The biologist Richard Dawkins explained this reasoning lucidly in his book *The Blind Watchmaker*. Dawkins notes that the fundamental problem of biology is to explain "complex design." The problem was appreciated well before Darwin. The theologian William Paley (1828) wrote:

> In crossing a heath, suppose I pitched my foot against a *stone*, and were asked how the stone came to be there; I might possibly answer, that, for anything I knew to the contrary, it had lain there for ever: nor would it perhaps be very easy to show the absurdity of this answer. But suppose I had found a *watch* upon the ground, and it should be inquired how the watch happened to be in that place; I should hardly think of the answer which I had before given, that for anything I knew, the watch might have always been there. (Cited in Dawkins 1986, 4)

Paley noted that a watch has a delicate arrangement of tiny gears and springs that function together to indicate the time. Bits of rock do not spontaneously exude metal that forms itself into gears and springs that in turn hop into an arrangement that keeps time. We are forced to conclude that the watch had an artificer who designed the watch with the goal of timekeeping in mind. But an organ like an eye is even more complexly and purposefully designed than a watch. The eye has a transparent protective cornea, a focusing lens, a light-sensitive retina at the focal plane of the lens, an iris whose diameter changes with the illumination, muscles that move one eye in tandem with the other and neural circuits that detect edges, colour, motion, and depth. It is impossible to make sense of the eye without noting that it appears to have been designed for seeing – if for no other reason than that it displays an uncanny resemblance to the man-made camera. If a watch entails a watchmaker, and a camera entails a camera-maker, then an eye entails an eyemaker, namely God. Biologists today do not disagree with Paley's laying out of the problem. They disagree only with his solution. Darwin is history's most important biologist because he showed how such "organs of extreme perfection and complication" could arise from the purely physical process of natural selection.

And here is the key point. No physical process *other* than natural selection can explain the evolution of a complex organ like the eye. The reason the choice is so stark – God or natural selection – is that structures that can do what the eye does are extremely low-probability arrangements of matter. By an unimaginably large margin, most objects thrown together out of generic stuff, even generic animal stuff, cannot bring an image into focus, modulate incoming light and detect edges and depth boundaries. The animal stuff in an eye seems to have been assembled with the goal of seeing in mind – but in whose mind, if not God's? How else could the mere *goal* of seeing well *cause* something to see well? The very special power of natural selection is to remove the paradox. What causes eyes to see well now is that they descended from a long line of ancestors that saw a bit better than their rivals, which allowed them to outreproduce those rivals. The small random improvements in seeing were retained and combined and concentrated over the eons, leading to better and better eyes. The ability of *many* ancestors to see a *bit* better in the *past* causes a *specific* organism to see *extremely* well *now*.

Another way of putting it is that natural selection is the only process that can steer a lineage of organisms along the path in the astronomically vast space of possible bodies leading from a body with no eye to a body with a functioning eye. The alternatives to natural selection can, in contrast, only grope randomly. The odds that the coincidences of genetic drift would result in just the right genes coming together to build a functioning eye are infinitesimally small. Gravity alone may make a flying fish fall into the ocean, a nice big target, but gravity alone cannot make bits of a flying fish embryo fall exactly into place to make a flying fish eye. When one organ develops, a bulge of tissue or some nook or cranny can come along for free, the way an S-bend accompanies an upright spine. But you can bet that such a cranny will not just happen to have a functioning lens and a diaphragm and a retina all perfectly arranged for seeing. It would be like the proverbial hurricane that blows through a junkyard and assembles a Boeing 747. For these reasons, Dawkins argues that natural selection is not only the correct explanation for life on earth, but is bound to be the correct explanation for anything we might be willing to call "life" anywhere in the universe.

And adaptive complexity, by the way, is also the reason that the evolution of complex organs tends to be slow and gradual. It is not that large mutations and rapid change violate some law of evolution. It is only that complex engineering requires precise arrangements of delicate parts, and if the engineering is accomplished by accumulating random changes, those changes had better be small. Complex organs evolve by small steps for the same reason that a watchmaker does not use a sledgehammer and a surgeon does not use a meat cleaver.

So we now know which biological traits to credit to natural selection and which ones to other evolutionary processes. What about language? In my mind, the conclusion is inescapable. Everything we have learned about the psychology and neurology of language has underscored the adaptive complexity of the language instinct. It is composed of many parts: syntax, with its discrete, combinatorial system that builds phrase structures; morphology, a second combinatorial system that builds words; a capacious lexicon; a revamped vocal tract; phonological rules and structures; speech perception; parsing algorithms and learning algorithms. Those parts are physically realized as intricately structured neural circuits, laid down by a cascade of precisely timed genetic events. What these circuits make possible is an extraordinary gift: the ability to dispatch an infinite number of precisely structured thoughts from head to head by modulating exhaled breath. The gift is obviously useful for reproduction. Anyone can benefit from the strokes of genius, lucky accidents and trial-and-error wisdom accumulated by anyone else, present or past. And actors can benefit by working in teams, their efforts co-ordinated by negotiated agreements. Randomly jigger a neural network or mangle a vocal tract, and you will not end up with a system with these capabilities. The language instinct, like the eye, is an example of what Darwin called "that perfection of structure and co-adaptation which justly excites our admiration," and as such bears the unmistakable stamp of nature's designer, natural selection.

If Chomsky maintains that grammar shows signs of complex design, but he remains sceptical that natural selection manufactured it, what alternative does he have in mind? What he repeatedly mentions is physical law. Just as the flying fish is compelled to return to the water and calcium-filled bones are compelled to be white, human brains might, for all we know, be compelled to contain circuits for Universal Grammar. Chomsky says:

> These skills [e.g., learning a grammar] may well have arisen as a concomitant of structural properties of the brain that developed for other reasons. Suppose that there was selection for bigger brains, more cortical surface, hemispheric specialization for analytic processing, or many other structural properties that can be imagined. The brain that evolved might well have all sorts of special properties that are not individually selected; there would be no miracle in this, but only the normal workings of evolution. We have no idea, at present, how physical laws apply when 10^{10} neurons are placed in an object the size of a basketball, under the special conditions that arose during human evolution. (Piatelli-Palmarini 1980)

We may not have any idea, just as we do not know how physical laws apply under the special conditions of hurricanes sweeping through junkyards, but the possibility that there is an undiscovered corollary of the laws of physics that causes human-sized and shaped brains to develop the circuitry for Universal Grammar seems unlikely for many reasons.

At the microscopic level, what set of physical laws could cause a surface molecule guiding an axon along a thicket of glial cells to co-operate with millions of other such molecules to solder together just the kinds of circuits that would compute something as useful to an intelligent social species as grammatical language? The vast majority of the astronomical ways of wiring together a large neural network would surely do something else: create bat sonar or nest-building or go-go dancing or, most likely of all, random neural noise.

At the level of the whole brain, the remark that there has been selection for bigger brains is, to be sure, common in writings about human evolution (especially from paleoanthropologists). Given that premise, one might naturally think that all kinds of computational abilities might come as a by-product. But if you think about it for a minute, you should quickly see that the premise has to have it backwards. Why would evolution ever have selected for sheer bigness of brain, that bulbous, hot-burning, oxygen-hungry organ? A large-brained creature is sentenced to a life that combines all the disadvantages of balancing a watermelon on a broomstick, running in place in a down jacket and, for women, passing a large kidney stone every few years. Any selection on brain size itself would surely have favoured the pinhead. Selection for more powerful computational abilities (language, perception, reasoning and so on) must have given us a big brain as a by-product, not the other way around!

But even given a big brain, language does not fall out the way that flying fish fall out of the air. We see language in humans whose heads are much smaller than a basketball (Lenneberg, 1967). We also see it in hydrocephalics whose cerebral hemispheres have been squashed into grotesque shapes, sometimes a thin layer lining the skull like the flesh of a coconut, but who are intellectually and linguistically normal (Lewin 1980). Conversely, there are Specific Language Impairment victims with normal basketball-sized and shaped brains, and with intact analytic processing (see the chapter by Gopnik in this volume, which describes one language-impaired boy who was fine with math and computers). All the evidence suggests that it is the precise wiring of the brain's microcircuitry that make language happen, not gross size, shape or neuron packing. The pitiless laws of physics are unlikely to have done us the favour of hooking up that circuitry so that we could communicate with each other in words.

Could Language Have Evolved Gradually?

To be fair, there are genuine problems in reconstructing how the language faculty might have evolved by natural selection, though Paul Bloom and I have argued that the problems are all resolvable (Pinker and Bloom 1990). As P.B. Medawar noted, language could not have begun in the form it supposedly took in the first recorded utterance of the infant Lord Macaulay, who after having been scalded with hot tea, allegedly said to his hostess "Thank you Madam, the agony is sensibly abated." If language evolved gradually, there must have been a sequence of intermediate forms, each useful to its possessor, and this raises several questions.

First, if language inherently involves another individual, who did the first grammar mutant talk to? One answer might be: the 50% of the brothers and sisters and sons and daughters who shared the new gene by common inheritance. But a more general answer is that the neighbours could have partly understood what the mutant was saying even if they lacked the new-fangled circuitry, just using overall intelligence. Though we cannot parse strings like *skid crash hospital*, we can figure out what they probably mean, and English speakers can often do a reasonably good job understanding Italian newspaper stories based on similar words and background knowledge. If a grammar mutant is making important distinctions that can be decoded by others only with uncertainty and great mental effort, it could set up a pressure for them to evolve the matching system that allows those distinctions to be recovered reliably by an automatic, unconscious parsing process. Natural selection can take skills that are acquired with effort and uncertainty, and hardwire them into the brain, a phenomenon called the Baldwin Effect (see Hinton and Nowlan 1987). Selection could have ratcheted up language abilities by favouring the speakers in each generation that the hearers could best decode, and the hearers who could best decode the speakers.

A second problem is what an intermediate grammar would have looked like. Bates and her collaborators ask:

> What protoform can we possibly envision that could have given birth to constraints on the extraction of noun phrases from an embedded clause? What could it conceivably mean for an organism to possess half a symbol, or three quarters of a rule? ... monadic symbols, absolute rules and modular systems must be acquired as a whole, on a yes-or-no basis – a process that cries out for a Creationist explanation. (Bates et al., 1991, 31)

The question is a bit odd, because it assumes that Darwin literally meant that organs must evolve in successively larger fractions (half, three quarters and so on). Bates's rhetorical question is like asking what it could conceivably mean for an organism to possess half a head or three quarters of an elbow. Darwin's real claim, of course, is that organs evolve in successively more complex forms. Grammars of intermediate *complexity* are easy to imagine: they would have symbols with a narrower range, rules that are less reliably applied, modules with fewer rules and so on. Derek Bickerton (1990) answers Bates even more concretely. He gives the term "protolanguage" to chimp signing, pidgins, child language in the two-word stage and the unsuccessful partial language acquired after the critical period by Genie and other wolf-children. Bickerton suggests that *Homo erectus* spoke in protolanguage. Obviously there is still a huge gulf between these relatively crude systems and the modern adult language instinct, and here Bickerton makes the jaw-dropping additional suggestion that a single mutation in a single woman, African Eve, simultaneously wired in syntax, resized and reshaped the skull and reworked the vocal tract (see Pinker 1992 for critical discussion). But we can extend the first half of Bickerton's argument without accepting the second half, which is reminiscent of hurricanes assembling jetliners. The languages of children, pidgin speakers, immigrants, tourists, aphasics, telegrams and headlines show that there is a vast continuum of viable language systems varying in efficiency and expressive power – exactly what the theory of natural selection requires.

A third problem is that each step in the evolution of a language instinct, up to and including the most recent ones, must enhance fitness. David Premack writes:

> I challenge the reader to reconstruct the scenario that would confer selective fitness on recursiveness. Language evolved, it is conjectured, at a time when humans or protohumans were hunting mastodons ... Would it be a great advantage for one of our ancestors squatting alongside the embers, to be able to remark: "Beware of the short beast whose front hoof Bob cracked when, having forgotten his own spear back at camp, he got in a glancing blow with the dull spear he borrowed from Jack"?
>
> Human language is an embarrassment for evolutionary theory because it is vastly more powerful than one can account for in terms of selective fitness. A semantic language with simple mapping rules, of a kind one might suppose that the chimpanzee would have, appears to confer all the advantages one normally associates with discussions of mastodon hunting or the like. For discussions of that kind, syntactic classes, structure-dependent rules, recursion and the rest, are overly powerful devices, absurdly so. (Premack 1985, 281–82)

The objection is a bit like saying that the cheetah is much faster than it has to be, or that the eagle does not need such good vision, or that the elephant's trunk is an overly powerful device, absurdly so. But it is worth taking up the challenge (see Burling 1986; Cosmides and Tooby 1992; Barkow 1992; Pinker and Bloom 1990).

First, bear in mind that selection does not need great advantages. Given the vastness of time, tiny advantages will do. Imagine a mouse that was subjected to a minuscule selection pressure for increased size, say, a 1% reproductive advantage for offspring that were 1% bigger. Some arithmetic shows that the mouse's descendants would evolve to the size of an elephant in a few thousand generations, an evolutionary eyeblink.

Second, if contemporary hunter-gatherers are any guide, our ancestors were not grunting cave men with little more to talk about than which mastodon to avoid. Hunter-gatherers are accomplished tool-makers and superb amateur biologists with detailed knowledge of the life cycles, ecology and behaviour of the plants and animals on which they depend. Language would surely have been useful in anything resembling such a lifestyle. It is possible to imagine a superintelligent solitary species whose isolated members cleverly negotiated their environment, but what a waste! There is a fantastic payoff in transmitting hard-won knowledge to kin and friends, and language is obviously a major means of doing so.

And grammatical devices designed for communicating precise information about time, space, objects and who did what to whom are not like the proverbial thermonuclear fly-swatter. Recursion in particular is extremely useful, and is not, as Premack implies, confined to phrases with tortuous syntax. Without recursion you cannot say *the man's hat* or *I think he left*. Recall that all you need for recursion is an ability to embed a noun phrase inside another noun phrase or a clause within a clause, which falls out of rules as simple as NP → det N PP and PP → P NP. With this ability a speaker can pick out an object to an arbitrarily fine level of precision. These abilities can make a big difference. It makes a difference whether a far-off region is reached by taking the trail that is in front of the large tree or the trail that the large tree is in front of. It makes a difference whether that region has animals that you can eat or animals that can eat you. It makes a difference whether it has fruit that is ripe or fruit that was ripe or fruit that will be ripe. It makes a difference whether you can get there if you walk for three days or whether you can get there and walk for three days.

Third, people everywhere depend on co-operative efforts for survival, forming alliances by exchanging information and commitments. This too puts complex grammar to good use. It makes a difference whether you understand me as saying that if you give me some of your fruit I will share meat that I will get, or that you should give me some fruit because I shared meat that I got, or that if you do not give me some fruit I will take back the meat that I got. And once again, recursion is far from being an absurdly powerful device. Recursion allows sentences like *He knows that she thinks that he is flirting with Mary* and other means of conveying gossip, an apparently universal human vice.

But could these exchanges really produce the rococo complexity of human grammar? Perhaps. Evolution often produces spectacular abilities when adversaries get locked into an "arms race," like the struggle between cheetahs and gazelles. Some anthropologists believe that human brain evolution was propelled more by a cognitive arms race among social competitors than by mastery of technology and the physical environment. After all, it does not take that much brain power to master the ins and outs of a rock or to get the better of a berry. But outwitting and second-guessing an organism of approximately equal mental abilities with non-overlapping interests, at best, and malevolent intentions, at worst, makes formidable and ever-escalating demands on cognition. And a cognitive arms race clearly could propel a linguistic one. In all cultures, social interactions are mediated by persuasion and argument. How a choice is framed plays a large role in determining which alternative people choose. Thus there could easily have been selection for any edge in the ability to frame an offer so that it appears to present maximal benefit and minimum cost to the negotiating partner, and in the ability to see through such attempts and to formulate persuasive counterproposals.

Finally, anthropologists have noted that tribal chiefs are often both gifted orators and highly polygynous – a splendid prod to any imagination that cannot conceive of how linguistic skills could make a Darwinian difference. I suspect that evolving humans lived in a world in which language was woven into the intrigues of politics, economics, technology, family, sex and friendship that played key roles in individual reproductive success. They could no more live with a Me-Tarzan-You-Jane level of grammar than we could.

The brouhaha over the uniqueness of language has many ironies. The spectacle of humans trying to ennoble animals by forcing them to mimic human forms of communication is one. The pains that have been taken to describe language as innate, complex and useful but not a product of the one force in nature that can make innate complex useful things is another. Why should language be considered so important? It has allowed humans to spread out over the planet and wreak large changes, but is that any more extraordinary than coral that build islands, earthworms that shape the landscape by building soil or the photosynthesizing bacteria that first released corrosive oxygen into the atmosphere, an ecological catastrophe of its time? Why should talking humans be considered any weirder than elephants, penguins, beavers, camels, rattlesnakes, hummingbirds, electric eels, leaf-mimicking insects, giant sequoias, venus fly-traps, echo-locating bats or deep-sea fish with lanterns growing out of their heads? Some of these creatures have traits unique to their species, others do not, depending only on the accidents of which of their relatives have become extinct. Darwin emphasized the genealogical connectedness of all living things, but evolution is descent *with modification*, and natural selection has shaped the raw materials of bodies and brains to fit them into countless differentiated niches (see Tooby and Cosmides 1989). For Darwin, such is the "grandeur in this view of life": "that whilst this planet has gone cycling on according to the fixed law of gravity, from so simple a beginning endless forms most beautiful and wonderful have been, and are being, evolved" (1859/1964, 484–85).

Acknowledgments

This chapter is adapted from S. Pinker (1994), *The Language Instinct*, New York: William Morrow. Preparation supported in part by NIH Grant HD 18381 and NSF Grant BNS 91–09766 and by the McDonnell-Pew Center for Cognitive Neuroscience at the Massachusetts Institute of Technology.

References

Bates, E., D. Thal and V. Marchman (1991). Symbols and syntax: A Darwinian approach to language development. In N.A. Krasnegor, D.M. Rumbaugh, R.L. Schiefelbusch and M. Studdert-Kennedy (eds.), *Biological and Behavioural Determinants of Language Development*. Hillsdale, NJ: Erlbaum

Barkow, J.H. (1992). Beneath new culture is old psychology: Gossip and social stratification. In J.H. Barkow, L. Cosmides and J. Tooby (eds.), *The Adapted Mind: Evolutionary Psychology and the Generation of Culture*. New York: Oxford University Press

Bickerton, D. (1990). *Language and Species*. Chicago: University of Chicago Press

Brandon, R. N., and N. Hornstein (1986). From icons to symbols: Some speculations on the origin of language. *Biology and Philosophy* 1: 169–89

Burling, R. (1986). The selective advantage of complex language. *Ethology and Sociobiology* 7: 1–16

Caplan, D. (1987). *Neurolinguistics and Linguistic Aphasiology*. New York: Cambridge University Press

Carrington, R. (1958). *Elephants*. London: Chatto and Windus

Chomsky, N. (1972) *Language and Mind*, 2nd ed. New York: Holt, Rinehart and Winston

——— (1988). *Language and Problems of Knowledge: The Managua Lectures*. Cambridge, MA: MIT Press

Corballis, M. (1991). *The Lopsided Ape*. New York: Oxford University Press

Cosmides, L., and J. Tooby (1992). Cognitive adaptations for social exchange. In J. Barkow, L. Cosmides and J. Tooby (eds.), *The Adapted Mind*. New York: Oxford University Press

Darwin, C.R. (1859/1964). *On the Origin of Species*. Cambridge, MA: Harvard University Press

Dawkins, R. (1986). *The Blind Watchmaker.* New York: Norton

Deacon, T.W. (1988). Evolution of human language circuits. In H. Jerison and I. Jerison (eds.), *Intelligence and Evolutionary Biology.* New York: Springer-Verlag

────── (1989). The neural circuitry underlying primate calls and human language. *Human Evolution* 4: 367–401

Dennett, D.C. (1983). Intentional systems in cognitive ethology: The "Panglossian Paradigm" defended. *Behavioral and Brain Sciences* 6: 343–90

Galaburda, A.M., and D.N. Pandya (1982). Role of architectonics and connections in the study of primate brain evolution. In E. Armstrong and D. Falk (eds.), *Primate Brain Evolution.* New York: Plenum

Gardner, B.T., and R.A. Gardner (1974). Comparing the early utterances of child and chimpanzee. In A. Pick (ed.), *Minnesota Symposium of Child Psychology,* Vol. 8. Minneapolis, MN: University of Minnesota Press.

Gardner, R.A., and B.T. Gardner (1969). Teaching sign language to a chimpanzee. *Science* 165: 664–72

Gould, J.L., and P. Marler (1987, January). Learning by instinct. *Scientific American*: 74–84

Gould, S.J. (1985). *The Flamingo's Smile: Reflections in Natural History.* New York: Norton

Gould, S.J., and R.C. Lewontin 1979. The spandrels of San Marco and the Panglossian program: A critique of the adaptationist programme. *Proceedings of the Royal Society of London* 205: 281–88

Greenfield, P.M., and E.S. Savage-Rumbaugh (1991). Imitation, grammatical development, and the invention of protogrammar by an ape. In N.A. Krasnegor, D.M. Rumbaugh, R.L. Schiefelbusch and M. Studdert-Kennedy (eds.), *Biological and Behavioral Determinants of Language Development,* 236–58. Hillsdale, NJ: Lawrence Erlbaum

Hinton, G.E., and S.J. Nowlan (1987). How learning can guide evolution. *Complex Systems* 1: 495–502

Hurford, J.R. (1989). Biological evolution of the Saussurean sign as a component of the language acquisition device. *Lingua* 77: 187–222

────── (1991). The evolution of the critical period in language acquisition. *Cognition* 40: 159–201

Lenneberg, E.H. (1967). *Biological Foundations of Language.* New York: Wiley

Lewin, R. (1980). Is your brain really necessary? *Science* 210: 1232–34

Lieberman, P. (1990). Not invented here. *Behavioral and Brain Sciences* 13: 741–42

Maynard Smith, J. (1984). Optimization theory in evolution. In E. Sober (ed.), *Conceptual Issues in Evolutionary Biology.* Cambridge, MA: MIT Press

────── (1986). *The Problems of Biology.* Oxford: Oxford University Press

────── (1988). *Games, Sex, and Evolution.* New York: Harvester Wheatsheaf

Mayr, E. (1982). *The Growth of Biological Thought.* Cambridge, MA: Harvard University Press

—— (1983). How to carry out the adaptationist program. *The American Naturalist* 121: 324–34

Myers, R.E. (1976). Comparative neurology of vocalization and speech: Proof of a dichotomy. In S.R. Harnad, H.S. Steklis and J. Lancaster (eds.), *Origin and Evolution of Language and Speech.* Special volume of *Annals of the New York Academy of Sciences* 280

Newmeyer, F. (1991). Functional explanation in linguistics and the origin of language. *Language and Communication* 11: 3–96

Paley, W. (1828). *Natural Theology.* 2nd ed. Oxford: J. Vincent

Petitto, L.A., and M.S. Seidenberg (1979). On the evidence for linguistic abilities in signing apes. *Brain and Language* 8: 162–83

Piatelli-Palmarini, M. (ed.) (1980). *Language and Learning: The Debate between Jean Piaget and Noam Chomsky.* Cambridge, MA: Harvard University Press

Pinker, S. (1992). Review of Bickerton's "Language and Species." *Language* 68: 375–82

—— (1994). *The Language Instinct.* New York: William Morrow

—— (1995). Facts about human language relevant to its evolution. In J.-P. Changeux and J. Chavaillon (eds.), *Origins of the Human Brain.* New York: Oxford University Press

Pinker, S., and P. Bloom (1990). Natural language and natural selection. *Behavioral and Brain Sciences* 13: 707–84

Premack, A.J., and D. Premack (1972, October). Teaching language to an ape. *Scientific American*: 92–99

Premack, D. (1985). "Gavagai!" or the future history of the animal language controversy. *Cognition* 19: 207–96

Robinson, B.W. (1976). Limbic influences on human speech. In S.R. Harnad, H.S. Steklis and J. Lancaster (eds.), *Origin and Evolution of Language and Speech.* Special volume of *Annals of the New York Academy of Sciences* 280

Sagan, C., and A. Druyan (1992). *Shadows of Forgotten Ancestors.* New York: Random House

Savage-Rumbaugh, E.S. (1991). Language learning in the bonobo: How and why they learn. In N.A. Krasnegor, D.M. Rumbaugh, R.L. Schiefelbusch and M. Studdert-Kennedy (eds.), *Biological and Behavioral Determinants of Language Development.* Hillsdale, NJ: Erlbaum

Seidenberg, M.S. (1986). Evidence from the great apes concerning the biological bases of language. In W. Demopoulos and A. Marras (eds.), *Language Learning and Concept Acquisition: Foundational Issues.* Norwood, NJ: Ablex

Seidenberg, M.S., and Petitto, L. A. (1979) Signing behavior in apes: A critical review. *Cognition* 7: 177–215

—— (1987) Communication, symbolic communication, and language: Comment on Savage-Rumbaugh, McDonald, Sevcik, Hopkins, and Rupert (1986). *Journal of Experimental Psychology: General* 116: 279–87

Terrace, H., R. Sanders, T.G. Bever and L.A. Petitto (1979). Can an ape create a sentence? *Science* 206: 891–902

Tooby, J., and L. Cosmides (1989). Adaptation versus phylogeny: The role of animal psychology in the study of human behavior. *International Journal of Comparative psychology* 2: 105–18

———— (1990). On the universality of human nature and the uniqueness of the individual: The role of genetics and adaptation. *Journal of Personality* 58: 17–67

Wallman, J. (1992). *Aping Language*. New York: Cambridge University Press

Williams, G.C. (1966). *Adaptation and Natural Selection*. Princeton, NJ: Princeton University Press

Williams, H. (1989). *Sacred Elephant*. New York: Harmony Books

Wilson, E.O. (1972, September). Animal communication. *Scientific American*: 52–60

10

A Neurobiological Approach to the Noninvariance Problem in Stop Consonant Categorization

Harvey M. Sussman

Perhaps the ultimate challenge for cognitive neuroscience is to meaningfully relate the abstract and formal domain of language to the physiological and electrochemical domain of the brain. Such an interface will be expedited if appropriate and matching levels from each domain are chosen for study. For example, the abstract formalisms of syntactic theory cannot, at this time, be related to actual neural mechanisms. Likewise, neurochemical events at the synapse cannot be systematically related to the structure or function of language. The level of analyses within both domains must be functionally compatible.

The outcome of a functional mismatch between the levels of analyses can be seen in the ongoing debate over the innateness issue (e.g., Pinker and Bloom 1990). Linguists who are concerned with the logical problem of language acquisition state that the "child is not a little linguist." Rather than assuming that environmental stimuli are the inductive base for language acquisition, formal linguists argue that the early language experiences of the child serve to trigger genetically endowed universal principles (Chomsky 1986). Unfortunately, the "innateness notion" has gradually taken on an explanatory role in language acquisition circles. In terms of neurobiological reality, however, it is simply a "default metaphor" placed over our ignorance (Jacobs and Schumann 1992, 286). Principles of Universal Grammar are not the proper level of language structure to establish a principled and data-based link between the brain and language. A lower and physically instantiated level of language structure would be more appropriate. The sound structure of language, its phonemic contrasts, is such a candidate to begin the quest to link language to the neural substrates.

All natural spoken languages are composed of a finite set of phonemes that form contrastive categories in a language's phonological inventory. The acoustic structure of these phonemic entities can be quantified and thus represented in acoustic/phonetic space. By providing a physical basis to a level of language structure we can add much needed flesh to the innateness notion. For just as children are not little linguists, they are also certainly not "little phoneticians." Auditory processing of burst spectra and formant transitions are not learned but rather develop from experiential sensory input working within genetically endowed processing guidelines. The crucial difference, however, between studying syntax and studying phonetic processing mechanisms is that only the latter possess a measurable sensory (physical) reality. When elements of language structure are physically represented, then, at minimum, a conceptual interface with neurobiological reality is possible. As stated by Churchland and Sejnowski (1989): "Whatever the basic principles of language representation, they are not likely to be utterly unrelated to the way or ways that the nervous system generates visual representations or auditory representations, or represents spatial maps and motor planning" (1989, 42).

In this chapter I will summarize research done over the last few years that is based on a relatively simple approach to bridging the elusive conceptual barrier between language function and brain function. This approach is based on using relevant findings from neuroethological studies as theoretical springboards to suggest, by way of analogy, similar mechanisms for human representation of an essential element of linguistic structure – the phonemic equivalence classes underlying the formation of stop consonantal categories.

Rationale for the Neuroethological Approach in Cognitive Science

There are several levels of justification for the use of the animal model to gain a better understanding of the human model. Most basic of all is the fact that the brain is a product of evolution, not engineering design. Evolution is the ultimate "tinkerer" (Jacob 1977), working within the design and architecture that is already in place and functioning. A basic assumption of my work is that speech perception abilities evolved epigenetically, building on the sound-processing capabilities common to various levels of the lineage ancestral to humans. Since evolution tends to have similar solutions for similar problems, a logical basis exists for linking documented animal processing algorithms to speculative human processing algorithms. A second justification is the strong degree of similarity of the brain, in both structure and function, across species. For example, non-human neural tissue is composed of the same types of neurons, has the same number of neurons within a cortical column, and has the same chemical neurotransmitters as are found in the human brain (Diamond 1988). Species biologically specialized for hearing, such as the bat and barn owl, would be expected to share many principles of auditory processing with the human brain.

Thus, the noninvariance problem in speech perception will be approached from the perspective of the processing system that has to deal with it and solve it, the brain. I will first briefly describe the noninvariance problem in speech research and then illustrate how the barn owl successfully resolves essentially the same ambiguity problem as faced by the human listener. Following this I will review several acoustic studies that provide, similar to the barn owl, an in-principle solution to the noninvariance dilemma. The studies utilize a new phonetic-based metric known as "locus equations."

Acoustic Variance and Perceptual Invariance

Categorization of stop place of articulation (e.g., [b], [d], [g] in English) has been described as the "litmus test" of invariance, for it illustrates how tolerant the human perceptual system is of coarticulatory induced variability in the speech waveform. The initial [d] in *deed, dead, dad, dude, did, etc.,* is perceived as the same alveolar stop [d] despite the fact that each instance of [d] is characterized by a physically distinct second formant (F2) transition. Human listeners ignore allophonic variations to invariantly establish perceptually based equivalence classes for stop consonants. The stop consonant equivalence class is established despite the fact that each consonant vowel (CV) token within a given stop place category is physically different in the direction and extent of the second formant transition (Liberman, Delattre, Cooper and Gerstman 1954). Different vowel contexts following (or preceeding) the stop create physically distinct acoustic signals as the coarticulatory gestures of the lips and tongue vary across each stop + vowel combination.

Non-human avian brains can also establish stop place categories. Kluender, Diehl and Killeen (1987) trained Japanese quail to respond to [d] followed by the four vowels: [i], [u], [ae], [a], and not to respond to initial [b] and [g] with the same vowels. It took the three quail many thousands of conditioning trials to eventually learn this task of discrimination and categorization. Generalization across other category-specific stimuli was subsequently demonstrated when the trained quail responded to presentations of [d] followed by novel vowel contexts, but not to [b] and [g] tokens. Connectionist models (e.g., Elman and Zipser 1987) have also accomplished [b d g] categorization across vowel contexts, but unfortunately the sorting rules of the hidden units remain hidden.

Despite intensive research over the last 50 years, speech scientists have not been able to find an absolute invariant cue or set of cues to account for human, non-human or machine sorting of stop place +

vowel tokens into invariant place of articulation categories. One short-
coming of past strategies dealing with the noninvariance issue has
been the scrutiny of single tokens as the unit of analysis and representation. In the work to be described below, the basic unit of analysis has
been enlarged to encompass a higher level of lingustic abstraction – the
phonological category.

To summarize, answers to the following questions were sought: (1)
How would an auditory system best categorize different F2 transitions
as manifestations of a single stop category? and (2) What feature of the
variable F2 transitions could be abstracted? The theoretical approach
to be described below hinges on the belief that the neural processing
mechanism somehow extracts relevant abstractions or commonalities
from the entire equivalence class.

In my search for the appropriate processing algorithm for stop place
categorization, I came across the elegant work of Mark Konishi and his
colleagues studying the sound localization system in the barn owl.
Strong similarities appeared between the two processing systems in
terms of the ambiguity obstacles needed to be overcome by both (the
barn owl and human listener) in order to establish unique commonalities spanning and unifying a category.

The Barn Owl's Sound Localization System:
Resolving Phase Ambiquity

The neuroethological studies of Mark Konishi and colleagues (e.g.,
Knudsen and Konishi 1977, 1978; Takahasi and Konishi 1986; Sullivan
and Konishi 1986; Wagner, Takahashi and Konishi 1987) provide an example of how specialized and hierarchically arranged neural circuits
resolve an encoding problem (sound source localization) in a way that
is not too different from phonemic categorization. The barn owl's hearing system is exquisitely organized to establish a map of auditory
space based on interaural time differences (ITD) and interaural inten-
sity differences (IID) of the sound wave arriving at the two ears. The
research to be reviewed below only deals with the resolution of ITDs.
This example is intended to illustrate how, at the neuronal level, an auditory system maps and categorizes temporally coded intervals that
are based on physical cues possessing overlapping and variable characteristics. The variation of F2 transitions within stop-place categories
bears a striking similarity to the barn owl's processing of ITDs.

Figure 1 schematically shows, in "bottom-up" order, the three signal
processing stages of this invariance-seeking algorithm: (1) the brain
stem site of the nucleus laminaris that initially introduces the ambiguous phase disparities between the two ears; (2) the central nucleus of

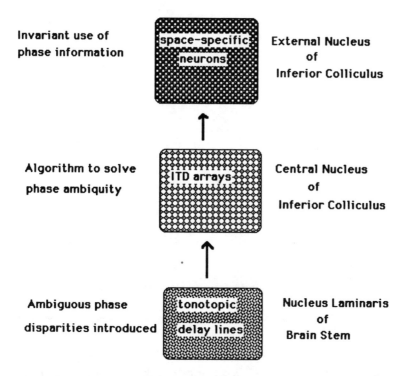

Figure 1: Resolving Phase Ambiguity in the Barn Owl's Sound Localization Processing System. Schematic showing three processing centres in barn owl's sound localization system where, from bottom to top (1) ambiguities are introduced, (2) resolved and (3) invariantly used in processing.

the inferior colliculus that provides the representational solution to the phase ambiguity dilemma; and (3) the external nucleus of the inferior colliculus that invariantly utilizes the phase information to form an accurate spatial azimuthal co-ordinate of the input target stimulus.

Tonotopic Delay Lines

Early theoretical speculation (Jeffress 1948) on a delay line mechanism for sound source localization has been neuroanatomically and neurophysiologically confirmed in the barn owl (Sullivan and Konishi 1986) and most recently in the chicken (Overholt, Rubel and Hyson 1992). Figure 2 presents a neural delay line based on the classic model of Jeffress (1948). Such delay lines are tonotopically arranged and its component neurons are phase-locked to the input stimulus. Neurons labelled A through G are best thought of as coincidence detectors that yield maximal discharge if stimulated by simultaneous arrival of

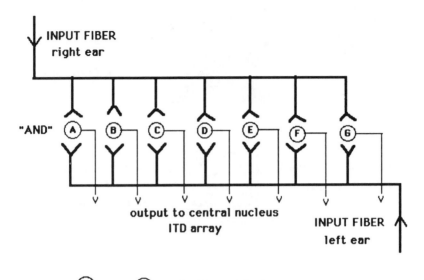

INPUT FIBER
right ear

"AND"

output to central nucleus
ITD array

INPUT FIBER
left ear

(A) thru (G) = coincidence detectors

Figure 2: Neural Delay Line Schematic. Schematic showing the neural delay line as en-
    visaged by L.A. Jeffress (1948), A place theory of sound localization, *Journal of Physio-
    logical Psychology* 41: 35–39.

binaural inputs. Right- and left-ear input pathways enter from opposite ends of the delay line. If the centre neuron *D* fires maximally, then
the sound source must be at midline, because signal paths are equal at
this place along the delay line circuit. If neuron *A* is to maximally respond it must be the case that the left ear input signal lead that of the
right ear by an interval that would permit the two signal paths to arrive simultaneously at *A*. These binaural delay disparities are place-
coded along each of the isofrequency delay lines and introduced to the
next processing station, the central nucleus.

ITD Arrays in the Central Nucleus: Resolving
the Phase Disparity Problem

Figure 3 shows a schematic of the organization of ITD arrays as
mapped by Wagner et al. (1987). Frequency and interaural phase differences (plotted as a percentage of a cycle) form a 2-D array that yield
the emergent-like property of interaural time difference (in microsec-
onds). The owl maps the phase equivalent of the interaural time difference, but it can be seen that a given interaural phase difference cannot
uniquely specify an ITD independent of frequency. For example, the
two stimpled areas show a 30% phase difference; one at 3kHz specifies

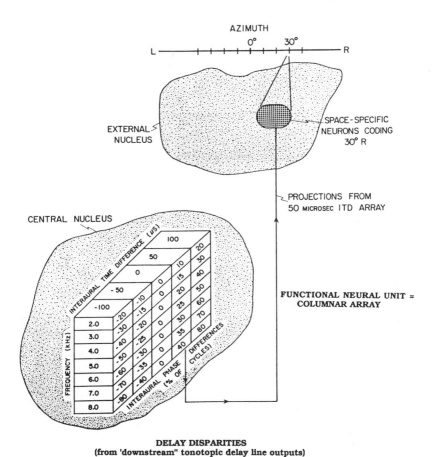

Figure 3: Mapping Interaural Time Differences (ITDS) as Percentage of Cycle in Phase: Disambiguation of Ambiguous Cues. Schematic representation of the barn owl's interaural time difference (ITD) arrays and their projection to space-specific target neurons mapping sound-source azimuth. (Adapted, by permission, from H. Wagner, T. Takahashi and M. Konishi (1987), Representation of interaural time difference in the central nucleus of the barn owl's inferior colliculus, *Journal of Neuroscience* 7: 3105–16).

a 100 microsecond ITD, while the other at 6kHz specifies a 50 microsecond ITD. Obviously the owl cannot depend on a single absolute phase difference to determine an ITD. To determine the organizational substrate of this 2-D array, Wagner et al. (1987) injected a radioactive tracer into a cluster of space-specific neurons in the external nucleus that were maximally sensitive, in this example, to stimuli originating 30 degrees to the right. As the external nucleus is the upstream target area for central nucleus projections, the radioactive tag was traced back to its synaptic origin in the central nucleus. The entire column coding a 50-microsecond right-ear lead "lit up" (30 degrees off centre is equivalent to a 50 microsecond ITD). Thus, the phase differences of 10%, 15%, 20%, 25%, 30%, 35% and 40%, across the frequency lamina 2kHz to 8kHz, had one thing in common: they all coded a 50-microsecond right-ear lead ITD, irrespective of frequency. The invariant coding of ITDs is neurally accomplished by virtue of the processing unit being the entire functional column, uniting all frequencies for the common goal of invariantly coding interaural temporal differences.

An Organizational Principle of Auditory Maps

The ITD arrays in the barn owl represent prototypical maps in auditory neural substrates. Similar organization has been found in the auditory cortex of the moustached bat (Suga, O'Neill, Kujirai and Manabe 1983). The biosonar echolocation system of the bat has been described previously in terms of its potential to reveal analogous human neural mechanisms capable of processing and normalizing steady-state vowels (Sussman 1986, 1988). For example, the bat establishes velocity information on in-flight target prey by systematically mapping Doppler-shifted frequencies from various combinations of constant frequency (CF) components of emitted versus echo harmonics. The pulse-echo frequency difference is mediated by specialized "combination-sensitive" neurons. Thus, frequency differences between orthogonally mapped CF harmonic pairs yield the effective equivalent of target velocity. Combinations of frequency modulated (FM) segments from pulse-echo pairs have been shown to yield odotopic maps coding target distance. Moreover, processing of FM-FM temporal differences are dependent on combination-sensitive neurons that are delay-tuned to differential time delays between emitted and returning FM components.

In both the avian (barn owl) and mammalian (bat) brain, auditory processing centres have been shown to map specific attributes of the complex input signal (viz., the "information bearing parameters"; see Suga et al. 1983, 1574). The schematic shown in Figure 4 captures an important generalization across auditory mapping systems as seen in the neuroethological studies of both the barn owl and bat. A 2-D map of two independent stimulus attributes, x and y, are laid out in a systematic (but not necessarily linear) order. More important ranges of variation within a given variable can be over-represented, as the second harmonic component in the bat's biosonar signal. Combination-sensitive neurons

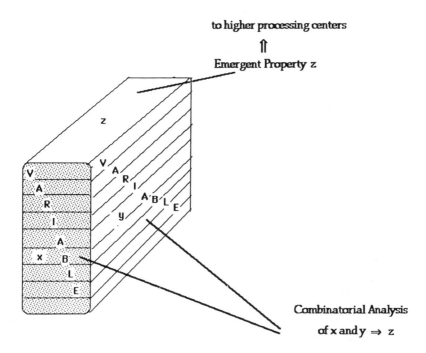

Figure 4: Schematic of auditory processing maps showing 2-D arrays of variables x and y yielding an emergent property z due to combination-sensitive processing of x and y parameters.

differentially process x_i and y_i combinations to yield an emergent property, z, that only exists by virtue of the combination of x and y. What appears as a general characteristic of such maps is that the emergent property z represents a coding or signalling characteristic that all x-y combinations possess. The insights gained from such neurophysiological studies can be speculatively applied to the intellectual thicket of the noninvariance problem in human speech perception.

A Phonetic Metric for Capturing
Stop Place of Articulation

There are two major cue sets for distinguishing stop place of articulation: the power spectra of the release burst and the dynamics of the F2 transition. Research on the former (e.g., Stevens and Blumstein 1978; Blumstein and Stevens 1979; Kewley-Port 1983; Lahiri, Gewirth and Blumstein 1984; Forrest, Weismer, Milenkovic and Dougall 1988) has contributed a great deal towards explicating how spectral cues serve to assist the listener in the categorization process. Spectral cues, however, do not work in isolation from second formant-based cues. The two cues are complementary and interactive (Dorman, Studdert-Kennedy and Raphael 1977). Studies focusing on the acoustic properties of the variable F2 transitions have not met with the same level of categorization success as found for burst spectra (e.g., Kewley-Port 1982). The phonetic metric to be reviewed below, locus equations, provides a new perspective to the study of F2 transitions in characterizing stop place of articulation. To date, the work has focused on the role of locus equations as a phonetic descriptor of stop place to provide a much needed taxonomic orderliness to the CV acoustic waveform. A widespread view in speech perception is that coarticulatory variability inherently masks any underlying acoustic invariance that might be contained in the speech signal (Liberman and Mattingly 1985). This view, known as the "Motor Theory of Speech Perception," would deny that phonetic categories can be acoustically represented. As stated by Liberman and Mattingly: "Putting together all the generalizations about the multiplicity and variety of acoustic cues, we should conclude that there is simply no way to define a phonetic category in purely acoustic terms" (1985, 12). It will be shown below that the systematic regularities of locus equations accomplish exactly that – the acoustic basis of non-overlapping stop consonantal categories.

Locus Equations

Locus equations are derived by making straight-line regression fits to co-ordinates formed by plotting onset frequencies of F2 transitions, measured at the first glottal pulse, on the ordinate, and their corresponding offset frequencies in the midvowel target nuclei on the abscissa. Locus equations of the form $F2_{onset} = k^*F2_{vowel} + c$ (where k = slope and $c = y$ intercept) were originally formulated by Lindblom (1963) and plotted for a single speaker of Swedish producing consonant-vowel-consonant (CVC) tokens where C = [b, d, g] and having eight medial vowel contexts. Scatterplots were reported to be extremely linear with slopes varying as a function of stop place of articulation. Work on locus equations ceased for over two decades and only recently has further work been reported (Krull 1988, 1989 for Swedish; and Nearey and Shamass 1987 for Canadian English).

Sussman, McCaffrey and Matthews (1991) analyzed 20 dialectally varied speakers of American English (10 male and 10 female) who produced [bVt], [dVt], [gVt] tokens with 10 medial vowel contexts [i, ɪ, ɛ, e, æ, a, ɔ, ʌ, o, u]. There were five repetitions of each, yielding a total of 50 tokens per stop place category. Figures 5a, 5b and 5c illustrate mean locus equation scatterplots for [b], [d], and [g] pooled across all vowel contexts for 10 male and 10 female speakers. A significant main effect

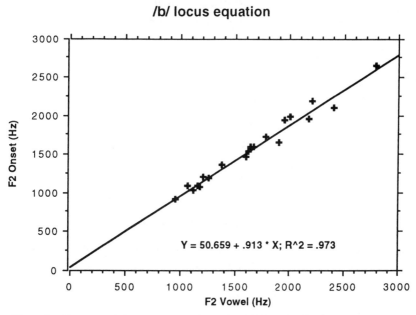

Figure 5a: Group mean locus equation for /b/ for 10 male and 10 female speakers.

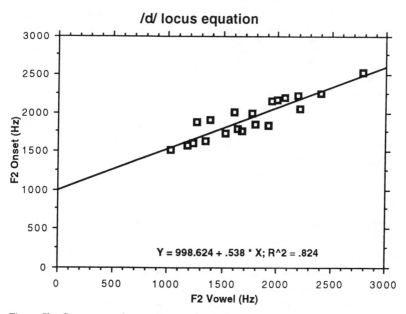

Figure 5b: Group mean locus equation for /d/ for 10 male and 10 female speakers.

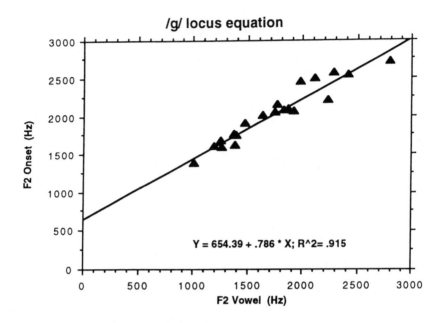

Figure 5c: Group mean locus equation for /g/ for 10 male and 10 female speakers.

for both slope and y-intercept was found as the mean labial slope was .87, alveolar slope was .41 and velar slope was .73. Data coordinates were consistently found to be tightly clustered around each regression function. A remarkable degree of linearity was shown for every speaker for every stop place. The mean R^2 value across all 60 locus equations (20 speakers × 3 stops) was .89, and frequently exceeded .95 in many individual cases. Thus, the linear locus equation functions were accounting for almost 90% of the total variance. A discriminant analysis procedure using higher order and derived parameters, slope and y-intercept, led to correct classification scores of 100% for the three stop place categories.

Slope and y-intercept parameters, as a function of stop place, can effectively serve as phonetic descriptors to taxonomically represent, in acoustic/phonetic space, non-overlapping stop-place categories. Locus equations clearly show that, in an *absolute* sense, there is nothing acoustically invariant about F2 onsets associated with stop place. However, in a *relational* sense, F2 onsets are systematically (linearly) related to their midvowel target frequencies. Relational invariance is revealed, not at the level of the individual token, where it is notoriously missing, but at a higher level of phonological abstraction, the entire consonantal category. Each linear and tightly clustered scatterplot across stop place categories depicts the lawful and well-defined relationship that ties together the variable F2 transitions. Locus equation co-ordinates, normalizing F2 transitions across vowel space, reflect the ensemble of allophonic variants that form the perceptually invariant stop place categories. Before a neural model is suggested that conceptually relates locus equations to the ITD arrays in the barn owl, additional validation of the locus equations will be provided in languages other than English.

Cross-linguistic Verification of Locus Equations

The locus equation metric has been extended to three additional languages: Thai, Cairene Arabic and Urdu. These languages have two, four and four stop-place contrasts respectively for syllable-initial voiced stops. Stop-vowel productions from 14 speakers (Thai = 6; Arabic = 3; Urdu = 5) were acoustically analyzed, and once again extremely linear regression functions were obtained for every stop place category with slopes and y-intercepts systematically varying as a function of stop place of articulation. Figures 6a and 6b, 7a to 7d and 8a to 8d show mean locus equation functions for the stop contrasts in Thai, Cairene Arabic and Urdu.

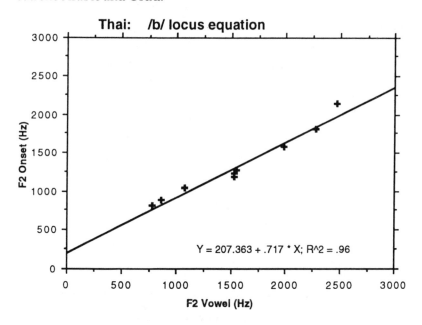

Figure 6a: Group mean locus equation for /b/ for six Thai speakers.

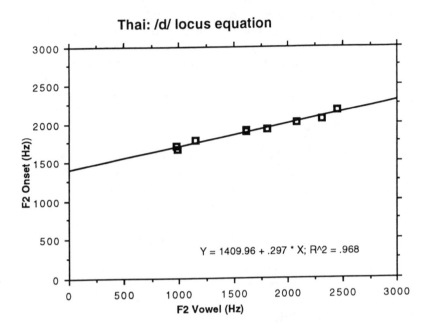

Figure 6b: Group mean locus equation for /d/ for six Thai speakers.

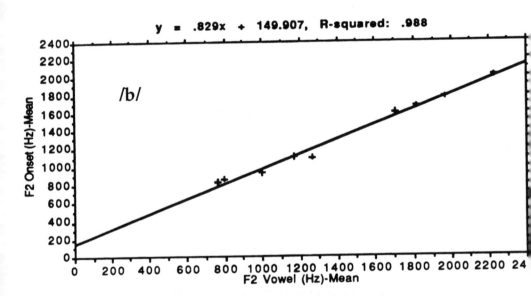

Figure 7a: Group mean locus equation for /b/ for five Urdu speakers.

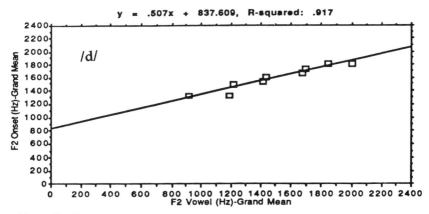

Figure 7b: Group mean locus equation for /d/ for five Urdu speakers.

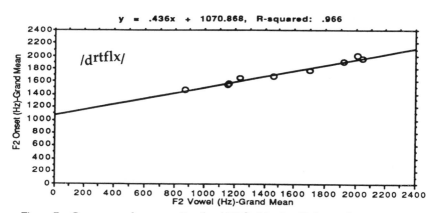

Figure 7c: Group mean locus equation for /d^{retroflex}/ for five Urdu speakers.

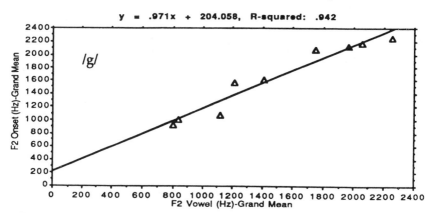

Figure 7d: Group mean locus equation for /g/ for five Urdu speakers.

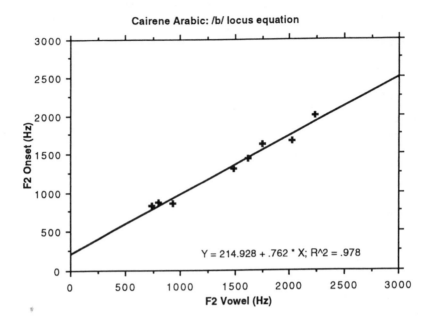

Figure 8a: Group mean locus equation for /b/ for three Cairene Arabic speakers.

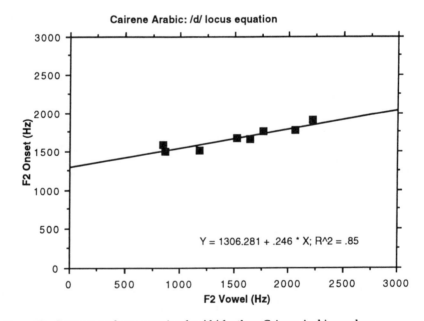

Figure 8b: Group mean locus equation for /d/ for three Cairene Arabic speakers.

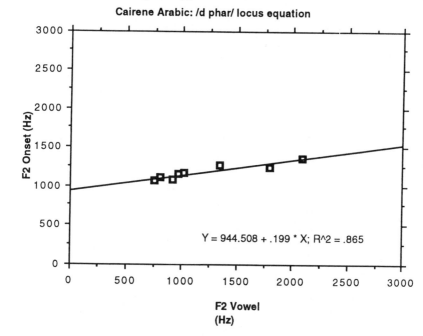

Figure 8c: Group mean locus equation for /d^{pharyngeal}/ for three Cairene Arabic speakers.

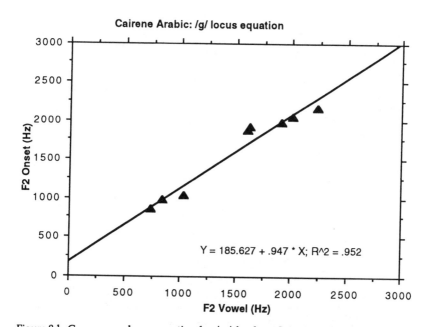

Figure 8d: Group mean locus equation for /g/ for three Cairene Arabic speakers.

Locus Equation Spectrotopic 2D Arrays
for Place of Articulation

Figure 9 presents a schematic illustrating hypothetical stop place arrays based on locus equation parameters. In analogous fashion to the ITD arrays in the barn owl, two orthogonal axes, F2 onset and F2 vowel frequencies, are systematically laid out for each stop place category. Each horizontal CV slab represents a given starting and ending frequency of an F2 transition. Similar to interaural phase differences in the barn owl, these individual F2 transitions are ambiguous and incapable of establishing identity of stop place by themselves. What all values of a given stop place array have in common is that their x-y co-ordinates

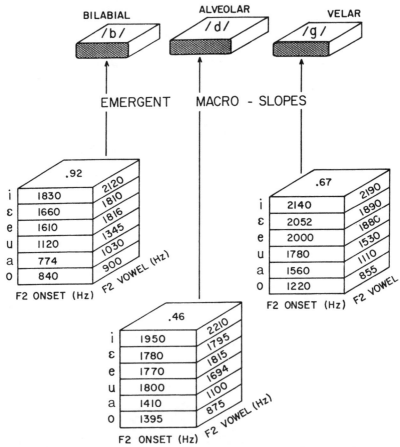

Figure 9: Stop Consonant Place of Production. Schematic showing locus equation arrays of F2 onsets plotted in relation to F2 midvowel targets to yield an emergent commonality of the whole array captured by the locus equation slope and y-intercept. (From Sussman 1989 *Psychological Review* 96, 631–42.)

lie along the same linear function as defined by the unique slope and y-intercept of the locus equation distribution in acoustic space (only locus equation slopes are shown in Figure 9). Similar to the schematic in Figure 4 this arrangement of locus equation values follows the organizational principles as documented in the auditory maps of the bat and barn owl. In the animal examples an emergent property, z, is established by combination-sensitive neurons tuned to specific x and y combinations. Neural maps are frequently represented in a Cartesian-looking "neural space" (Suga 1984). If the human nervous system encodes an equivalent map of locus equation scatterplots, as shown in acoustic/phonetic space, then the conceptual neural equivalent of what I am calling "slope and y-intercept" of the regression functions can be considered the emergent commonality linking all the vowel-specific CV tokens together into a class of abstracted phonological equivalents. In essence, the extreme linearity of the locus equation distributions in combination with the differential distributional appearance of each stop place function, suggests a Cartesian-like neural representation for stop + vowel combinations.

The specific combination-sensitive neuron class that would be needed for such a coding operation has already been documented in the mustached bat (Suga 1984; 1988; Olson and Suga 1991). FM-FM combination-sensitive neurons are sensitive to the brief downward sweeps at the end of a pulse or echo harmonic component. Such neurons have been shown to be delay-tuned as much as 30 msec in the bat. In other words they respond maximally to a pulse-echo pairing of specific frequencies separated by a specific temporal delay. The bat uses such delay-tuned neurons to establish target range maps (odotopic representation) in an FM-FM area of the medial geniculate (Olsen and Suga 1991). It thus appears that neurons used by the mustached bat to process its species-specific signals are very much of the type that the locus equation model of stop consonant perception would predict are necessary to form neural representations of contrastive sound categories in the human auditory system. The basic requirement would be an auditory system capable of detecting the coincidence of specific frequencies sampled at different times. CV transitions in speech would necessitate longer time intervals than those seen for bat distance coding. Rather than iso-velocity or iso-range maps as documented in the bat, iso-stop fields could be mapped. Multiple arrays, both complementary and redundant, will be necessary for complete stop place encoding, as locus equation functions for [b d g] have a few areas of overlap with each other across various vowel contexts. In this regard two-dimensional maps of F3 onsets plotted with respect to F2 vowel frequencies can resolve [d, g] overlap for back vowel contexts (Sussman et al.

1991). One would also expect information about the stop burst to be integrated with the CV transition at an early stage of processing.

A Neuronal Model for On-line
Single Token Classification

A major difference exists between ITD arrays in the barn owl and hypothesized "locus equation" arrays in humans: the former contains cotemporal frequency components and the latter does not. Spectral analysis of the complex input sound for sound source localization in the owl results in the simultaneous presence of multiple, harmonically related, frequency components. On-line speech perception is obviously composed of successive sampling periods where one CV at a time is processed. How does a single CV input activate an entire stop place array? The neuronal model shown in Figure 10 attempts to reconcile on-line single token processing with the categorical (as opposed to token level) nature of the locus equation metric. One key characteristic of the linear locus equation function is the inherent accuracy of the independent variable, F2 vowel (Hz), to predict the dependent variable, F2 onset (Hz), which in reality is the stop consonantal locus.

To illustrate how the model works, I will step through the processing of a [d æ] input. A tri-tier input segmentation is shown in Figure 10 to include, from top to bottom, the burst spectra, F2 onset, and F2 vowel. Combination-sensitive (And/Or gate) neurons are located in between each tier. The topmost combination-sensitive layer is tuned to maximally respond to spectral burst + F2 onset frequency information. Output projections go to another layer of And/Or gate neurons that signal stop place (input #1 in Figure 10). The F2 onset detector neurons also project to this layer (input #2) as well as the layer predicting an alternative and competing stop place category, labial stop onsets (which is only partially activated). By this time F2 vowel information can be used to predict F2 onset. Predicted F2 onset arrives at the same And/Or gate (input #3) as the previous inputs from the on-line F2 onset (#2) and the combination-sensitive burst + F2 onset And/Or gate (input #1). F2 vowel input also partially activates the potential labial tier, but no converging input verifications arrive at this tier, and hence it does not trigger a response. Thus a multiple convergence of redundantly coded inputs, based on initial burst cues and F2 transition dynamics, combine to signal stop place. Operational steps in labial place signalling is shown, by comparison, in the bottom schematic of Figure 10.

From the viewpoint of neurogenesis of phonology, such CV isostop categorical maps would serve to establish primordial phonological primitives. The software controlling the exact wiring of the neural hardware is the sensory input patterns of the ambient natural language(s).

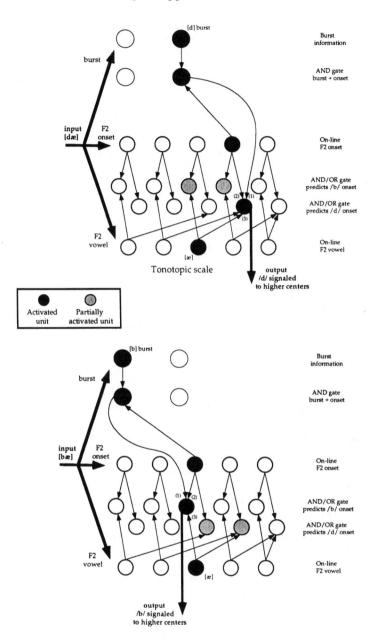

Figure 10: Schematic of a neuronal model showing processing of [dae] versus [bae]. Each input token provides burst, F2 onset, F2 vowel information and combination-sensitive processing of these parameters plus comparison of predicted to actual F2 onsets provides convergent inputs to signal stop place of articulation.

What gets encoded is what is heard. Fine-tuning of phonological forms gradually occurs as thousands and thousands of input samples are continually processed. Lexical entities are gradually formed by hierarchical combinations of basic prototypical CVs ("daddy") and increasing syllable slot expansions to include initial and final consonant clusters (Sussman 1984).

Continuing work with the locus equation metric will explore potential categorical constancies for other manner class consonants such as glides [w], [j] and liquids [r], [l] across vowel contexts. Reduced coarticulatory effects across the consonant-vowel interface for approximates compared to stops appear to allow the locus equation parameters, slope and y-intercept, to differentiate these classes [w, j, r, l] from more heavily coarticulated stops [b d g] in acoustic phonetic space. The metric is also applicable to the study of disordered speaking populations, such as aphasic, apraxic and hearing-impaired.

References

Blumstein, S.E., and K.N. Stevens (1979). Acoustic invariance in speech production: Evidence from measurements of the spectral characteristics of stop consonants. *Journal of the Acoustic Society of America* 66: 1001–17

Chomsky, N. (1986). *Knowledge of Language: Its Nature, Origin, and Use.* New York: Praeger

Churchland, P.S., and T.J. Sejnowski (1989). Neural representation and neural computation. In L. Nadel, L.A. Cooper, P. Culicover and R.M. Harnish (eds.), *Neural Connections, Mental Computations,* 15–48. Cambridge, MA: MIT Press

Diamond, M.C. (1988). *Enriching Heredity: The Impact of the Environment on the Anatomy of the Brain.* New York: Free Press

Dorman, M.F., M. Studdert-Kennedy and L. Raphael (1977). Stop consonant recognition: Release bursts and formant transitions as functionally equivalent, context-dependent cues. *Perception and Psychophysics* 22: 109–22

Elman, J.L., and D. Zipser (1987). Learning the hidden structure of speech. (ICS Report No. 8701). San Diego, CA: University of California

Forrest, K., G. Weismer, P. Milenkovic and R.N. Dougall (1988). Statistical analysis of word-initial voiceless obstruents: Preliminary data. *Journal of the Acoustical Society of America* 84:, 115–23

Jacob, F. (1977). Evolution and tinkering. *Science* 196: 1161–66

Jacobs, B., and J. Schumann (1992). Language acquisition and the neurosciences: Towards a more integrative perspective. *Applied Linguistics* 13: 282–301

Jeffress, L.A. (1948). A place theory of sound localization. *Journal of Comparative Physiological Psychology* 41: 35–39

Kewley-Port, D. (1982). Measurement of formant transitions in naturally produced stop consonant-vowel syllables. *Journal of the Acoustical Society of America* 72: 379–89

——— (1983). Time-varying features as correlates of place of articulation in stop consonants. *Journal of the Acoustical Society of America* 73: 322–35

Kluender, K.R., R.L. Diehl and P.R. Killeen (1987). Japanese quail can learn phonetic categories. *Science* 237: 1195–97

Knudsen, E., and M. Konishi (1977). A neural map of auditory space in the owl. *Science* 200: 795–97

——— (1978). Space and frequency are represented separately in auditory midbrain of the owl. *Journal of Neurophysiology* 41: 870–84

Krull, D. (1988). Acoustic properties as predictors of perceptual responses: A study of Swedish voiced stops. *PERILUS (Phonetic Experimental Research at the Institute of Linguistics, University of Stockholm)* 7: 66–70

——— (1989). Second formant locus patterns and consonant-vowel coarticulation in spontaneous speech. *PERILUS (Phonetic Experimental Research at the Institute of Linguistics, University of Stockholm)* 10: 87–108

Lahiri, A., L. Gewirth and S.E. Blumstein (1984). A reconsideration of acoustic invariance for place of articulation in diffuse stop consonants: Evidence from a cross-language study. *Journal of the Acoustical Society of America* 76: 391–404

Liberman, A.M., P.C. Delattre, F.S. Cooper and L.J. Gerstman (1954). The role of consonant-vowel transitions in the perception of the stop and nasal consonants. *Psychological Monographs* 68: 1–13

Liberman, A.M., and I.G. Mattingly (1985). The motor theory of speech perception revised. *Cognition* 21: 1–36

Lindblom, B. (1963). On vowel reduction. Report No. 29, The Royal Institute of Technology, Speech Transmission Laboratory, Stockholm, Sweden.

Nearey, T.M., and S.E. Shammass (1987). Formant transitions as partly distinctive invariant properties in the identification of voiced stops. *Canadian Acoustics* 15: 17–24

Olsen, J.F., and N. Suga (1991a). Combination-sensitive neurons in the medial geniculate body of the mustached bat: encoding of relative velocity information. *Journal ofNeurophysiology* 65: 1254–74

——— (1991b). Combination-sensitive neurons in the medial geniculate body of the mustached bat: encoding of target range information. *Journal of Neurophysiology* 65: 1275–96

Overholt, E.M., E.W. Rubel and R.L. Hyson (1992). A circuit for coding interaural time differences in the chick brainstem. *Journal of Neuroscience* 12: 1698–1708

Pinker, S., and P. Bloom. (1990). Natural language and natural selection. *Behavioral and Brain Sciences* 13: 707–84

Stevens, K.N., and S.E. Blumstein (1978). Invariant cues for place of articulation in stop consonants. *Journal of the Acoustical Society of America* 64: 1358–68

Suga, N. (1984). The extent to which biosonar information is represented in the bat auditory cortex. In G.M. Edelman, W.E. Gall and W.M. Cowan (eds.), *Dynamic Aspects of Neocortical Function*, 315–73. New York: John Wiley

—————— (1988). Auditory neuroethology and speech processing: complex sound processing by combination-sensitive neurons. In G.M. Edelman, W.E. Gall and W.M. Cowan (eds.) *Auditory Function*, 679–720. New York: John Wiley

Suga, N., W.E. O'Neill, K. Kujirai and T. Manabe (1983). Specificity of combination-sensitive neurons for processing of complex biosonar signals in auditory cortex of the mustached bat. *Neurophysiology* 49: 1573–1627

Sullivan, W.E., and M. Konishi (1986). Neural map of interaural phase difference in the owl's brainstem. *Proceeedings of the National Academy of Sciences, USA* 83: 8400–8404

Sussman, H.M. (1984). A neuronal model for syllable representation. *Brain and Language* 22: 167–77

—————— (1986). A neuronal model of vowel normalization and representation. *Brain and Language* 28: 12–23

—————— (1988). The neurogenesis of phonology. In H. Whitaker (ed.), *Phonological Processes and Brain Mechanisms*, 1–23. New York: Springer-Verlag

Sussman, H.M., H.A. McCaffrey and S.A. Matthews (1991). An investigation of locus equations as a source of relational invariance for stop place categorization. *Journal of the Acoustical Society of America* 90: 1309–25

Takahashi, T., and M. Konishi (1986). Selectivity for interaural time difference in the owl's midbrain. *Journal of Neuroscience* 6: 3413–22

Wagner, H., T. Takahashi and M. Konishi (1987). Representation of interaural time difference in the central nucleus of the barn owl's inferior colliculus. *Journal of Neuroscience* 7: 3105–16